KINGDOM COMING

The Rise of Christian Nationalism

Michelle Goldberg

W. W. Norton & Company
New York   London

For Matt, of course.

Manufacturing by Courier Westford
Book design by Rhea Braunstein
Production manager: Amanda Morrison

Library of Congress Cataloging-in-Publication Data

Goldberg, Michelle, 1975–
Kingdom coming : the rise of Christian nationalism / Michelle
Goldberg.— 1st ed.
p. cm.
Includes bibliographical references and index.
ISBN-13: 978-0-393-06094-2 (hardcover)
ISBN-10: 0-393-06094-2 (hardcover)
1. Dominion theology. 2. Christianity and politics. I. Title.
BT82.25.G65 2006
277.3'083—dc22
2005036593

ISBN 978-0-393-32976-6 pbk.

W. W. Norton & Company, Inc.
500 Fifth Avenue, New York, N.Y. 10110
www.wwnorton.com

W. W. Norton & Company Ltd.
Castle House, 75/76 Wells Street, London W1T 3QT

1 2 3 4 5 6 7 8 9 0

ACKNOWLEDGMENTS

This book was born in a Brooklyn coffee shop during the summer of 2004. I was talking to my soon-to-be agent, the indefatigable Larry Weissman, about another idea entirely, when the conversation veered towards the parallel culture—an amalgam of extreme nationalism and apocalyptic religion—that seemed to be ascendant in much of America. Again and again while reporting for Salon, I'd had the sense that liberals and conservatives no longer merely had divergent values—they occupied different realities, with contradictory facts, histories and epistemologies. As I remember it, I grew increasingly animated, until finally Larry interjected that that's the book I should write. So I did, but it never would have happened without him.

I'd already had the opportunity to delve into the culture and politics of the right thanks to my editors at Salon, who give their writers the rare freedom to follow their curiosity wherever it leads. I'm particularly grateful to Joan Walsh, who took a gamble on hiring me four years ago. Without the priceless reporting opportunities she offered me, I could never have developed the ideas that became *Kingdom Coming*.

Many people helped me with my research. Chip Berlet of Political Research Associates, an invaluable resource for anyone who studies the right, offered me insight, archival materials and a home-cooked dinner. I'm also indebted to Al Ross of the Institute for Democracy Studies; Dan Quinn of the Texas Freedom Network; Adrienne Verrilli of the Sexuality Information and Education Council of the United States; and Rob Boston of Americans United for Separation of Church and State. The Reverend Don Wilkey, pastor of First Baptist Church in Onalaska,

Texas, gave me access to his considerable files and an inspiring reminder that Christian nationalism and Christianity are two very different things. I learned an enormous amount about the religious right from the pioneering work of Frederick Clarkson and Sara Diamond, who were both too far ahead of their time to get all the credit they deserve for their prescience.

My good friend Cassi Feldman read these chapters as they were written and gave me both crucial suggestions and constant encouragement. Morgen Van Vorst, my wonderful editor, rescued this project, and my sanity, at a particularly hazardous juncture and made it far more lucid than it would be otherwise. I'm enormously thankful to Trent Duffy, my fabulous copyeditor, who saved me from several mortifying mistakes.

Like almost everything worthwhile in my life, this book would never have been possible without the support of my husband, Matt Ipcar. Our chance meeting over a decade ago—also in a coffee shop where I'd gone with other plans—remains the only miracle I believe in.

Contents

KINGDOM
COMING

INTRODUCTION

Taking the Land

M ichael Farris, the founder and president of the evangelical Patrick
Henry College, calls his campaign to turn Christian homeschooled students into political cadres Generation Joshua. The name
has a very specific biblical and martial meaning. Joshua was Moses's
military commander and successor as leader of the Israelites; while
Moses brought his people out of Egypt, Joshua led them in seizing the
holy land. Farris's Generation Joshua has a less bloody mission, but it is
imbued with an Old Testament dream of exile redeemed by conquest.
The holy land is America as Farris imagines it. The enemy is America as
it exists right now.

A veteran right-wing activist and the nation's premier advocate of
homeschooling, Farris was speaking at 2005's annual Christian Home
Educators of Colorado convention. Thousands of parents had converged on the sprawling Denver Merchandise Mart, a conference and
exhibition center, for three days of lectures and workshops with titles
like "Conquering Corrupt Culture by Raising Christian Communica-
tors" and "Restoring American Values." The parking lot teemed with
SUVs bearing Bush/Cheney decals, metallic Jesus fish, and magnetic
Support Our Troops ribbons. Inside, several women wore stickers saying "I'm Married to the World's Greatest Principal."

Farris refers to these parents and their peers nationwide as the
Moses generation, because they have successfully led their children out
of the bondage of the godless public schools. But permanent exile from

1

the American mainstream was never the goal. As Farris wrote in his book *Generation Joshua*, the homeschooling movement "will succeed when our children, the Joshua Generation, engage wholeheartedly in the battle to take the land."

He admits it's a large task. "This is the land of MTV, Internet porn, abortion, homosexuality, greed, and accomplished selfishness," he observed. Giants stalk America, "giants that live in the fields of law, government, journalism, and history. And we are going to look in depth at the elite colleges and universities of our nation. The enemies of freedom and truth dominate these institutions and thereby dominate our nation."[1]

What Farris wants is a cultural revolution. He's trying to train a generation of leaders, unscathed by secularism, who will gain political power in order to subsume everything—entertainment, law, government, and education—to Christianity, or their version of it. That might sound like fantasy, but it's worth pondering what Farris has achieved so far.

Short and boyishly handsome, with a full head of sandy hair, Farris is in his fifties but appears much younger. A protégé of Tim LaHaye, author of the best-selling apocalyptic *Left Behind* novels, Farris was chief counsel for Concerned Women for America, the organization founded by LaHaye's wife, Beverly, before becoming a full-time homeschool advocate in 1983, when he founded the Home School Legal Defense Association. In 1982, when he and his wife, Vickie, started teaching the first of their ten kids at home, they didn't know anyone else who was doing it. In many states, it was against the law. Now, thanks in large part to Farris's activism, homeschooling is a legal right in every state. The practice has become a badge of authenticity and commitment among Christian conservatives, with somewhere between 1.1 and 2.1 million kids, most of them evangelicals, being homeschooled nationwide.[2]

The influence of these kids, trained from infancy to be Christian culture warriors, is already making itself felt. Farris's Patrick Henry College, located in rural Virginia, caters specifically to homeschooled evangelical students. It has existed only since 2000, and accepts fewer than one hundred students a year, yet in 2004's spring semester it provided 7 percent of the White House's interns. Twenty-two conservative congressmen have employed one or more Patrick Henry interns, and a Patrick Henry graduate works on Karl Rove's staff.[3]

Through Generation Joshua, launched in 2004 to involve homeschooled teenagers in politics, children are becoming Republican foot soldiers before they can vote. In its first year, Generation Joshua paid all the travel and living expenses for hundreds of homeschooled students who volunteered on right-wing political campaigns nationwide, rewarding the most productive with scholarships to Patrick Henry. It sent teams to work for the Bush campaign in various swing states and dispatched other students to help Senate candidates like Oklahoma's Tom Coburn (who has called for the death penalty for abortionists) and South Carolina's Jim DeMint (who has said he would like to ban gays and unmarried pregnant women from teaching in public schools). Both DeMint and Coburn won their races, as did all but one of the candidates supported by Generation Joshua.

Generation Joshua's director is Ned Ryun, a former speechwriter for George W. Bush and the homeschooled son of Kansas congressman Jim Ryun. He's in his early thirties, with dark receding hair and glasses. Like Farris, he's a biblical literalist who is fluent in the worldly dynamics of Washington, D.C., and, as he explained to the parents on the first day of the Denver conference, one of his responsibilities is training homeschoolers to bridge the two worlds.

According to Generation Joshua's philosophy, Christianity holds the answer to every public and private dispute. But because the American people do not yet accept this, Christian ideas need to be rationalized in secular terms. Ryun teaches thousands of protégés this rhetorical two-step through online seminars, chats, and book clubs.

"A lot of time in the public debate, Christians will say, 'Well, the Bible says so,' or 'God says this is wrong'" Ryun explained. "And that's true. God is not for same-sex marriages. God believes that the Bible protects life." In public, though, "usually you have to use terms and facts that the other side accepts as reasonable. What I'm trying to do with young people is, let's take the Bible and the Constitution, and let's look at current events. What does the Bible have to say about it? Let's get a firm, solid biblical worldview, and then learn how to communicate that in terms that the other side accepts."

Farris and Ryun foresee a government filled with people who think this way. "Homeschoolers will be inordinately represented in the highest levels of leadership and power in the next generation," said Ryun. "You're starting to see them all around the Hill, as staffers on Capitol Hill." His homeschooled sister, he noted, works in the White House's Office of Faith-Based and Community Initiatives, which is in charge of channeling hundreds of millions of federal dollars to religious charities.

"There are two worldviews that are very much in conflict right now, especially in Washington, D.C.," Ryun explained. The first, he said, is Judeo-Christian. "It starts with God as the creator, but then it also protects life, it's about traditional marriage, one man, one woman," he said. "On the other side, you have secular humanism, which starts with man as the center of all things. There are no absolute standards, it's all morally relative, anything goes as long as it has to do with sex."

According to Ryun, everything the government does derives from one of these systems. "You look at all the various laws that affect us, tax laws, social security, the life issue, the marriage issue, all these various laws and policy, you can trace them back to one of these two worldviews," he said.

Thus every political issue—indeed, every disputed aspect of our national life—is a struggle between good and evil.

When Ryun finished speaking to the conventioneers, most of them wandered out into a vast exhibition hall to shop for school supplies. The cavernous space—all thirty thousand square feet of it—was crowded with booth after booth selling Christian curricula, videos, and educational games for students of every age. There were great piles of Bible-themed coloring books and creationist science textbooks, countless adventure stories about intrepid missionaries, instruction manuals for raising chaste, submissive girls and vigorous, capable boys, and dense, scholarly tomes of history and biblical exegesis.

Artifacts of our ongoing culture wars were everywhere. One table sold *Of Pandas and People*, an anti-evolution biology text that was introduced into a public high school in Dover, Pennsylvania, in 2004, making headlines worldwide. Several vendors had the new book by Roy Moore, the former chief justice of the Alabama Supreme Court who lost his job after refusing to remove the two-and-a-half-ton Ten Commandments monument he'd installed in his court building. Another peddled *How to Dethrone the Imperial Judiciary* by Edwin Vieira, who had recently gained notoriety when, at a conference attended by numerous prominent Republicans, he approvingly alluded to Stalin's purges as a way of dealing with liberal judges.

In sum, the mountains of media at the Denver Merchandise Mart presented a vision of reality utterly at odds with that of the secular world. The history texts described a past in which America was founded as a Christian nation, only to be subverted and debased by God-hating liberals bent on perverting the country's heritage. A CD lecture lauded the Christian kindness the Puritans showed to Native Americans. Science videos claimed that leading researchers have discredited evolution, and some offered evidence that dinosaurs and men lived together in the Garden of Eden. Astronomy textbooks explained that the universe was created six thousand years ago with the appearance of age, which is why starlight only *seems* as if it has traveled millions of years to reach the Earth.

Many volumes were packed with footnotes referencing books for sale at other tables, all of them confirming each other's claims. Reading through them one after another, I sometimes felt I was in a novel by Jorge Luis Borges, drifting through a parallel reality contained in a monumental library of lies.

The people who live inside this reality often call it the "Christian worldview." The phrase is based on the conviction that true Christianity must govern every aspect of public and private life, and that all—

government, science, history, culture, and relationships—must be understood according to the dictates of scripture. There are biblically correct positions on every issue, from gay marriage to income tax rates, and only those with the right worldview can discern them.

This is Christianity as a total ideology. It's an ideology adhered to by millions of Americans, some of whom are very powerful. It's what drives a great many of the fights over religion, science, sex, and pluralism that are now dividing communities all over the country. It is a conscious refutation of Enlightenment rationalism, and it is an ideology that people like Ryun and Farris want to see guiding every decision the government makes.

I call this totalistic political ideology Christian nationalism, and in *Kingdom Coming* I attempt to show how it is reshaping America. The homeschooling movement represents Christian nationalism's vanguard, but it's also promulgated by countless churches, lobbying groups, politicians, law firms, professional associations, student clubs, and media outlets. These organizations are intricately linked together, creating a movement that is both incredibly disciplined and amorphous. It is a hydra-headed thing, sometimes contradictory but unified enough to be called by a single name.

The United States has always been a pious country, given to bursts of spiritual fervor, but Christian nationalism is qualitatively different from earlier religious revivals. Like America's past Great Awakenings, the Christian nationalist movement claims that the Bible is absolutely and literally true. But it goes much further, extrapolating a total political program from that truth, and yoking that program to a political party. It is a conflation of scripture and politics that sees America's triumphs as confirmation of the truth of the Christian religion, and America's struggles as part of a cosmic contest between God and the devil. It claims supernatural sanction for its campaign of national renewal and speaks rapturously about vanquishing the millions of Americans who would stand in its way.

The motivating dream of the movement is the restoration of an imagined Christian nation. With a revisionist history that claims the founders never intended to create a secular country and that separation of church and state is a lie fostered by conniving leftists, Christian nationalism rejects the idea of government religious neutrality. The movement argues that the absence of religion in public is itself a religion—the malign faith of secular humanism—that must, in the interest of fairness, be balanced with equal deference to the Bible.

As I hope to illustrate in the following chapters, however, the ultimate goal of Christian nationalist leaders isn't fairness. It's dominion. The movement is built on a theology that asserts the Christian right to rule. That doesn't mean that nonbelievers will be forced to convert. They'll just have to learn their place.

Like all ideologies, Christian nationalism tells a story. It's a tale about a godly country, blessed for its piety, that began to go wrong in the nineteenth century and sank to unimagined lows in the twentieth. Charles Darwin's theory of evolution eroded people's faith in man's dignity and God's supremacy. The great universities that once saw Christianity as the root of all knowledge turned away from scripture and toward the secular philosophies of a decadent Europe, which put man at the center of the universe. Franklin Delano Roosevelt's New Deal brought socialism to America and began the process by which government, rather than churches, became the guarantors of social welfare.

A generation of intellectuals and attorneys, educated to discount the centrality of God, fought a vicious campaign against America's Christian heritage. Atheist judges scorned the Lord by outlawing prayer in public school, striking down bans on contraception, and, most ignominiously, forcing the states to legalize abortion with 1973's *Roe v. Wade.*

An angry God began to withdraw his favor. Crime and discord increased. Children turned against their parents and wives against their husbands. Hedonism and licentiousness ruled. In the last decades of the twentieth century, the forces of darkness threatened to turn America into Sodom. Homosexuals, symbols of everything unnatural and decadent, marched out of the closet, spreading perversion and disease. Even as they cavorted in public, Christianity was banished to the private sphere, an exile encouraged by liberal pastors in mainline churches whose worldliness blinded them to the pure truth of God's word.

But God didn't give up on America. He changed the hearts of a few people, and before long, there was a great revival in the country. Conservative evangelical churches mushroomed. Believers shed their apathy, got organized, and elected godly men.

Yet God's enemies remained strong, abroad and at home. On September 11, they struck. Domestic traitors abetted the terrorists, first weakening the country with their moral laxity and then undermining it when it was under attack. For America to triumph, it would have to purify itself, restore God to the center of public life, and finally vanquish liberalism.

In the aftermath of September 11, only two significant American public figures blamed the country for bringing the calamity on itself. On September 13, Jerry Falwell appeared on *The 700 Club*, Pat Robertson's television show, and said, "I really believe that the pagans, and the abortionists, and the feminists, and the gays and the lesbians who are actively trying to make that an alternative lifestyle, the ACLU, People for the American Way, all of them who have tried to secularize America. I point the finger in their face and say 'you helped this happen.'"

"Well," Robertson replied, "I totally concur."

The Christian nationalist movement does not represent a majority of Americans—it does not even represent a majority of all evangelicals—but it does represent a significant and highly mobilized minority. White evangelicals constitute around a quarter of the country's population, but according to a 2004 study by political scientist John Green, only 12.6 percent of Americans describe themselves as "traditionalist evangelicals," the group, Green wrote, that comes "closest to the 'religious right' widely discussed in the media." As Green described them, this group is overwhelmingly Republican and tends to reject pluralism. A majority of them, for example, disagree with the statement that "homosexuals should have the same rights as other Americans."[4]

George Barna, a respected evangelical pollster, defines "evangelicals" more narrowly as a fundamentalist subset of born-again Christians.* By his measures, almost 40 percent of Americans are born-again Christians, but only 7 percent are true evangelicals. Among both cohorts, there is substantial support for amending the United States Constitution to make Christianity the country's official religion—66 percent of evangelicals endorse the idea, as do 44 percent of other born-again Christians.

Numbers, of course, can only approximate the size of a movement. Ideas aren't confined to demographic phyla, and ideologies are never monolithic—people take what speaks to them and overlook what doesn't. There are many Catholics and even a tiny handful of Jews, Moonies, and others who are deeply involved in the Christian nationalist movement, and a considerable number of theologically traditional Christians who believe passionately in the separation of church and state.[5]

Around the movement's core, there is a penumbra of vague supporters who sympathize with its aims without considering themselves part of it, and many more who can be mobilized by appeals to family, faith, and flag. In polls, majorities of Americans say they favor some legal recognition for gay relationships, yet in many states people have voted overwhelmingly to strip same-sex couples of any partnership benefits, often after campaigns warning them their families and children were under attack by sexual degenerates.

---

* Rather than relying on self-definition, Barna classifies respondents by asking them a series of questions about their religious beliefs and practices. He classifies those who say they have a personal relationship with Jesus Christ and accept him as their personal savior as born-again Christians. Evangelicals, according to his definition, meet these conditions and six others—they "say their faith is very important in their life today; believe they have a personal responsibility to share their religious beliefs about Christ with non-Christians; believe that Satan exists; believe that the eternal salvation is possible only through grace, not works; believe that Jesus Christ lived a sinless life on earth; and describe God as the all-knowing, all-powerful, perfect deity who created the universe and still rules it today."

If Christian nationalists don't predominate in the population, they do dominate the Republican party, for reasons that have more to do with their organization than their numbers. A 2002 study published in *Campaigns & Elections* found the religious right had a strong influence in eighteen state Republican parties and a moderate influence in twenty-six others. The study's authors concluded, "On balance, the perceived influence of Christian conservatives in state Republican parties has expanded since 1994 . . . the Christian right has been 'spreading out' across the states, especially in the South, Midwest and West. Thus, Christian conservatives have become a staple of politics nearly every-where."[6] It is likely that their control has only expanded since then.

Their hold on state Republican parties, coupled with the overrepre-sentation of less populated states in the Senate, has helped Christian nationalists win influence in Congress in excess of their actual num-bers. In 2004, the Christian Coalition gave 42 out of 100 senators rat-ings of 100 percent, meaning they took the group's position on every significant issue. More than half of senators achieved ratings of at least 83 percent. And that was before the 2004 election, which brought in new ultra-right lawmakers like Coburn and DeMint.

To understand how the Christian nationalists have consolidated so much power, it is necessary to trace some recent history.

The movement has several antecedents, most obviously the funda-mentalist preachers (and Nazi sympathizers) Gerald B. Winrod and Gerald L. K. Smith. Depression-era demagogues who railed against communism, modernism, and big government (and, in Winrod's case, Darwinism), both peddled a right-wing gospel conflating Christianity and patriotism. Smith was the founder of a group called the Christian Nationalist Crusade, whose magazine, *The Cross and the Flag,* pro-claimed, "Christian character is the basis of all real Americanism."[7]

Today's Christian nationalism also has roots in the anti-Communist John Birch Society, a conspiracy-minded grassroots group founded in 1958. As I'll illustrate in chapter 6, Christian nationalist arguments and campaigns often precisely echo Birch propaganda, and movement leaders like Tim LaHaye began as Birch organizers.

Yet, insofar as Christian nationalism has become a partisan political force, it developed out of the modern religious right born in the late 1970s. That's when a group of right-wing strategists including Paul Weyrich, Richard Viguerie, and Howard Phillips—all veterans of the Barry Goldwater campaign—recruited a somewhat obscure Baptist televangelist named Jerry Falwell to found the Moral Majority. Their idea was to use issues like abortion as a wedge to split social traditionalists from the Democratic party, and to harness the energy of the evangelical movement to the GOP.

It worked. Sara Diamond, one of the leading scholars of the American right, wrote in her 1995 book *Roads to Dominion: Right-Wing Movements and Political Power in the United States*, "Not only did evangelical Christians contribute significantly to Reagan's vote totals, but New Right-assisted organizations Christian Voice and the Moral Majority took credit for routing a slate of veteran liberal Senators and Representatives."[8] Among the most prominent of the vanquished progressives were Senators George McGovern of South Dakota and Frank Church of Idaho. It was the beginning of a massive political realignment in Middle America that Democrats have yet to cope with.

In 1981, a group of right-wing activists including Tim LaHaye, an original board member of the Moral Majority, formed the Council for National Policy (CNP), intended as the religious right's answer to the Council on Foreign Relations.* The organization is the stuff of liberal nightmares—it meets thrice yearly in secret, bringing together powerful evangelical activists, Republican politicians, and wealthy donors to

---

* The Council on Foreign Relations sits at the center of many right-wing conspiracy theories. Pat Robertson wrote in *The New World Order*, "A single thread runs from the White House to the State Department to the Council on Foreign Relations to the Trilateral Commission to secret societies to extreme New Agers. There must be a new world order. It must eliminate national sovereignty. There must be world government, a world police force, world courts, world banking and currency, and a world elite in charge of it all."

make plans to pull the country to the right. Over the years, its membership rolls have included James Dobson, Pat Robertson, Michael Farris,
former House Majority Leader Tom DeLay, and former Senator Jesse
Helms, along with forthright theocrats like R. J. Rushdoony, whom
we'll learn more about in chapter 1. The CNP still exists and remains
powerful. George Bush has refused to release a copy of the speech he
gave to the group in 1999, and during his presidency, both Dick Cheney
and Donald Rumsfeld have attended CNP meetings.[9]

The Christian right needs an enemy, and throughout the Reagan
administration, the Soviet Union stood in for Satan. Thus many
thrilled to the president's apocalyptic rhetoric and enthusiastically supported his policies in Latin America and Africa. Both Christian broadcasting star Pat Robertson and Concerned Women for America founder
Beverly LaHaye raised money for the contras in Nicaragua. Robertson
was also an enthusiastic supporter of the brutal Guatemalan dictator
Efrain Ríos Montt and of the government of El Salvador, which was
then deploying death squads against its political enemies. Jerry Falwell
used his position to speak out in favor of the apartheid regime in South
Africa, considered an anti-Communist bulwark.[10]

But the Reagan administration disappointed the Christian right on
the domestic front. Reagan appointed a few of the movement's activists
to prominent jobs in his administration, but expended little political
capital on Christianizing the country. Besides, even with Reagan's support, the House of Representatives was under Democratic control, so
many of the religious right's initiatives never had a chance.

Realizing it wasn't enough to win the White House, the Christian
right expanded its focus on grassroots politics (even as a small fringe
turned toward anti-abortion terrorism). Activists began taking over
the Republican party precinct by precinct, running for local offices
and becoming party delegates. Pat Robertson's 1988 presidential campaign taught many evangelicals the nuts and bolts of local party
organizing. The nationwide infrastructure that grew out of that campaign would become the Christian Coalition, which entered the political scene in 1989.

The founder of the Christian Coalition, Pat Robertson is a crucial figure in the development of Christian nationalism. A media titan whose Christian Broadcasting Network airs TV and radio programs in seventy-one languages to almost every country in the world, he has an unthreatening, grandfatherly mien. Yet there's a fierce totalitarian streak in his writing, which draws liberally on crackpot anti-Semitic conspiracy theories.[11] His 1991 book *The New World Order* tells of scheming Illuminati and shadowy Jewish bankers manipulating world events for their own monetary gain. Robertson castigated "cosmopolitan, liberal, secular Jews" for their "assault on Christianity" and compared liberals' persecution of Christians to Nazi propaganda campaigns.[12]

Robertson helped put dominionism—the idea that Christians have a God-given right to rule—at the center of the movement to bring evangelicals into politics. Dominionism is derived from a theocratic sect called Christian Reconstructionism, which advocates replacing American civil law with Old Testament biblical law. Most Christian Reconstructionist theology—a very strict Calvinism that mandates the death penalty for a long list of moral crimes, including homosexuality and apostasy—has little appeal to outsiders and is controversial even among Christian conservatives. But dominionism, its political theory, has been hugely influential in the broader evangelical movement, thanks in part to Robertson.

As the historian Garry Wills has noted, Robertson recycles dominionist ideas in his writing. "Entrepreneurial evangelicals are always edgy about the competition," Wills wrote. "But one clearly derivative aspect of Robertson's book [*The Secret Kingdom*] is his view of 'dominion.' . . . 'Dominion theologians,' as they are called, lay great emphasis on Genesis 1:26–27, where God tells Adam to assume dominion over the animate and inanimate world. When man fell, his control over creation was forfeited; but the saved, who are restored by baptism, can claim again the rights given Adam. Thus the true inheritors and custodians of this world are Christians who can 'name it and claim it' by divine right."[13]

Some Christian nationalists, including Ralph Reed, the Christian Coalition's telegenic former executive director, have thought it wise to publicly disavow Christian Reconstructionism. Robertson has had fewer qualms, though he disputes aspects of the theology. He hosted the leaders of the Reconstructionist movement on his television show, *The 700 Club*, and their work has been required reading for some classes at his school, Regent University.[14]

Far more important than Robertson's embrace of dominionist rhetoric (or Reed's rejection of it), however, is the way the Christian Coalition put it into practice.

Reconstructionist theory calls for a stealth strategy to Christianize politics and culture. In a 1981 article from *The Journal of Christian Reconstruction*, Gary North, one of the movement's key theorists, wrote of the need for activists to penetrate secular institutions to "smooth the transition to Christian political leadership. . . . Christians must begin to organize politically within the present party structure, and they must begin to infiltrate the existing institutional order."[15]

The Christian Coalition specialized in this kind of dispersed political warfare. While the Moral Majority had focused on direct mail and large rallies, the Christian Coalition trained activists and candidates on the local level. They ran in school board races and learned how to become Republican delegates. Crucially, Christian Coalition manuals urged candidates to keep their religious agenda quiet until after they were elected. Supporters would learn who the local Christian Coalition candidates were through voter guides distributed at evangelical churches, but the general public was often in the dark. " I want to be invisible," Ralph Reed told the *Norfolk Virginian-Pilot* in 1991. "I paint my face and travel at night. You don't know it's over until you're in a body bag. You don't know until election night."

The Christian Coalition's grassroots, under-the-radar strategy was hugely effective, so that by 1992 religious activists had more influence in writing the GOP's platform than the party's presidential candidate,

George H. W. Bush. Nearly half the delegates at the 1992 party convention were evangelical Christians, and despite Bush's objections, they succeeded in getting a plank in the platform calling for a constitutional amendment to ban abortion without exception.

The Christian Coalition has been in serious decline since the late 1990s. Ralph Reed left in 1997 to become a political consultant (and, in 2006, a candidate for lieutenant governor of Georgia). In 1999 the group lost its nonprofit status for violating Federal Election Commission rules on partisan politicking. According to the liberal group People for the American Way, contributions to the Christian Coalition dropped from $26.5 million in 1996 to an estimated $3 million in 2000. Robertson stepped down as president in 2001, saying he wanted to devote more attention to his ministry.

Yet even as the Christian Coalition atrophied, other organizations proliferated and the Christian nationalist movement expanded. Most significantly, James Dobson, the evangelical psychologist at the head of Focus on the Family, grew increasingly visible in partisan politics. Dobson has been active in public life and conservative causes since the 1970s, but until the last decade he was best known for his advice on child rearing and Christian family life, dispensed in best-selling books like *Dare to Discipline* and on widely heard radio programs.

In the 1990s, Dobson leapt into the political fray to fight gay rights, getting heavily involved in the campaign for Amendment 2, a Colorado ballot initiative to overturn laws banning discrimination against gay people. As the Southern Poverty Law Center reported, "When Dobson began pushing Amendment 2, its organizers had been struggling to get enough signatures to qualify for the ballot. Overnight, the campaign was flooded with volunteers and money. Amendment 2 won by a 53%–47% margin."

By 2004, Dobson was so inflamed by the specter of gay marriage and other ostensible threats to the American family that he cast aside his former pretense of partisan neutrality for good. He started a separate organization, Focus on the Family Action, devoted to political combat, and campaigned ardently for Bush's reelection.

Dobson is as influential as Falwell or Robertson ever was, but it would be incorrect to say he replaced either of them. Rather than concentrate its energies in a single group, the Christian nationalist movement has developed multiple power centers, creating a potent combination of organization and diffusion. Its center of gravity shifts constantly, and coalitions are forever forming and dissolving. There are no indispensable leaders. Any of the movement's figureheads or political allies could fall tomorrow and Christian nationalism would thrive undiminished.

The movement's decentralized, overlapping organizations focus on multiple issues simultaneously. They act as both a goad and an auxiliary to the Republican party and create an echo chamber that turns outlandish claims into conventional wisdom for large parts of the country.

George W. Bush has brought Christian nationalism into the government in an unprecedented way. High-profile appointees like the stridently religious former attorney general John Ashcroft have gotten lots of attention, but in some ways Bush's obscure appointments are more significant. Veterans of the Christian nationalist movement occupy positions throughout the federal bureaucracy, making crucial decisions about our national life according to their theology. This is part of the reason for the terrifying chasm between the evidence of science and history, and some of the passionately averred declarations of our government.

There is no way to know how much Bush really shares the Christian worldview, although he gives every indication of believing that God personally installed him in the White House. But whatever his beliefs, much of the movement is convinced he's one of them. Christian nationalist books and videos celebrate the president's piety; David W. Balsiger, a former member of the Council for National Policy, produced and directed a seventy-minute hagiography, *George W. Bush: Faith in the White House*, telling the story of Bush's midlife transformation from hard-drinking hellion to righteous Christian leader.[16] (A pivotal moment in his conversion was a 1984 Midland, Texas, meeting with a roving evangelist named Arthur Blessitt, who has carried a twelve-foot crucifix around the world, winning both souls to Christ and a citation in the Guinness Books of Records for "World's Longest Walk.") By all accounts, the Bush White House is saturated with evangelical Christianity: "Nobody spends more time on his knees than George W. Bush," said one BBC reporter. The president's public statements teem with evangelical references, thanks in part to speechwriter Michael Gerson, a former theology student who once worked for Charles Colson, the born-again Watergate felon who became an evangelical celebrity after emerging from prison and founding Prison Fellowship Ministries.

Bush clearly has faith in the wonder-working power of a devoted base. He has given the Christian nationalist movement government authority and access to billions of taxpayer dollars. The movement, in turn, ensured his reelection, along with a strengthened Republican majority in Congress.

Yet the Christian nationalists are neither sated nor complacent. Indeed, one of the most striking things about the movement is that, for all its influence, its cries of oppression have increased during the last few years, and its demands for dominion have become more insistent. It has become common for Christian nationalist leaders and the Republican politicians they support to speak of any attempts to defend church/state separation as part of a "war" on believers.

In the spring of 2005, there was a scandal at the Air Force Academy in Colorado Springs, just across the interstate from Focus on the Family's headquarters. According to numerous reports, a climate of Christian nationalism saturated the academy, occasionally leading to outright religious bigotry. Students who refused to attend chapel during basic cadet training were marched back to their dormitories in what was called a "heathen flight." Some faculty members introduced themselves to their classes as born-again Christians and encouraged their charges to find Jesus. There were numerous reports of upperclassmen using their authority over undergraduates to proselytize and insult those who wouldn't convert; one Jewish cadet was slurred as a Christ killer.[17]

The Christian nationalist response to the situation was telling. Almost immediately, the movement's leaders declared evangelical Christians the victims. When Democratic Congressman David Obey proposed an amendment to a defense appropriations bill calling for an investigation into religious bias at the academy, Republican John Hostettler stood up on the House floor and said, "The long war on Christianity in America continues today on the floor of the House of Representatives," later adding, "Democrats can't help denigrating and demonizing Christians."

A week later, James Dobson hosted Hostettler on his radio show. Dobson began the segment by announcing, "Liberal forces in this country want to squelch the freedoms of evangelical Christians throughout the culture, but now it's popped up at the Air Force Academy." He praised Hostettler for having "the courage to stand up and be counted."

Hostettler then declared, "I am just sick and tired of the moniker of evangelical Christian being equated to an epithet, and that is why I could not hold my tongue on the floor of the House."

The refrain that Christians are under siege creates a sense of perpetual crisis among the movement's grass roots. Talk of persecution is common. I've heard well-spoken, kind believers—people who say they long for empathy and understanding to replace the harsh divisiveness in America—worry that one day in the future, the American government might start rounding up Christians and executing them.

"Take missionaries—many have been killed," said Wayne Markegard, a fifty-six-year-old U.S. Department of Agriculture employee from North Dakota. "They're killing them every day because of their faith. Ultimately they're dying for their faith." Someday, he feared, the same thing will happen in America.

"I think it will," he said. "The events that we're seeing, I can't say for sure, but when you start spinning and keep spinning in this direction, unless God intervenes—and God will intervene someday, that's been written—but ultimately mankind will get to that point."

Just look, he said, at what's happening in Canada, where "a pastor who reads from the Bible regarding scriptures that talk about homosexuality can go to jail. That's the first step or the second or third step that ultimately leads to worse."

I met Markegard and his forty-eight-year-old brother, David, on a Saturday tour of Focus on the Family's headquarters. Wayne was visiting David, who lives in Colorado, and they were spending the day sightseeing. After Focus on the Family, they were heading to the Air Force Academy.

Dobson's lair, a sprawling brick office park on manicured grounds, is a big tourist draw in Colorado Springs, with its own sign on the highway and its own zip code. According to the Focus on the Family Web site, the campus has seen more than a million visitors since the 1994 opening of its welcome center, an airy space filled with exhibits paying tribute to the Dobson clan and the GOP. When I visited, framed photos of George W. Bush with James Dobson and his wife, Shirley, hung near a wall-mounted video monitor playing a constant loop of one of the president's National Day of Prayer speeches. A framed letter from Bush thanked Dobson for his support of the administration's stem cell policy and for "the leadership you bring to efforts to refocus the Nation on values and morality."

In a nearby alcove was a life-size statue of James Dobson's father, a traveling evangelist, kneeling in prayer. Displayed on the wall was the crimson coat Dobson *père* liked to wear on Christmas.

There were about fifteen of us on the free tour, including a homeschooling family on vacation together before the teenage son left for army boot camp. Our perky blonde tour guide asked us all to introduce ourselves—I said I was there researching a book—before taking us through the administration building. She showed us the warren of putty-colored cubicles where counselors compose answers to the thousands of letters Focus receives each day; we saw the "chapelteria," a teal-carpeted auditorium that combines a worship area and a commissary. In one of the building's hallways, our guide pointed out mounted maps with pins marking locales in thirty different countries where Focus on the Family broadcasts are heard.

We saw the well-appointed radio broadcast studio, filled with plants and bookshelves and set in front of rows of stadium seating for a live audience, as well as a smaller room set up for satellite feeds, allowing Dobson to appear as a talking head on live TV without leaving the grounds.

The tour took about an hour, and when it was finished, David Markegard approached me in the building's foyer. He was curious about my book, and we started talking about the cultural divide between the coasts and the interior, about the role of Christianity in government, and about the struggles he and his brother see in the families around them. Both brothers spoke of wanting Americans to come together, to respect one another despite their religious and political differences, to end the acrimony that makes the public atmosphere so toxic. I agreed with them, and as we stood talking in the almost empty building, I began to wonder whether I had overestimated the gap between my reality and the one inhabited by Dobson's followers.

Wayne Markegard, a grandfather with a soft, flat Midwestern voice, praised Dobson not as a politician, but as a trusted counselor. "I think people are looking for answers to a lot of the questions life brings us," he said. "As we go through life, we find there are a lot of things that we don't understand, that don't make sense, and this ministry and this organization help people find answers. They talk about someone committing suicide, or some gal who's going to have a baby and doesn't know what to do about it."

He believes that Americans are suffering from a kind of materialistic malaise. The question, he said, is "What is it that I want out of life? Do I want a nice house, do I want all these nice things, or do I want my children to inherit all the wisdom that I have, and be able to use that as they go on to experience life on their own?"

That seemed to me an important thing for people to ask themselves.

But for the Markegard brothers, the answers were bound up with a restoration of public faith, as if through asserting Christianity, the anxieties and disappointments of American life would be replaced by transcendent certainties. They longed for a Christian community, not as a subculture, but as *the* culture.

David, indignant, mentioned attempts to ban nativity scenes from public squares. "I firmly believe that we'll be a minority," added Wayne. By "we," he meant Christians. "There is a battle going on," he said. "There always will be. We as Christians have to recognize that there is a force that's working in this world—the god of this world is working to destroy Christianity. So we have to always be wary."

On a personal level, many of the people involved in the Christian nationalist movement are as thoughtful and amiable as Wayne and David Markegard. Researching *Kingdom Coming* took me all over America—from the lush and febrile deep South to the surreally homogeneous exurbs on the edges of Midwestern cities; from Washington, D.C., to Austin, Texas, and almost a dozen states in between. Nearly everywhere I went, I was treated with remarkable openness and hospitality, even by those who knew how much our politics differed. I'm a secular Jew and an ardent urbanite, and I started this book in part because I was terrified by America's increasing hostility to the cosmopolitan values I cherish. Traveling the country and talking to people about their beliefs, I was quiet about my own, but I told the truth when I was asked. While many Christian conservatives tried to convert me, very few attacked me. Instead, in some of America's reddest corners, at churches, rallies, and conferences, I met many people eager to engage in passionate discussion about the meaning of life, and about how we understand morality and reality. I saw the searching spirit that motivates many who find their way to the movement, their existential longings, and craving for a place in the world.

Sometimes it's hard to reconcile this benignancy with the violence of the movement's rhetoric. It's tempting to think that all the talk of war, of taking the land, subduing God's enemies and building the Christian nation, is just harmless hyperbole. But it is wrong, I think, to assume that people must not mean what they say just because they're friendly.

Before I began this book, I did some reporting in the Middle East. There, too, I was usually received warmly and treated with humbling generosity. It would be a mistake to conclude from that, however, that the region's antipathy toward Jews and Americans is not real and dangerous. In my experience, people are often kinder than their ideologies, and always more complicated. Yet individual decency can dissolve when groups are mobilized against diabolized enemies, especially when they believe they're under attack.

America is full of good people, but something dark is loose. There's a free-floating anxiety that easily metastasizes into paranoia and hatred for the same enemies always targeted by authoritarian populist movements—homosexuals, urbanites, foreigners, intellectuals, and religious minorities. Rationality is losing its hold; empirical evidence is discounted as the product of a secular worldview or a scheming liberal elite.

In such an atmosphere, most mainstream sources of information are assumed to be deceptive, so many people find ascertaining the true state of things very difficult. Thus trusted authorities—preachers, politicians, radio demagogues—hold enormous sway. All truth except biblical truth becomes relative, and biblical truth is entwined with American history and national destiny. Democracy suffocates in this atmosphere, and space opens up for something else to supplant it. In her 1951 masterpiece *The Origins of Totalitarianism*, Hannah Arendt wrote, "Before they seize power and establish a world according to their doctrines, totalitarian movements conjure up a lying world of consistency which is more adequate to the needs of the human mind than reality itself. . . . The force possessed by totalitarian propaganda—before the movements have the power to drop iron curtains to prevent anyone's disturbing, by the slightest reality, the gruesome quiet of an entirely imaginary world—lies in its ability to shut the masses off from the real world."[18]

I am not arguing that America is on the cusp of religious totalitarianism. Yet there are totalitarian elements in the Christian nationalist movement, particularly its attacks on decadent internal enemies and its drive to replace society's apprehension of reality with its parallel version. As Christian nationalism gains influence, it is changing our country in troubling ways, and its leaders say they've only just begun. It is up to all Americans to decide how far they can go.

CHAPTER 1

This Is a Christian Nation

A teenage modern dance troupe dressed all in black took their places on the stage of the First Baptist Church of Pleasant Grove, a suburb of Birmingham, Alabama. Two dancers, donning black overcoats, crossed their arms menacingly. As a Christian pop ballad swelled on the speakers, a boy wearing judicial robes walked out. Holding a Ten Commandments tablet that seemed to be made of cardboard, he was playing former Alabama Supreme Court justice Roy Moore. The trench-coated thugs approached him, miming a violent rebuke and forcing him to the other end of the stage, sans Commandments.

There, a cluster of dancers impersonating liberal activists waved signs with slogans like "No Moore!" and "Keep God *Out*!! *No* God in Court." The boy Moore danced a harangue, first lurching toward his tormentors and then cringing back in outrage before breaking through their line to lunge for his monument. But the dancers in trench coats—agents of atheism—got hold of it first and took it away, leaving him abject on the floor. As the song's uplifting chorus played—"After you've done all you can, you just stand"—a dancer in a white robe, playing either an angel or God himself, came forward and helped the Moore character to his feet.

The performance ended to enthusiastic applause from a crowd that included many Alabama judges and politicians, as well as Roy Moore himself, a gaunt man with a courtly manner and the wrath of Leviticus in his eyes. Moore has become a hero to those determined to remake the

United States into an explicitly Christian nation. That reconstructionist dream lies at the red-hot center of our current culture wars, investing the symbolic fight over the Ten Commandments—a fight whose outcome seems irrelevant to most peoples' lives—with an apocalyptic urgency.

On November 13, 2003, Moore was removed from his position as chief justice of the Alabama Supreme Court after he defied a judge's order to remove the 2.6-ton Ten Commandments monument he'd installed in the Montgomery judicial building. On the coasts, he seemed a ridiculous figure, the latest in a line of grotesque Southern anachronisms. After all, Moore is a man who, in a 2002 court decision awarding custody of three children to their allegedly abusive father over their lesbian mother, called homosexuality "abhorrent, immoral, detestable, a crime against nature, and a violation of the laws of nature and of nature's God upon which this Nation and our laws are predicated," and argued, "The State carries the power of the sword, that is, the power to prohibit conduct with physical penalties, such as confinement and even execution. It must use that power to prevent the subversion of children toward this lifestyle, to not encourage a criminal lifestyle."[1] He's a man who writes rhyming poetry decrying the teaching of evolution and who fought against the Alabama ballot measure to remove segregationist language from the state constitution.

To the growing Christian nationalist movement, though, Roy Moore is a martyr, cut down by secular tyranny for daring to assert God's truth.

It's a role he seems to love. The battle that cost Moore his job wasn't his first Ten Commandments fight. In 1995, the ACLU sued Moore, then a county circuit judge, for hanging a Ten Commandments plaque in his courtroom and leading juries in prayer. As Matt Labash recalled in an adulatory *Weekly Standard* article, "The conflict's natural drama was compounded when the governor, Fob James, announced that he would deploy the National Guard, state troopers, and the Alabama and Auburn football teams to keep Moore's tablets on the wall."[2]

That case reached an ambiguous conclusion in 1998, when the state supreme court threw out the lawsuit on technical grounds. By then, Moore had become a star of the right. Televangelist D. James Kennedy's Coral Ridge Ministries raised more than $100,000 for his legal defense fund, and Moore spoke at a series of rallies that drew thousands. His right-wing fame helped catapult him to victory in the 2000 race for chief justice of the state supreme court.

Moore installed his massive Ten Commandments monument on August 1, 2001, and from the beginning, he and his allies used it to stir up the Christian nationalist faithful. He gave videographers from Coral Ridge Ministries exclusive access to the courthouse on the night the monument was mounted, and on October 14, D. James Kennedy started hawking a $19 video about Moore's brave, covert installation on his television show.

As the controversy over the statue ignited, Moore's fame grew. At rallies across the country, he summoned the faithful to an ideal that sounded very much like theocracy. "For forty years we have wandered like the children of Israel," he told a crowd of three thousand supporters in Tennessee. "In homes and schools across our land, it's time for Christians to take a stand. This is not a nation established on the principles of Buddha or Hinduism. Our faith is not Islam. What we follow is not the Koran but the Bible. This is a Christian nation."[3]

By the time he was removed as chief justice, Moore had sparked a movement, and his monument was an icon. In the days before officials came to cart the Commandments away, hundreds flocked to Montgomery to rally on the courtroom steps. Some slept there and imagined themselves the nucleus of a new civil rights movement.

Thomas Bowman, a bearded Christian folk singer from Kentucky who wears a knit Rasta hat, wrote an anthem called "Montgomery Fire" celebrating the demonstrations: "We had love in our hearts that no man could ever remove / but with the whole world we watched as they hauled the Commandments away." When I met him a year later at First Baptist, he referred to the protesters, romantically, as the "ragamuffin warriors" fighting for God against the atheist state. During the controversy, he said, he'd felt the Lord's call, and driven six and a half hours from Louisville. In Montgomery, he met others like him, who'd felt compelled to take a stand against secularism.

"The opposing side, the anti-God side, the do-whatever-you-want side, the judicial side, just kept pushing and pushing and pushing for the last forty years," Bowman said. "They keep moving that line back." Finally, he said, God called on Christians to defend themselves.

After the Commandments were removed, a group of retired military men from Texas who called themselves American Veterans in Domestic Defense spent months taking the monument—now affectionately called "Roy's Rock"—on tour all over the country, holding more than 150 viewings and rallies in churches, at state capitols, even in Wal-Mart parking lots. Moore also found powerful supporters in statehouses and in Congress who proposed laws to radically restrict the power of federal courts to enforce the separation of church and state. In solidarity, another Alabama judge, Ashley McKathan, had the Ten Commandments embroidered onto his robe. Christian homeschool catalogues offered copies of a video titled *Roy Moore's Message to America*. When Moore suggested he might run for Alabama governor, state polls showed him with a double-digit lead.

One Nation Under Jesus

Moore's message—that biblical injunctions are more binding than secular law—is one with a growing currency in this country. As the 2004 Texas Republican party platform said, "The Republican Party of Texas affirms that the United States of America is a Christian nation, and the public acknowledgement of God is undeniable in our history. Our nation was founded on fundamental Judeo-Christian principles based on the Holy Bible." The Texas GOP incubated many of our country's most powerful leaders and political operatives, including George W. Bush, Karl Rove, Tom DeLay, and Alberto Gonzales.

The Christian nation is both the goal of the religious right and its fundamental ideology, the justification for its attempt to overthrow the doctrine of separation of church and state. It's what divides the religious right from those who see America as a product of Enlightenment secularism. The church/state legal developments that liberals and secularists think of as progress—from the disestablishment of religion in the states to bans on school prayer and classroom Bible reading—strike the evangelical right as a tyrannical suppression of America's Christian character. They see the forces of secularism as internal enemies who must be defeated so that they can declare, in the words of former attorney general John Ashcroft, that America has no king but Jesus.

The fight between secular modernity and religious authority is an old one, and it has raged with varying intensity throughout the country's history. Right now, however, is high tide for theocratic fervor. Ultra-conservative churches are expanding so fast many can barely find space to contain all their worshippers, while many moderate, mainline congregations are withering.[4] There's an inchoate sense of crisis in parts of the country, a fierce longing for national renewal coupled with a rejection of pluralism. In January 2005, the research group Public Agenda released findings of its latest survey about religion in public life: compared with four years ago, it found "a smaller number of Americans who believe that deeply religious elected officials sometimes have to compromise in the political arena, with major decreases among those who attend religious services weekly." The majority of evangelicals disagreed with the statement that, on social issues like gay rights and abortion, religious politicians "should be willing to compromise with others whose views are different."

Growing numbers of right-wing Christians are learning, in their churches, private schools, home schools—and even a few public schools—that religious pluralism itself is nothing more than a plot cooked up by devious liberals to undermine America. Rick Scarborough, a high-profile Texas pastor and close ally of Tom DeLay, has published a monograph titled *In Defense of . . . Mixing Church and State*. In it, he claims that separation of church and state is "a lie introduced by Satan and fostered by the courts. Unfortunately, it is embraced by the American public to our shame and disgrace, and that lie has led us to the edge of the abyss."[5]

Thus the struggle over a granite rock in Alabama—and other Ten

Commandments statues and plaques nationwide—has taken on the intensity of a crusade for the soul of America. Scarborough has gone so far as to call Roy Moore the victim of a "crucifixion." Presumably, that makes the federal courts executioners.

The feverish rhetoric only increased after two 2005 Supreme Court decisions on Ten Commandments cases. The pair of 5–4 rulings dealt with a Ten Commandments monument erected on the grounds of the Austin statehouse in 1961 and with framed copies of the Commandments put up in Kentucky court houses in 1999. The court ruled the Texas monument permissible but the Kentucky Commandments unconstitutional, reasoning that one was part of a historical display, the other an attempt to promote a religious message.

There was something in the ruling to displease both sides, but the rage on the right eclipsed any protests from the left. The day after the decision, the Family Research Council, the D.C. spin-off of James Dobson's Focus on the Family, sent out an e-mail inviting a group of pastors to participate in an "urgent conference call." Preachers from all over the country called in, and Family Research Council President Tony Perkins told them, "It's no longer a question of whether or not we'll join the fight, because they have brought the fight to us. . . . This is a direct attack on Christianity in this country and we must respond."

Because this is a war over semiotics, it's tempting to dismiss its significance. Why worry about what Roy Moore puts in his courtroom while George Bush shreds the safety net and war rages in the Middle East? Aren't the symbolic prizes Republicans give to their base trivial compared to the billion-dollar ones their cronies get?

In his influential book *What's the Matter with Kansas?*, Thomas Frank described culture war skirmishes like that over Moore's monument as part of the bait and switch the corporate right pulls on its benighted Christian foot soldiers. "The leaders of the backlash may talk Christ, but they walk corporate. Values may 'matter most' to voters, but they always take a backseat to the needs of money once the elections are won," Frank wrote. "Abortion is never halted. Affirmative action is never abolished. The culture industry is never forced to clean up its act."[6]

Frank was right about many things, but he underestimated the successes that Christian nationalists have had—and continue to have—in transforming America. Besides stripping gay people of hard-won rights and science of its authority, the religious right has secured hundreds of millions of dollars in government grants for itself, thanks to Bush's faith-based initiative. Cultural conservatives have succeeded in making abortion unavailable in much of the country and are moving ever closer to their dream of outlawing it altogether. Bush has filled the federal bench and national bureaucracy with judges and officials who think very much like Roy Moore.

None of these right-wing triumphs would be possible without the ideology of the Christian nation. Large segments of the American public are convinced that separation of church and state is a myth, and they see the posting of the Ten Commandments as an affirmation of that conviction. Secularists could decide simply to let them have their plaques and statues, since battles over religious imagery only help the right rally its troops. Whenever the principle of separation is breached, though, it makes it that much harder to hold the line against the rest of the Christian nationalist agenda.

Several times in our history, apparently innocuous references to God have been injected into public life during national crises, only to be used later to legitimate further erosions of church/state separation. "It is not true that the founders designed a Christian commonwealth, which was then eroded by secular humanists and liberals; the reverse is true," historians Isaac Kramnick and R. Laurence Moore write in their 1996 book *The Godless Constitution*. "The framers erected a godless federal constitutional structure, which was then undermined as God entered first the U.S. currency in 1863, then the federal mail service in 1912, and finally the Pledge of Allegiance in 1954."[7] Advocates of the Christian nation, in turn, often cite these precedents to argue that America has no true legacy of secularism.

One of the most crucial current questions for progressives is how to preserve that embattled legacy without further alienating their over-whelmingly pious fellow citizens. The stakes are high. Those who aren't Christian—or who aren't the right kind of Christian—can never be full citizens of the country the Christian nationalists want to create. The birth of the Christian nation means the destruction of the pluralist beacon that inspires the often anguished love of liberal patriots. America is not yet close to becoming a theocracy, but it is in danger of turning into a place where only conservative Christians really belong.

The Ten Commandments, after all, are not ecumenical rules for living. While some of them, like, "Thou shalt not kill," are part of every religious system, four others are sectarian injunctions against worshipping other gods, working on the Sabbath, and taking God's name in vain. The second commandment (at least in the Protestant version, which differs from the Hebrew and Catholic version) forbids depictions of living things: "Thou shalt not make unto thee any graven image, or any likeness *of any thing* that *is* in heaven above, or that *is* in the earth beneath, or that *is* in the water under the earth. Thou shalt not bow down thyself to them, nor serve them: for I the Lord thy God *am* a jealous God, visiting the iniquity of the fathers upon the children unto the third and fourth *generation* of them that hate me; and shewing mercy unto thousands of them that love me, and keep my commandments."

There is a similar prohibition on graven images in Islamic law. The Taliban enforced it, which is why they banned movies and dynamited the ancient Buddha statues in Bamiyan province. I asked a man at a Ten Commandments rally in Texas what it would mean to enforce the Second Commandment in America—would it also require the end of cinema? "That's a good question," he replied.

Most American evangelicals don't want to establish a Christian Taliban, but their version of tolerance is often very different from the secular equality most liberals see as America's heritage. At best, leaders of the religious right tend to envision a nation where non-Christians can worship as they please but where Christianity is privileged. In 2000, when

Venkatachalapathi Samuldrala became the first Hindu priest to offer an invocation before Congress, the Family Research Council issued the following apoplectic statement:

> While it is true that the United States of America was founded on the sacred principle of religious freedom for all, that liberty was never intended to exalt other religions to the level that Christianity holds in our country's heritage. . . . Our Founders expected that Christianity—and no other religion—would receive support from the government as long as that support did not violate peoples' consciences and their right to worship. They would have found utterly incredible the idea that all religions, including paganism, be treated with equal deference.

In fact, Thomas Jefferson likely would have found this statement itself incredible. After all, his famous 1786 statute establishing religious freedom in Virginia is widely considered to be the inspiration for the First Amendment. In his autobiography, he wrote that an amendment to the statute referring to Jesus Christ as the source of religious liberty was "rejected by the great majority, in proof that they meant to comprehend, within the mantle of its protection, the Jew and the Gentile, the Christian and Mohammedan, the Hindoo and Infidel of every denomination."

Nevertheless, the Family Research Council needn't have worried—in America, all religions certainly aren't treated with equal deference. Thanks to Bush's faith-based programs, the government now funds a number of social service agencies that hire only Christians. In conservative states, government officials regularly disparage non-Christians. At the Alabama rally, State Senator Hank Irwin boomed, "The Ten Commandments remind us that there is a God, that he is real. That we do not have a nation or any kind of a world that's built on secular whatever-you-want-to-believe Jell-O. . . . [T]here is a God and he has made himself known, and I will say this to you, his name is not Allah, his name is not Wicca, his name is the Lord God of the Bible."

Such talk isn't reserved for obscure provincials—the president himself speaks the language of Christian nationalism, although much more mildly than Irwin. In January 2005 Bush told the *Washington Times* that, while religious freedom is essential to America, "On the other hand, I don't see how you can be president, at least from my perspective, how you can be president, without a relationship with the Lord."[8] A personal "relationship with the Lord," of course, is a central tenet of evangelical Christianity, although not of many other faiths. Assuming he meant what he said, the president's statement implies that only evangelicals are qualified for his job.

Unfortunately, Bush wasn't asked whether there should be a similar religious prerequisite for any other public positions. But evangelical Christianity certainly seems to help people fit in in Bush's administration. As David Frum, Bush's former speechwriter, wrote in his book *The Right Man*, the first words he heard in the Bush White House were "Missed you at Bible study." Frum, who is Jewish, continued a few paragraphs later, "The news that this was a White House where attendance at Bible study was, if not compulsory, not quite *uncompulsory*, either, was disconcerting to a non-Christian like me."[9]

Our government is becoming more and more like a born-again ministry. The very fact that Bush tends to speak in evangelical code, using phrases that initiates recognize as references to biblical verses, is a sign that in his America, religious insiders are privileged.

So far, these are small insults, little diminutions. Still, as Christian nationalists assert their right to rule, a deep anxiety stalks the country's more cosmopolitan corners. There are intimations of religious authoritarianism, but because they're only intimations, they're hard to discuss without sounding shrill and hyperbolic.

A few days before Bush's second inauguration, *The New York Times* carried a story headlined "Warning from a Student of Democracy's Collapse" about Fritz Stern, a refugee from Nazi Germany, professor emeritus of history at Columbia, and scholar of fascism. It quoted a speech he had given in Germany that drew parallels between Nazism and the American religious right. "Some people recognized the moral perils of mixing religion and politics," he was quoted saying of prewar Germany, "but many more were seduced by it. It was the pseudo-religious transfiguration of politics that largely ensured [Hitler's] success, notably in Protestant areas."

It's not surprising that Stern is alarmed. Reading his forty-five-year-old book *The Politics of Cultural Despair: A Study in the Rise of the Germanic Ideology*, I shivered at its contemporary resonance. "The ideologists of the conservative revolution superimposed a vision of national redemption upon their dissatisfaction with liberal culture and with the loss of authoritative faith," he wrote in the introduction. "They posed as the true champions of nationalism, and berated the socialists for their internationalism, and the liberals for their pacifism and their indifference to national greatness."[10]

Fascism isn't imminent in America. But its language and aesthetics are distressingly common among Christian nationalists. History professor Roger Griffin described the "mobilizing vision" of fascist movements as "*the national community rising Phoenix-like after a period of encroaching decadence which all but destroyed it*" (his italics).[11] The Ten Commandments has become a potent symbol of this dreamed-for resurrection on the American right.

True, our homegrown quasi-fascists often appear so absurd as to seem harmless. Take, for example, American Veterans in Domestic Defense, the organization that took the Ten Commandments on tour. The group says it exists to "neutralize the destructiveness" of America's "domestic enemies," which include "biased liberal, socialist news media," "the ACLU," and "the conspiracy of an immoral film industry."

To do this, it aims to recruit former military men. "AVIDD reminds all American Veterans that you took an oath to defend the United States against all enemies, 'both foreign and domestic,'" its Web site says. "In your military capacity, you were called upon to defend the United States against foreign enemies. AVIDD now calls upon you to continue to fulfill your oath and help us defend this nation on the political front, against equally dangerous domestic enemies."

According to Jim Cabaniss, the seventy-two-year-old Korean War veteran who founded AVIDD, the group now has thirty-three chapters across the country. It's entirely likely that some of these chapters just represent one or two men, and as of 2005, AVIDD didn't seem large enough to be much of a danger to anyone.

Still, it's worth noting that thousands of Americans nationwide have flocked to rallies at which military men don uniforms and pledge to seize the reigns of power in America on behalf of Christianity. In many places, local religious leaders and politicians lend their support to AVIDD's cause. And at least some of the people at these rallies speak with seething resentment about the tyranny of Jews over America's Christian majority.

"People who call themselves Jews represent maybe 2 or 3 percent of our people," Cabaniss told me after a January 2005 rally in Austin. "Christians represent a huge percent, and we don't believe that a small percentage should destroy the values of the larger percentage."

I asked Cabaniss, a thin, white-haired man who wore a suit with a red, white, and blue tie and a U.S. Army baseball cap, whether he was saying that American Jews have too much power. "It appears that way," he replied. "They're a driving force behind trying to take everything to do with Christianity out of our system. That's the part that makes us *very* upset."

Ed Hamilton, who'd come to the rally from San Antonio, interjected, "There are very wealthy Jews in high places, and they have significant control over a lot of financial matters and some political matters. They have a disproportionate amount of influence in our financial structure."

We were standing outside the Texas Capitol building on a sunny Saturday morning. A few hundred people from across the state had turned out for the rally, which began at 10 A.M. Three or four men in military uniforms sat with their wives on chairs at the top of the Capitol steps. Next to them sat an old man dressed as Uncle Sam in a tall Stars and Stripes top hat, a red, white, and blue suit, and a pointy white beard. Four other men supported tall, coffin-shaped signs labeled with the names of objectionable Supreme Court rulings.

The crowd was full of teenagers who'd come on church buses and families with young children. A white-bearded man in a leather biker vest dragged a ten-foot-tall cedar crucifix painted red, white, and blue. One woman wore a T-shirt with a photograph of Moore's monument. Another held a handwritten sign saying:

Ban Judges
<u>Not</u> God
God Rules

Rick Scarborough, one of the headline speakers, called for a "million Roy Moores" who will "stand up, speak up, and refuse to give up." A former football player at Stephen F. Austin State University, Scarborough is a thick man with white hair, black eyebrows, and a surprisingly high voice. In recent years, he's positioned himself as a comer in the Christian nationalist movement, riding church/state controversies to ever higher prominence. In 2002, he left his post as pastor of Pearland First Baptist Church—where he had mobilized members of his flock in that Houston suburb to try to take over the city council and school board—to form Vision America, a group dedicated to organizing "patriot pastors" for political action. The same year, Jerry Falwell christened him as one of the new leaders of the Christian right. The courts that martyred Moore are Scarborough's bête noire, and as 2005 progressed, he emerged as one of most vehement right-wing denunciators of the federal judiciary.

Also speaking was John Eidsmoe, a retired lieutenant colonel in the Air Force who wore full military dress. A professor at Thomas Goode Jones School of Law, a Christian school in Montgomery, Alabama, Eidsmoe has authored a number of Christian nationalist books including *Christianity and the Constitution: The Faith of Our Founding Fathers*, which argues that Calvinism inspired America's founding document. He's a proponent of a Confederate doctrine called interposition, which holds that states have the right to reject federal government mandates they deem unconstitutional. "Implementation of the doctrine may be peaceable, as by resolution, remonstrance or legislation, or may proceed ultimately to nullification with forcible resistance," he wrote in a manifesto titled "A Call to Stand with Chief Justice Roy Moore."

When the speeches were finished, the four black-coffin signs were knocked down and four white doves were released from behind them, to awed gasps and cheers from the crowd. Moore's monument sat on the back of a flatbed truck parked several yards away. An American flag flew on one side. On the other was a flag with a fierce-looking eagle perched upon a bloody cross.

The Rise of Dominionism

Roy Moore and Rick Scarborough are Baptists, D. James Kennedy is a fundamentalist Presbyterian, and John Eidsmoe is a Lutheran. All of them, however, have been shaped by dominion theology, which asserts that, in preparation for the second coming of Christ, godly men have the responsibly to take over every aspect of society.

Dominion theology comes out of Christian Reconstructionism, a fundamentalist creed that was propagated by the late Rousas John (R. J.) Rushdoony and his son-in-law, Gary North. Born in New York City in 1916 to Armenian immigrants who had recently fled the genocide in Turkey, Rushdoony was educated at the University of California at Berkeley and spent over eight years as a Presbyterian missionary to Native Americans in Nevada. He was a prolific writer, churning out dense tomes advocating the abolition of public schools and social services and the replacement of civil law with biblical law. White-bearded and wizardly, Rushdoony had the look of an Old Testament patriarch and the harsh vision to match—he called for the death penalty for gay people, blasphemers, and unchaste women, among other sinners.*

---

* One of the most telling (and amusing) anecdotes about the Reconstructionists' view of justice appeared in the libertarian magazine *Reason* in 1998: "For connoisseurs of surrealism on the American right, it's hard to beat an exchange that appeared about a decade ago in the Heritage Foundation magazine *Policy Review*. It started when two associates of the Rev. Jerry Falwell wrote an article which criticized Christian Reconstructionism, the influential movement led by theologian Rousas John (R. J.) Rushdoony, for advocating positions that even they as commit-

Democracy, he wrote, is a heresy and "the great love of the failures and cowards of life."[12]

Reconstructionism is a postmillennial theology, meaning its followers believe Jesus won't return until after Christians establish a thousand-year reign on earth. While other Christians wait for the messiah, Reconstructionists want to build the kingdom themselves. Most American evangelicals, on the other hand, are premillenialists. They believe (with some variations) that at the time of Christ's return, Christians will be gathered up to heaven, missing the tribulations endured by unbelievers. In the past, this belief led to a certain apathy—why worry if the world is about to end and you'll be safe from the carnage?

Since the 1970s, though, in tandem with the rise of the religious right, premillenialism has been politicized. A crucial figure in this process was the seminal evangelical writer Francis Schaeffer, an American who founded L'Abri, a Christian community in the Swiss Alps where religious intellectuals gathered to talk and study. As early as the 1960s, Schaeffer was reading Rushdoony and holding seminars on his work.[13] Schaeffer went on to write a series of highly influential books elucidating the idea of the Christian worldview. *A Christian Manifesto*, published in 1981, described modern history as a contest between the Christian worldview and the materialist one, saying, "These two world views stand as totals in complete antithesis to each other in content and also in their natural results—including sociological and government results, and specifically including law."[14]

Schaeffer was not a theocrat, but he drew on Reconstructionist ideas of America as an originally Christian nation. In *A Christian Manifesto*, he warned against wrapping Christianity in the American flag, but added, "None of this, however, changes the fact that the United

---

ted fundamentalists found 'scary.' Among Reconstructionism's highlights, the article cited support for laws 'mandating the death penalty for homosexuals and drunkards.' The Rev. Rushdoony fired off a letter to the editor complaining that the article had got his followers' views all wrong: They didn't intend to put *drunkards* to death."

States was founded upon a Christian consensus, nor that we today should bring Judeo-Christian principles into play in regard to government."[15] Schaeffer was one of the first evangelical leaders to get deeply involved in the fight against abortion, and he advocated civil disobedience and the possible use of force to stop it. "It is time we consciously realize that when *any office* commands what is contrary to God's Law it abrogates its authority," he wrote.[16]

Tim LaHaye, who is most famous for putting a Tom Clancy gloss on premillenalist theology in the *Left Behind* thrillers that he co-writes with Jerry Jenkins, was heavily influenced by Schaeffer, to whom he dedicated his book *The Battle for the Mind*. That book married Schaeffer's theories to a conspiratorial view of history and politics, arguing, "Most people today do not realize what humanism really is and how it is destroying our culture, families, country—and, one day, the entire world. Most of the evils in the world today can be traced to humanism, which has taken over our government, the UN, education, TV, and most of the other influential things of life.

"We must remove all humanists from public office and replace them with pro-moral political leaders," LaHaye wrote.[17]

As premillenialists grew to embrace the goal of dominion, they made alliances with Reconstructionists. In 1984, Jay Grimstead, a disciple of Francis Schaeffer, brought important pre- and post-millenialists together to form the Coalition on Revival (COR) in order to lay a blueprint for taking over American life. Tim LaHaye was an original member of COR's steering committee, along with Rushdoony, North, creationist Duane Gish, D. James Kennedy, and the Reverend Donald Wildmon of the influential American Family Association.

Between 1984 and 1986, COR developed seventeen "worldview" documents, which elucidate the "Christian" position on most aspects of life. Just as political Islam is often called Islamism to differentiate the fascist political doctrine from the faith, the ideology laid out in these papers could be called Christianism. The documents outline a complete political program, with a "biblically correct" position on issues like taxes (God favors a flat rate), public schools (generally frowned upon), and the media and the arts ("We deny that any pornography and other blasphemy are permissible as art or 'free speech'").

In a 1988 letter to supporters, Grimstead announced the completion of a high school curriculum "using the COR Worldview Documents as textbooks." Since then, there's been a proliferation of schools, books, and seminars devoted to inculcating the correct Christian worldview in students and activists. Charles Colson accepts one hundred people annually into his yearlong "worldview training" courses, which include meetings in Washington, D.C., online seminars, "mentoring," and several hours of homework each week. "The program will be heavily weighted towards how to think," Colson's Web site says. It's intended for those who work in churches, media, law, government, and education, and who can thus teach others to think the same way.

Those who don't have a year to spare can attend one of more than a dozen Worldview Weekend conferences held every year in churches nationwide. Popular speakers include the revisionist Christian nationalist historian David Barton, David Limbaugh (Rush's born-again brother), and evangelical former sitcom star Kirk Cameron. In 2003, Tom DeLay was a featured speaker at a Worldview Weekend at Rick Scarborough's former church in Pearland, Texas. He told the crowd, "Only Christianity offers a comprehensive worldview that covers all areas of life and thought, every aspect of creation. Only Christianity offers a way to live in response to the realities that we find in this world. Only Christianity."[18]

Speaking to outsiders, most Christian nationalists say they're simply responding to anti-Christian persecution. They say that secularism is itself a religion, one unfairly imposed on them. They say they're the victims in the culture wars. But Christian nationalist ideologues don't want equality, they want dominance. In his book *The Changing of the Guard: Biblical Principles for Political Action*, George Grant, former executive director of D. James Kennedy's Coral Ridge Ministries, wrote:

Christians have an obligation, a mandate, a commission, a holy responsibility to reclaim the land for Jesus Christ—to have dominion in civil structures, just as in every other aspect of life and godliness.

But it is dominion we are after. Not just a voice.

It is dominion we are after. Not just influence.

It is dominion we are after. Not just equal time.

It is dominion we are after.

World conquest. That's what Christ has commissioned us to accomplish. We must win the world with the power of the Gospel. And we must never settle for anything less. . . .

Thus, Christian politics has as its primary intent the conquest of the land—of men, families, institutions, bureaucracies, courts, and governments for the Kingdom of Christ.[19]

As a multimedia empire, Coral Ridge Ministries is one of the country's most important popularizers of dominion theology. Its founder, D. James Kennedy, is a leader in the Presbyterian Church in America, a schismatic sect that broke with the mainline Presbyterian church over its theological liberalism. The Presbyterian Church in America is home to many influential Christian Reconstructionists, and Kennedy serves as one of the bridges connecting them to the larger evangelical world.

An original board member of the Moral Majority, Kennedy isn't as famous as Tim LaHaye or Jerry Falwell, but he's nearly as influential, with millions of people either watching him on TV or listening to him on the radio every week. His television show, *The Coral Ridge Hour*, is the third-most-widely syndicated Christian program in the country, airing on more than 600 TV stations and the Armed Forces Network. His radio show, *Truths That Transform*, is broadcast on more from 700 stations. In 2005, Kennedy was inducted into the National Religious Broadcasters Hall of Fame.

Kennedy has a lobbying group, the Center for Reclaiming America, and a D.C. operation, the Center for Christian Statesmanship, which is devoted to evangelizing people on Capitol Hill. Each month, the latter group hosts private luncheons for members of Congress and their staffers, usually featuring speeches by Republican politicians. Along with James Dobson, Kennedy is one of the founders of the Alliance Defense Fund, an important Christian Nationalist legal organization. He also runs a K-12 school, Westminster Academy, with around 1300 students, and Knox Theological Seminary, both in Ft. Lauderdale.

Kennedy's projects are intended to foster Christian rule over the country and, eventually, the world. He finds biblical sanction for Christian rule in Genesis 1:28: "And God blessed them, and God said unto them, Be fruitful, and multiply, and replenish the earth, and subdue it: and have dominion over the fish of the sea, and over the fowl of the air, and over every living thing that moveth upon the earth."

"Would God be saying to unregenerate people today that they are to rule the earth? I don't think so," Kennedy wrote in his 1994 book *Character and Destiny: A Nation in Search of Its Soul.* "He is speaking to those of us who have been recreated into the image of God and who are being refashioned by him."[20] God has given believers dominion over all. It's their duty to seize it.

Kennedy is more radical than some of his better-known peers, but his style is more polished and sober. He wears well-cut gray suits and has the stately good looks, blow-dried silver hair, and stentorian voice of a senator in a Hollywood movie. He studied at the Columbia Theological Seminary, Chicago Graduate School of Theology, and New York University, where he earned a Ph.D. and refined his horror of secular, cosmopolitan society. His appeal is more intellectual than emotional. He offers a carefully worked out theory of history and philosophy to justify the political goals of dominion.

Other Christian nationalist writers are implicitly opposed to the Enlightenment; Kennedy is explicitly against it. He's no fan of the Renaissance, either, due to its taste for pagan Greek philosophers. Like many dominionists, Kennedy's lodestar is the Calvinist theocracy of sixteenth-century Geneva. "[T]oday, we are still enduring the age-old conflict in Western society between Reformation and Renaissance beliefs," he wrote in *Character and Destiny*. "Clearly, the Enlightenment in France was another expression of the Renaissance's bearing bitter fruit. Had they known their historical models, the men and women of the Enlightenment could have had a preview of coming attractions by simply looking back at the fruits of secular ideology in ancient times. In Greece and Rome, as well as in the succession of wars and disasters ever after, they could have had a portrait of the ghastly results their vision has produced."[21]

How does Kennedy reconcile his abhorrence of classicism and the Enlightenment with his love of America, one of the Enlightenment's proudest legacies? Simply by denying that that legacy exists. That's where the idea of America as a Christian nation, a staple of Christian Reconstructionism, comes in. In this revisionist history, the foundations of our country lay not in the Constitution, but in the New England theocracies of the 1600s.*

That belief allows Kennedy to deny the fact that the Constitution in fact represented a decisive break with the type of theocracy erected by the Puritans, who prescribed the death penalty for witchcraft, blasphemy, sodomy, homosexuality, and adultery, among other crimes. Christian nationalist history lets dominionists present their agenda, which seeks to resurrect some aspects of Puritan society, as the restoration of the founders' principles, rather than a wholesale rejection of them.

Making History

Kennedy didn't invent this revisionist version of America's past. He got it from a host of Christian nationalist writers and self-styled historians whose work has been percolating through the religious right for years. One of the most important is David Barton, a frequent guest on Kennedy's radio show who has done more to popularize Christian

---

* "It is, of course, the contention of probably most people that this nation began basically as a Christian nation," Kennedy wrote in *Character and Destiny*. "The Mayflower Compact was the first draft of the United States Constitution."

nationalist history than anyone else. Barton's work is cited constantly by conservative leaders and rank-and-file Republicans alike to "prove" that separation of church and state is a myth. In February 2005, *Time* magazine cited him as one of the country's twenty-five most important evangelicals.

A graduate of Oral Roberts University and a former math teacher, Barton is the founder and president of WallBuilders, a Texas-based organization devoted to remaking America as a Christian nation. (The name is a reference to the Old Testament book of Nehemiah's passage about rebuilding the walls of Jerusalem). His books and videos argue that separation of church and state is a myth fostered by God-hating secularists, that most of the founding fathers shared the beliefs of today's religious right, and that they intended Christianity to be central to American government.

This of course runs contrary to most available evidence and mainstream history. While many of America's founders were Christians, others were deists. Thomas Jefferson, for example, admired Jesus' teachings, but rejected his divinity, resurrection, and virgin birth. The Constitution contains not a single mention of either God or Christianity. That wasn't lost on earlier generations of Christian conservatives, who decried America's founding document as an affront to the Lord.*

Since the late 1980s, Barton has made a career of rewriting this history. His most famous works are the book *The Myth of Separation* and the video *America's Godly Heritage.* In them, he combs through history, stringing together statements about the founders' religious beliefs to imply that they wanted Christianity to serve as the foundation of gov-

---

* "The nation has offended Providence," Reverend Timothy Dwight, president of Yale College, said in 1812. "We formed our Constitution without any acknowledgement of God; without any recognition of His mercies to us, as a people, of His government or even of His existence. The [Constitutional] Convention, by which it was formed, never asked even once, His direction, or His blessings, upon their labours. Thus we commenced our national existence under the present system, without God."[22]

ernment. He also traffics in more contemporary revisionism—for example, "Democrats and Republicans: In Their Own Words," a twenty-eight-page document available on the WallBuilders Web site, compares the platforms of the parties throughout the years in an attempt to paint today's Democrats as racist. The study conveniently ends in 1964, the year when the most bigoted elements among the Democrats began their mass exodus to the GOP. Barton does mention that Dixiecrat presidential candidate Strom Thurmond later became a Republican, but attributes the switch, amazingly, to his supposed "dramatic change of heart on civil rights issues," as if Thurmond fled the Democrats because of their support for segregation, not their opposition to it.

Throughout the 1990s, Barton's books and videos were marketed by every major Christian right church and organization, including the Christian Coalition, Focus on the Family, and Coral Ridge Ministries. In 1994, then House Minority Whip Newt Gingrich praised Barton's *The Myth of Separation* as "wonderful" and "most useful." Barton claims to deliver four hundred talks a year to church groups, conferences, and political gatherings and appears frequently on right-wing radio and TV shows.

Barton has recently made efforts to reach out to black conservatives, but in the past he was embraced by the racist far right, addressing at least two Christian Identity gatherings. (Christian Identity maintains that Anglo-Saxons are the true children of Israel, while blacks are "mud people" and Jews are the spawn of Satan). Pete Peters, the head of the Christian Identity group Scriptures for America, praises neo-Nazi skinheads as the "S.O.S. troops of the right." Like Jim Cabaniss, he uses the phrase "people who call themselves Jews" to talk about Jewish people, suggesting that they are, in fact, something else entirely. In July 1991, Barton addressed Scriptures for America's summer retreat. Other speakers included Holocaust denier Malcolm Ross and white supremacist Richard Kelly Hoskins. A few months later, Barton spoke at another Christian Identity gathering in Oregon.[23] He later claimed he didn't know he was talking to hate groups.

This blot on his record didn't stop Barton from becoming a player in the GOP. In 1997, he was elected vice chairman of the Texas Republican party. He's since become an important link between Republicans in Washington and the Christian nationalist grass roots. In 2002, pastors around the country received an invitation to a policy briefing with White House and congressional leaders printed on WallBuilders stationery. The letter didn't say what the briefing was about, only that it would feature "a number of administration officials in the White House," as well as Congressmen Tom DeLay, Dick Armey, and Chris Smith, and Senators Sam Brownback and James Inhofe. It concluded, "In prayer that our government will once against rest upon *His* shoulders, and that we will again become one nation *under* God." It was signed by Barton and Congressman J. C. Watts.

During Bush's 2004 campaign for reelection, Barton was hired by the Republican National Committee to give a series of get-out-the-vote speeches to groups of clergy around the country. They were closed to the press, but a journalist for *The Oregonian* reported that one hundred pastors showed up for one event in Eugene.

The next spring, Senate Majority Leader Bill Frist invited all one hundred senators on a private tour of the Capitol led by Barton. The invitation promised a "fresh perspective on our nation's religious heritage."

Against the Courts

Meanwhile, Barton's ideas were driving a right-wing congressional push to exempt Roy Moore and officials like him from the authority of the Supreme Court. In February 2004, Senator Zell Miller, a Christian nationalist Democrat from Georgia, gave a speech to the Senate praising several bills designed to weaken federal courts, including the Constitution Restoration Act.

This piece of legislation was drafted by Roy Moore himself and Herb Titus, a Christian Reconstructionist and former dean of the law school at Pat Robertson's Regent University. Introduced in both houses of Congress in 2004, it would strip federal courts of their power to hear cases dealing with any state or local government's "acknowledgement of God as the sovereign source of law, liberty, or government." A radical curtailment of both church/state separation and judicial authority, it's intended as a way to nullify the kind of court decisions that led to Moore's removal.

"I highly recommend a great book entitled *Original Intent* by David Barton," Miller said from the Senate floor. "It really gets into how the actual members of Congress, who drafted the First Amendment, expected basic biblical principles and values to be present throughout public life and society, not separate from it." In supporting the Constitution Restoration Act, Miller said, "I stand shoulder to shoulder not only with my Senate co-sponsors and Chief Justice Roy Moore of Alabama but, more importantly, with our Founding Fathers in the conception of religious liberty and the terribly wrong direction our modern judiciary has taken us in."

It seems bizarre that Congress could override the Supreme Court without amending the Constitution, but there is at least some legal justification for Moore's bill. It relies on Article III of the Constitution, which gives Congress power to make exceptions to the Supreme Court's appellate jurisdiction. Article III, however, has never been used to say that the Supreme Court can't enforce its interpretation of the Bill of Rights. That's essentially what the Constitution Restoration Act would do, since its language implies that the First Amendment as it's currently understood doesn't apply to the states. That's a break with sixty years of legal precedent, but it's a bedrock principle of many Christian nationalists. Thus in recent years, court-stripping initiatives have been all the rage on the right—there are similar plans afoot to strip the courts of their power to rule on same-sex marriage and school prayer.

Some Republicans have suggested that court rulings offensive to right-wing Christians could be simply ignored. At the 2004 Christian Coalition meeting, Indiana Congressman John Hostettler said, "When the courts make unconstitutional decisions, we should not enforce them. Federal courts have no army or navy. . . . The court can opine, decide, talk about, sing, whatever it wants to do. We're not saying they can't do that. At the end of the day, we're saying the court can't enforce its opinions."[24]

Hostettler's language was mild compared to what followed in 2005, when the right grew enraged over Terri Schiavo and the Democratic filibuster of Bush's judicial nominees. By then, Christian nationalists started calling for the mass impeachment of every judge to the left of Antonin Scalia. A few went further and hinted that liberal judges deserved violent retribution.

With supporters like Hostettler, the Constitution Restoration Act passed the House in 2004. It stalled in the Senate, despite the support of powerful Republicans including Brownback, South Carolina's Lindsey Graham, Colorado's Wayne Allard, and Mississippi's Trent Lott, the former Senate majority leader. In 2005, it was reintroduced in both houses. The 2004 GOP platform explicitly endorsed the ideas behind the Constitution Restoration Act, saying, "A Republican Congress, working with a Republican president, will restore the separation of powers and re-establish a government of law. There are different ways to achieve that goal, such as using Article III of the Constitution to limit federal court jurisdiction; for example, in instances where judges are abusing their power by banning the use of 'under God' in the Pledge of Allegiance or prohibiting depictions of the Ten Commandments, and potential actions invalidating the Defense of Marriage Act (DOMA)."

Even if it's unlikely to survive a court challenge and become law, the Constitution Restoration Act is significant for what it says about current right-wing attitudes toward the separation of powers and the Bill of Rights. The campaign surrounding it reveals the extent to which Barton and Moore's thinking permeates the party in power, and it shows how eager the right is to dispense with decades of legal precedent and government practice in their quest for the Christian nation.

At the Alabama rally, Roy Moore compared the Constitution Restoration Act to the discipline one would mete out to a thieving housekeeper. "It's kind of like if you had a maid who was coming into your house to clean for twenty years, and you find out she was stealing from you all this time. What would you tell her? Just don't take any more of my silverware? Or would you fire her, and kick her out of your house and say don't come back? That's what we need to do to the courts! Put them in the proper jurisdiction, which is interpreting the laws of the Constitution."

Then he read a poem that he wrote about America's degeneration, line after rhyming line condemning the nation for its hedonism and blasphemy. He recited:

Too soft to place a killer in a well deserved tomb,
But brave enough to kill that child before he leaves the womb.
You think that God's not angry? This land's a moral slum!
How much longer will it be before His judgment comes?

It sounded like Moore hated the very nation he wanted to save. But of course, he just hates it as it is now. He's awaiting its glorious resurrection, the day America arises, Phoenix-like, from the ashes of liberalism.

CHAPTER 2

Protocols of the Elders of San Francisco:
The Political Uses of Homophobia

On a Sunday morning just over three weeks before the 2004 election, a purple curtain rose on the stage of the 12,000-member World Harvest Church in Columbus, Ohio, to reveal a purple- and white-robed choir standing on a bridge several stories above the ground. Beneath them, a row of gospel singers in black suits sang soft-rock worship anthems. A black backdrop behind them sparkled with pinpricks of light like a starry sky. Colored lights swept over the singers, and two huge monitors showed close-ups of the ecstatic faces of thousands of churchgoers who were about to hear how Jesus wanted them to save marriage from the hell-spawned forces of homosexuality on November 2.

On the monitors flanking the stage, words to a simple, chantlike hymn appeared for people to sing along:

You are a mighty God
You are a mighty God
Mighty God mighty God
Yes you are a mighty God

Two pianists played and electric guitar riffs sizzled through the air. In the pews—row after row of them—there was an ecstasy of singing and dancing, people swaying with their hands in the air or turning in small circles. The verse was repeated over and over, slightly modified— "You are an awesome God; You are a holy God." The song ended with cheers and applause from an audience that continued to grow as latecomers trickled into the amphitheaterlike chapel.

A man with a neat silver pompadour took the stage to warm up for Pastor Rod Parsley, a faith-healing televangelist who, like Rick Scarborough, is positioning himself as one of the evangelical right's next generation of leaders. Calling Parsley a "prophet" and an "oracle of God," the warm-up preacher said, "Tomorrow he's got eighteen years of marital bliss. He's not only preaching it, he's living it. Marriage—one man, one woman." The crowd shouted its approval.

Parsley, a broad-shouldered, dark-haired white man with narrow eyes and ripe, fleshy lips, appeared onstage. "The nation has never been more divided and the choices have never been more clear," he declared. "Everyone asks, 'Why is it so close?' The light is getting lighter and the dark is getting darker. These two opponents are not just opponents. This is a values situation. This is lightness and darkness!"

He would say much more about marriage, but not until his flock was looser and giddy with music and movement. "Reach over and slap someone a high five and tell them it's gonna get better!" he said, and people happily complied. As the music rose, Parsley enjoined the worshippers to dance harder. "You need to abandon yourself! Don't let those aisles separate you!"

At his words, people started dancing in the aisles.

Parsley called headache sufferers to the front of the auditorium. But as people watched them line up, he cried out, "Don't stop worshipping Him! Don't stop worshipping Him! Don't become a spectator!" As thousands in the crowd kept dancing, he moved among those who came forward, putting his hand on their foreheads. "In the presence of God I rebuke it," he said. "In the presence of God I rebuke it. In Jesus, I rebuke it. Lose it. Lose it. In the name of Jesus. In the name of Jesus. Lose that."

The choir kept singing and Parsley kept preaching, spewing glossolalia as he laid his hands on his flock. Some people fell back and were caught by ushers standing behind them. One woman paced the aisle, her hands above her head, looking up and sobbing.

Nearly an hour and a half passed before Parsley started preaching in earnest to a crowd that was by then happily worn out and receptive. He told his audience that Christianity was under siege. Interlopers from out of state had come to Ohio, "going door to door, knocking on doors so we can continue to murder babies and further strip the church of its First Amendment rights through hate crimes legislation." Gay marriage, he said, heralds "the annihilation of a civilization."

He started to sweat. An organ trilled behind him as he said, "On November 2, I see people marching like a holy army to the voting booth. I see the holy spirit anointing you as you vote for life, as you vote for marriage, as you vote for the pulpit!"

Three and a half weeks later, on November 3, a dozen or so volunteers for Americans Coming Together (ACT)—the "interlopers" of Parsley's sermon, who had come to Ohio to turn out the progressive vote—slumped stunned in front of a TV in their suddenly deserted Columbus headquarters. Off to the side, a blonde girl sobbed quietly. Bush had won. Anti-gay-marriage initiatives, many of which also banned domestic partnerships and other legal recognition for gay couples, had passed resoundingly in all eleven states where they were on the ballot, including Ohio. The far right had made gains in the House and the Senate. It was a debacle for the Democrats, and many hadn't seen it coming.

All through October, the mood among Democratic volunteers was ebullient. ACT had mounted one of the largest, most well-financed get-out-the-vote drives in the history of American politics, dispatching thousands of paid workers and impassioned volunteers to canvass voters in swing states. On Ohio's residential streets, ACT people seemed to be everywhere, along with volunteers from the Kerry campaign and the unions. There was no visible Republican equivalent.

In *The New York Times Magazine*, Matt Bai wrote of Steve Bouchard, ACT's Ohio director, and his colleague Tom Lindenfeld: "What gnawed at Bouchard was that nowhere we went in Franklin County, a vigorously contested swing county, did we see any hint of a strong Republican presence—no signs, no door-knockers, no Bush supporters handing out leaflets at the polls. This seemed only to increase Lindenfeld's confidence. . . . For Bouchard, however, the silence was unsettling. How could there be such a thing as a stealth get-out-the-vote drive?"

The drive wasn't happening in stealth. It was happening in churches, especially megachurches, temples of religious nationalism where millions of Americans gather every week for exultant sermons that mingle evangelical Christianity, self-help, and right-wing politics. Bush's brigades were hidden in plain sight in a parallel culture, an America that's both mainstream and invisible to many on the coasts, an America that had been set alight by the intolerable threat posed by gay marriage.

November 2 was just the beginning. In the months that followed, state and local lawmakers across the country attempted to strip gay people of a host of legal protections, including the right to share health insurance, adopt children, and become foster parents. An Alabama lawmaker introduced a bill to prevent school libraries from buying books by gay authors or with gay characters. He said the move was necessary to protect Alabama's children from "the homosexual agenda."[1] Commissioners in Rhea County, Tennessee—famous as the site of the Scopes trial—voted to urge state lawmakers to criminalize gay sex. "We need to keep them out of here," said Commissioner J. C. Fugate, who also asked the Rhea County attorney how they might ban homosexuals from living in the county at all.[2] (The commissioners later retreated from their position after a national outcry.)

Homosexuality has become *the* mobilizing passion for much of the religious right. A populist movement needs an enemy, but one reason the Christian nationalists are so strong is that they've made peace with many old foes, especially Catholics and African-Americans. Gay people have taken the place of obsolete demons.

For the right, gays are living signifiers of decadence and corruption. They're seen as both repulsive and tempting, their mere existence sparking some deep primordial panic among much of straight America. A great many of the anxieties stalking the country—fears about social dysfunction, family breakdown, cultural decay, and decreasing status—have been projected onto homosexuals and their ostensible "agenda." Books and videos chronicle the homosexual plots to take over America's schools, children, churches, and government.

In their widely promoted 2003 book *The Homosexual Agenda*, Craig Osten and Alan Sears (president of the Alliance Defense Fund, the major Christian nationalist legal outfit) write breathlessly of a national conspiracy that, under the cover of fighting for civil rights, aims to steal the souls of children and silence the church. "Overt efforts are made by many to lead young men and women into homosexual behavior, many for simple, base reasons that have nothing to do with political agendas," they wrote. "Instead, the new recruits are 'fresh meat' and sources of new cash, new sex partners, and new profit."[3]

In the past, this kind of demonization has been a precursor to horror. There are some inescapable parallels between the rhetoric of cultural purity in 1930s Germany and in our America. One of the first things the Nazis did upon coming to power was crack down on gays as part of a broader family values campaign. As Richard J. Evans wrote in *The Coming of the Third Reich*, "The Nazis moved with the approval of conservatives and Catholics alike to destroy every branch of Weimar Germany's lively and intricately interconnected congeries of pressure-groups for sexual freedom, the reform of the abortion law, the decriminalization of homosexuality, the public dispensing of contraceptive advice and anything else that they thought was contributing to the continued decline of the German birth rate."[4]

Social conservatism is not in itself fascistic, of course. But the combination of repression, populism, and paranoia, the fear of decadence as a monstrous plot against the nation, carries frightening echoes. The Nazis saw sexual liberation movements as part of a Jewish conspiracy to subvert the German family and thus Germany as a whole. Today's right attributes a similar scheme to gays. In their introduction, Sears and Osten wrote, "We will outline how the homosexual agenda touches every area of our lives, from the media to education to families to corporate America and to government [*sic*]. We will document how the religious freedoms of all Americans are under attack from radical homosexual activists."[5] The homosexual agenda canard is to Christian nationalists what the *Protocols of the Elders of Zion* was to earlier generations of authoritarians.

Just as anti-Semites deny the Holocaust, some Christian nationalists argue that stories about the Nazi victimization of gay people are lies devised to further the homosexual agenda and disarm its opposition. In their revisionist history *The Pink Swastika*, Scott Lively and Kevin Abrams make the astonishing charge that Nazism was a primarily homosexual movement, that today's gay rights movement is its direct descendant, and that claims to the contrary are simply part of the homosexual conspiracy. Being ruthless, those behind the "homosexual agenda" must be treated ruthlessly. "Like their Nazi predecessors, today's homosexualists lack any scruples," wrote Lively and Abrams. "Homosexuality is primarily a predatory addiction striving to take the weak and unsuspecting down with it. The 'gay' agenda is a colossal fraud; a gigantic robbery of the mind. Homosexuals of the type described in this book have no true idea of how to act in the best interests of their country and fellow man. Their intention is to serve none but themselves."[6]

Lively and Abrams are not solitary cranks: their contention that gays were perpetrators rather than victims of the Holocaust is common among Christian nationalists. Among those who've endorsed *The Pink Swastika* is Steve Baldwin, executive director of the Council for National Policy, one of the most powerful right-wing groups in America. Lively, the president of the Pro-Family Law Center in Sacramento, California, serves as California state director of Donald Wildmon's American Family Association and has been a guest on Fox News, James Dobson's radio show, *The 700 Club*, and a host of other programs, and his work is referenced in many books on the "homosexual agenda."

The demonology these men peddle—repeated endlessly at churches, on right-wing TV and radio, at rallies, and by politicians—helps explain how in 2004 millions of Americans decided that, in a time of war and economic uncertainty, there was no issue more urgent than keeping gay people from getting married.

The role that gay marriage played in the 2004 election—and continues to play in American politics—has been confused by competing hyperbole. In the days after November 2, conventional wisdom held that the election represented the triumph of right-wing culture warriors, who wasted no time claiming a mandate. On November 3, William Bennett, the former Reagan drug czar famous for political sanctimony and compulsive gambling, wrote in the *National Review Online*, "Having restored decency to the White House, President Bush now has a mandate to affect policy that will promote a more decent society, through both politics and law. . . . Now is the time to begin our long, national cultural renewal . . . no less in legislation than in federal court appointments."

Culture warriors pointed to the much quoted exit poll in which 22 percent of voters cited "moral values" as their chief concern, exceeding those who pointed to Iraq (15 percent) or the economy and jobs (20 percent) as priorities. Eighty percent of voters who said they cared most about moral values choose Bush. ("Moral values," of course, is widely understood as a euphemism for opposition to gay marriage and abortion rights.)

In one way, the significance of this poll was overstated. Yes, more voters pointed to "moral values" than any of the other issues listed, but that's partly because of the way the question was worded. Nineteen percent of respondents said the most important issue in the election was terrorism. Add that to Iraq, and you have 34 percent of voters making their decision based on foreign policy.

As a percentage of the electorate, the evangelical vote was no higher in 2004 than it was in 2000. Yet evangelicals were the most active and cohesive part of the campaign, outmatching the unprecedented progressive mobilization on behalf of John Kerry. As Marvin Olasky wrote in the evangelical magazine *World*, "President Bush won because moral issues were more important than any others for one fifth of the voters, and the president won that fifth by at least a 4–1 majority. To put it another way, Senator Kerry probably received about 56 percent of the vote from people most concerned with foreign policy or economic issues, the traditional subjects for presidential campaigns."[7]

While the 2004 election wasn't won on the culture war alone, it revealed the growing size and strength of the Christian nationalist movement that's been building in this country for decades. The cadres of the religious right are the foot soldiers of the Republican party, the people who man phone banks and organize their neighbors. Not all Republican voters believe that gay marriage portends the death of the nation, but ones who do were key to Bush's victory, and they're now driving America's social policy.

Megachurch Machines

Nowhere was the influence of the cultural right starker than in the election-deciding state of Ohio.

The first Bush term wasn't good to Ohio. Between 2000 and 2004, the state lost a quarter of a million jobs—the second worst record in the country. Under Bush, Cleveland became America's poorest big city, according to a report from the U.S. Census Bureau. Young people were leaving the state in droves. In August 2004, Brent Larkin, editorial-page director of the *Cleveland Plain Dealer*, wrote about Ohio's "raging brain drain."

But even as the state's economy decayed, its evangelical churches thrived. Drive down Interstate 75 toward Cincinnati and the parade of neon-lit crosses flickering by from roadside churches is hypnotic. Christian talk shows, Christian pop, and portentous sermons crowd the radio dial. Near the town of Monroe, a recently erected sixty-two-foot-tall bust of Jesus made of plastic foam and fiberglass beseeches onlookers from the front of the Solid Rock Church, its thick white hands raised up to heaven.

All over America, megachurches—generally defined as churches with more than two thousand members—are multiplying. There were about 10 such churches in 1970. Today there are upward of 880.[8] Such churches still represent only 1 percent of American congregations, but they're growing as older churches atrophy. John N. Vaughn, founder of the research and consultancy firm Church Growth Today, has estimated that a new megachurch opens its doors every two days.[9]

These churches are usually located on the sprawling edges of cities, in new exurban developments that almost totally lack for public space—squares, parks, promenades, or even, in some places, sidewalks. With their endless procession of warehouselike chain stores and garish profusion of primary-colored logos, the exurbs are the purest of ecosystems for consumer capitalism. Yet the brutal, impersonal utilitarianism of the strip mall and office park architecture—its perversely ascetic refusal to make a single concession to aesthetics—recalls the Stalinist monstrosities imposed on Communist countries. The banality is aggressive and disorientating. Driving through many of these places in states from Pennsylvania to Colorado, I've experienced more than a few moments of vertiginous panic where I literally could not remember where I was.

Because most exurbs are so new, none of the residents grew up in them; everyone is from somewhere else and there are few places for them to meet. In such locales, megachurches fill the spiritual and social void, providing atomized residents instant community. Besides worship services, they offer dinners and parties, family counseling and summer camp, even sports leagues, gyms, and weight-loss programs. There's a McDonald's inside the Brentwood Baptist Church in Houston, and a Starbucks in the Covenant Celebration Church in Tacoma, Washington. The congregations are often organized into small groups of people who monitor one another's spiritual progress, developing intimate relationships in the process.

While megachurches *look* like everything else in the newly developing parts of America—they're usually enormous, unadorned boxy buildings, designed to resemble shopping malls or multiplexes and surrounded by acres of asphalt parking lots—they provide an outlet for energies that aren't rational, productive, or acquisitive, for furies and ecstasies that don't otherwise fit into suburban life. Spiritual marketplaces, they are both the apotheosis of the prefab exurban lifestyle and the antidote to its dissatisfactions. They're where all the weirdness comes out.

Walk into a megachurch during the height of a Sunday service and you'll see staid suburbanites bouncing and swaying as strobe lights strafe the air and bombastic anthems crescendo; for a secular urbanite, the closet comparison is the dizzy ecstasy of a rock concert or the dawn communion of an all-night dance club. The preacher usually tells everyone to greet their neighbors, and worshippers of every race and age turn toward one another and exchange blessings with radiant smiles. Nowhere else in America is so indiscriminately welcoming.

It can be beautiful and, to those wary of Christian nationalism, terrifying. Because megachurches don't just serve as exurban versions of town squares and community centers. In many cases they're also tightly organized right-wing political machines. Small group leaders often report to church officials above them, and so on up the hierarchy. The churches are themselves organized and networked together, and literally get marching orders from Washington, D.C. Every month, the Family Research Council hosts a conference call for sympathetic pastors. The group's president, former Louisiana state representative Tony Perkins, gives participants an update of his latest conversations with the White House and the congressional leadership, and tells the preachers which issues to bring to their flocks' attention.

I signed up for the Family Research Council's e-mail newsletter for pastors, and soon I started getting invitations for these calls. I'd RSVP, receive a toll-free phone number and password, and dial in. The calls begin with prayer. Then Perkins briefs his listeners on a few issues and gives them instructions to pass on to their congregants. On a typical call in April 2005, the conversation was all about the filibuster of judicial nominees. "The message that's being sent is if you are a person, in particular a Christian, if you are someone of strong Christian faith, to the point where you would actually live out your faith, you'll have to choose between that and serving on the courts in this country," Perkins said. A few days later, Perkins would host an antifilibuster rally and simulcast called Justice Sunday, featuring Senate Majority Leader Bill Frist. During the conference call, he encouraged all the pastors to participate, and to have their congregations contact their senators the next day. "We are striking deep in enemy territory by taking on the judicial system in this country," he said.

Perkins also reminded his listeners of an upcoming three-day "pastors' policy briefing" in D.C. More than four hundred pastors had already registered. "I know the Lord's going to use it to bless these pastors, to encourage them, to equip them and prepare them for these battles that are raging before us," Perkins said.

Such briefings take place several times a year and feature off-the-record talks by GOP leaders; at the previous gathering in March, Tom DeLay informed the preachers that Terri Schiavo, the brain-dead Florida woman and Christian right cause célèbre, was a gift from heaven. "I tell you, ladies and gentlemen, one thing that God has brought to us is Terri Schiavo, to elevate the visibility of what's going on in America, that Americans would be so barbaric as to pull a feeding tube out of a person that is lucid and starve them to death for two weeks," he said.*

The Family Research Council is only one of the groups marshaling the megachurch brigades on behalf of conservative politics. Rick Scarborough has organized a nationwide network of more than 3000 so-called patriot pastors to keep their flocks permanently mobilized. "I've been calling pastors to be involved politically, and get involved in the moral, civil arenas, speaking to the great issues of the day, debunking the myth of separation," he told me. He was referring, of course, to the myth of the separation of church and state. Rod Parsley is involved in the "Ohio Restoration Project," which has mustered nearly 1000 preachers in an effort to take over the state's politics and fight what one

---

* Contrary to the claims of the religious right, an autopsy proved Schiavo was in a persistent vegetative state with no hope of recovery. See "Schiavo Autopsy Shows Irreversible Brain Damage," Associated Press, June 15, 2005.

of the group's leaders called "secular jihadists." Similar efforts are afoot in other states.[10]

Not surprisingly, pastors have much to gain from these networks, and they develop clout in them through their political activism. Jerry Johnston, pastor of the 3000-member First Family Church in Overland Park, Kansas, was relatively obscure until he started speaking out against gay marriage. Now he's being initiated into the Christian nationalist movement's most elite circles.

First Family is an eight-year-old church set on fifty-one acres in a well-off suburb of Kansas City. During his first several years there, Johnston says he stayed out of politics. "Like so many megachurch pastors, I was busy building my church," he told me. But the threat of gay marriage roused him, and soon he was attending meetings with hundreds of other similarly worried Kansas preachers and organizing to get an anti-gay-marriage amendment on the Kansas ballot. "I have never seen the cooperation, ever, as I have on the marriage amendment," he said.

Shortly before the 2004 election, Johnston gave a sermon titled "Same Sex Marriage vs. Marriage God's Way." As is his practice, he gave his congregation "Sermonar" booklets with fill-in-the-blank sentences to complete as he spoke. One sentence read, "The legalization of homosexual marriage will quickly _____ traditional marriage and families." (The answer, according to the key printed on the back, is "destroy.") Another read, "Similar to the disobedient nations of the Old Testament, America could experience the _____ of God." (The answer is "judgment.")

"Same Sex Marriage vs. Marriage God's Way" was a hit, and received a lot of attention from evangelicals nationwide. CD copies were sent to 2800 pastors in Oregon, one of the states with an anti-gay-marriage amendment on the November ballot. "We did a lot of different programs—O'Reilly, you name it, Scarborough," Johnston said. "I don't know how this thing really caught on like it did, but it did."

Johnston's punchy sermon brought him to the attention of some of the religious right's kingmakers. When I spoke to him in March 2005, he was about to leave for Los Angeles, where he was talking with the Trinity Broadcasting Network, owner of more than 6000 Christian TV stations, about anchoring what he described as a "Sean Hannity–equivalent television program." In addition, he said, he was being inducted into the Council for National Policy, the secretive Christian nationalist group comprised of the top tier of conservative Republicans, right-wing lobbyists and donors, and famous televangelists.

Besides inflaming individual pastors, gay marriage has been important in activating church-based political machines on behalf of the GOP. As of this writing, IRS rules deem that preachers endorsing candidates from the pulpit will lose their tax-exempt status (the religious right is trying hard to change that rule—by the time you read this, they may have succeeded). Preachers are free, however, to take stands and mobilize their flocks behind ostensibly nonpartisan issues like gay marriage. Anti-gay-marriage amendments on state ballots gave them an opening to pour their energies and resources into politics.

In Ohio, the signatures to put the anti-gay-marriage amendment Issue 1 on the ballot were counted and sorted inside the Potters House, a sprawling fundamentalist church on Columbus's outskirts. Voter registration drives and get-out-the-vote phone banks were organized out of Rod Parsley's church. According to *USA Today*, Parsley "assembled a list of 100,000 Ohio acolytes, all of whom were to be called by the World Harvest Church on the eve of the election, reminding them to vote."[11]

Family Emergencies

Of the eleven state constitutional amendments that were adopted in 2004 to ban gay marriage and other legal recognition for gay couples, Ohio's Issue 1 was the strictest. While the first sentence simply decreed that marriage is between a man and a woman, the second said, "This state and its political subdivisions shall not create or recognize a legal status for relationships of unmarried individuals that intends to approximate the design, qualities, significance or effect of marriage."

Thus Issue 1 could force Ohio's cities and universities to stop offering domestic partner benefits, including health insurance. Such benefits had been available to people who worked for the city of Columbus, Miami University outside Cincinnati, Ohio University, and Ohio State University, the largest university in America. Cleveland Heights had a domestic partnership registry, and some Ohio public schools gave gay employees family leave to care for ailing partners. Issue 1 was expected to put all that to an end.

Watching the Issue 1 juggernaut, a lot of the state's gay citizens were terrified. A minority courted by no one, they were blindsided by the campaign against them. Many felt like they were under siege. Talk of moving to a friendlier state or country was widespread.

Julie Reeves and Leigh Mamlin lived in a split-level, stucco-and-brick house in a Columbus suburb with their two children, eighteen-month-old Frannie and three-year-old Charlie. Reeves, forty-five, worked full-time as an administrator at Ohio State University, her alma mater, while forty-year-old Mamlin, the children's biological mother, stayed home. A gray minivan was parked in the driveway and baby books were piled on the coffee table. Sitting in their cozy living room on a Sunday evening a few weeks before the election, they were the picture of suburban domesticity, Frannie nestled in Mamlin's lap while Charlie perched on Reeves's knee.

Because Ohio already didn't allow two-parent gay adoptions, Reeves had to go through a lengthy legal process to become Frannie and Charlie's legal co-parent. Her lawyer told her that if Issue 1 passed, her parental rights could be nullified. If that happened, not only Mamlin would lose her health insurance—the kids would, too.

Like many gay couples, Reeves and Mamlin had a raft of documents designed to "approximate" marriage, and no way of knowing which ones the courts might decide Ohio couldn't "recognize." Would agreements allowing them to make medical decisions for each other still be valid? Would their wills?

"It's such a personal assault," said Mamlin. "We feel violated, misunderstood, misrepresented, and hated by people who are ignorant of who we truly are."

A few weeks earlier, Reeves was horrified when the Republican

National Committee mailed her a voter registration form attached to a four-color flyer about "protecting marriage." The front pictured a bride and groom and the words, "One Man One Woman." Inside it said, "One vote could make a difference in making sure it stays that way." The mailer warned that "Traditional values are under attack from the radical left," which seeks to "destroy traditional marriage by legalizing gay marriage," "support abortion on demand and partial birth abortion," and "declare the Pledge of Allegiance unconstitutional because of its reference to God."

Mamlin said she always felt accepted and welcomed by her neighbors, but suddenly she sensed prejudice massing just outside the door. "When you get a flyer like the one we got in the mail and you see the polls, you know it's there," she said. "I'm glad my children are young enough not to catch on." Incredulously, she asked, "Who out there believes it is their right to vote on my life?"

Phil Burress does. Founder of an Ohio group called Citizens for Community Values and a driving force behind Issue 1, Burress made no apologies for the fact that Mamlin and her kids might lose their health insurance. "Ohio State and Miami University, Columbus and Cleveland Heights, are all taxpayer-funded institutions," he told me. "They're using taxpayer money and giving out the benefits of marriage when they have no right to do so."

Burress, a thrice-married Cincinnati man, described himself as a former pornography addict redeemed by Jesus. He has spent much of the last decade fighting gay rights—one of his first victories was getting Cincinnati to pass a 1994 amendment to its city charter that made it the only metropolis in the country to ban laws protecting gays and lesbians. (He's also been active in trying to get Ohio hotels to stop offering pay-per-view porn.)

Burress first began thinking about the threat of gay matrimony in 1995, when Mike Gabbard, a friend in Honolulu (and failed 2004 Republican congressional candidate), warned him that the same-sex-marriage fight that had erupted there could spread to the mainland. In January 1996, Burress called a meeting of about twenty-five national "pro-family" activists in Memphis to discuss strategy. Those activists, who call themselves the D.C. group, continue to meet every three months to plan antigay legislation. Burress is also part of the Arlington group, a coalition of 53 antigay organizations with three full-time staffers in Washington, D.C. The Arlington group, which is run out of the offices of the Family Research Council, is primarily focused on amending the federal constitution to ban both gay marriage and domestic partnerships.

The very mention of gay couples as a part of society seems to collide with Burress's sense of reality. When I referred to Issue 1 as an anti-gay-marriage amendment, he snapped at me, "There's no such thing as gay marriage, so how can there be anti–gay marriage?"

Polls show that many Americans—32 percent, according to a November 2004 CBS News/New York Times survey—support civil unions, which would provide gay couples with many of the economic and legal benefits of marriage. Add that to the 21 percent who support gay marriage, and it suggests that a slim majority of the population favor legal recognition for gay couples. That's an enormous victory for gay rights—after all, thirty years ago gay people were scarcely acknowledged in public. (The American Psychiatric Association classified homosexuality as a mental disorder until 1973.)

But this growing acceptance has led to a mounting militancy among the significant minority of Americans who hate and fear homosexuality. As a whole, America may be moving fitfully forward toward gay equality. Beneath that aggregate progress, though, parts of the country are veering in radically different directions. America's big cities and some of its Northeastern states are increasingly making marriage or something like it available to gay couples. That in turn has helped turn gay people and their relationships into devil figures for the Christian nationalist movement, which sets the agenda for much of the Republican party. The headline of a 2004 Washington Post story about the intensity of the fight called gay marriage "the new abortion."

To celebrate heterosexual matrimony, a woman from the Traditional Values Coalition, one of the nation's most vocal antigay lobbies, donned a white wedding dress and served cake to guests at the 2004 Conservative Political Action Conference (CPAC). Drawing thousands every year, CPAC is ground zero of the vast right-wing conspiracy, the place where in 1994 Paula Jones was first introduced to the world. It brings together the grass roots—boys in blue blazers, soignée blonds in short skirts, and portly Southerners in T-shirts with slogans like "Fry Mumia"—with organizers, celebrities, and politicians. Dick Cheney gave the opening addresses in 2003, 2004, and 2005. Much of the Republican leadership attends, along with people like Phyllis Schlafly, Ann Coulter, and National Rifle Association CEO Wayne LaPierre. It's a gathering animated by a quaking, obsessive loathing of all things liberal—feminists, environmentalists, internationalists. In 2004, however, one foe predominated. All the culture warriors were talking about gay marriage.

Obviously, right-wing homophobia is nothing new—Jerry Falwell was fulminating against the possibility of gay marriage in 1980—but in recent years the right's focus on homosexuality has sharpened, and its language has grown ever more apocalyptic. In October 2004, James Dobson told an Oklahoma rally that gay marriage "will destroy the Earth." The Reverend Lou Sheldon, chairman of the Traditional Values Coalition, compares the legalization of gay marriage in Massachusetts to the attack on Pearl Harbor.

At 2004's CPAC, Sheldon, a plump, pink man with snowy white hair, presided over a makeshift carnival game called "Tip a Troll," in which players were invited to throw gray beanbags at toy trolls representing various right-wing nemeses. Some had the heads of villains like Osama bin Laden, Saddam Hussein, and Hillary Clinton. One held a sign that read "The Homosexual Agenda."

Sheldon, who claims to have a weekly conference call with the White House to discuss gay issues, is convinced that if America allows gay marriage, the country will fall from God's grace and become Babylon, the whorish metropolis of Revelation, symbol, he said, of "promiscuity, hedonism, and homosexuality."

People in the so-called blue states can be forgiven for not seeing the crisis in the American family. After all, theirs are more likely to be intact. Conservatives often paint the Democratic-voting coastal states as decadent enclaves of vice and perversion, but in fact these states lead the nation in many quantifiable measures of moral fitness. In comparison, the so-called heartland, where protecting marriage is an abiding passion, is a dissolute swamp, making many of the people who live there desperate for renewal.

"What about the heartland's much-vaunted moral qualities?" *The Economist* asked in 2002. "Here again the image of small-town piety bears little relation to reality in rural America. The states that Mr. Bush won in 2000 boast slightly higher rates for murder, illegitimacy and teenage childbirth than the supposedly degenerate states that voted for Mr. Gore."[12]

The contrast is especially stark when it comes to marriage. As *The New York Times* reported shortly after Bush's reelection, "The lowest divorce rates are largely in the blue states: the Northeast and the upper Midwest. And the state with the lowest divorce rate was Massachusetts, home to John Kerry, the Kennedys and same-sex marriage. In 2003, the rate in Massachusetts was 5.7 divorces per 1,000 married people, compared with 10.8 in Kentucky, 11.1 in Mississippi and 12.7 in Arkansas."[13]

Such numbers make red state cultural chauvinism particularly grating, but more than just hypocrisy is at play. People in the most right-wing states see their families and those around them falling apart, and are flailing wildly for ways to save them. James Dobson's radio show, which has 7 million listeners, attracts its audience less with politics than with its attention to personal unhappiness—it's full of discussions about women who've fallen out of love with their husbands and men who ignore their wives. The many cruelties and insecurities of contemporary relationships are interpreted as a spiritual crisis that must be resolved before people can feel safe in their own commitments. When evangelicals talk about preserving marriage's "sanctity," they're also talking about preserving its security.

In 2000, Arkansas governor Mike Huckabee declared "a marital emergency" in his state and pledged to halve the divorce rate in a decade. He hasn't had much success, but he did win lots of right-wing accolades on Valentine's Day 2005, when he and his wife, Janet, held a mass ceremony at Little Rock's Alltel Arena to convert their union into a "covenant marriage," one of the Christian nationalists' favorite panaceas for family breakdown.

Such marriages, which exist in Louisiana and Arizona as well as Arkansas, are harder to end than ordinary unions and, as public policy, they're intended to reduce divorce. "Only when there has been a complete and total breach of the marital covenant commitment may a party seek a declaration that the marriage is no longer legally recognized," says Arkansas's 2001 Covenant Marriage Act. Such a breach can include physical abuse, imprisonment, or "habitual drunkenness for one year." The author of the Louisiana law was the Family Research Council's Tony Perkins, who was then a state legislator.

Before the Valentine's Day rally, Governor Huckabee toured the state with the co-host of the event, Dennis Rainey, head of an Arkansas-based division of the Campus Crusade for Christ. Together, they encouraged pastors to refuse to perform noncovenant marriages in their churches. The churches, in turn, organized fleets of buses to take their congregants to Alltel for a kind of religious revival as scripted by Hallmark.

The highlight of the night was the Huckabees' conversion of their marriage and restatement of their vows, including Janet's pledge to "submit" to Mike. When they were done, they invited the audience to repeat their promises. Thousands of wives, some in evening gowns or wedding veils, vowed to submit to thousands of husbands, and then thousands of couples kissed and cheered.

Though the rally was billed only as a celebration of straight marriage, many sensed an antigay subtext. I met people at the Alltel rally who didn't know what covenant marriage was but who had come to stand against homosexuality. "Why don't they go get back in their closet?" asked one man in a wide-shouldered black suit and black cowboy hat. "It ain't logical. It's against nature." His son, who also wore a cowboy hat, pointed proudly to his pregnant wife and said, "They can't do that."

As I walked away, the son called out, "Remember, Sodom and Gomorrah got boiled in oil because they were gay."

Moving Targets

Overall, the feeling in Alltel was more saccharine than sulphurous, but the cozy unity inside depended on the enemy without. Christian nationalism, like most militant ideologies, can exist only in opposition to something. Its sense of righteousness depends on feeling besieged, no matter how much power it amasses. Conservatives control almost the entire federal government, along with an enormous Christian counterculture, but go to any right-wing gathering, and you'll hear speaker after speaker talk about being under attack, about yearning to "take the country back," about the necessity of fighting ever harder.

Needing to see their foe as equal to their hatred, they exaggerate its strength. So gay people become a threat to the most important thing conservatives have—their families. In standing up to that threat, they see themselves as heroes. Their loathing is transformed into virtue.

This is a familiar phenomenon, one Richard Hofstadter described in his seminal 1964 essay "The Paranoid Style in American Politics": "Since the enemy is thought of as being totally evil and totally unappeasable, he must be totally eliminated—if not from the world, at least from the theater of operations to which the paranoid directs his attention," Hofstadter wrote. "Even partial success leaves him with the same sense of powerlessness with which he began, and this in turn only strengthens his awareness of the vast and terrifying quality of the enemy he opposes."[14]

While the paranoid style is perennial, the enemy keeps changing. Throughout the nineteenth and twentieth centuries, American right-wing movements were fueled by fear and hatred of Catholics, a loathing coupled with a perverse fascination with the supposed debaucheries of the convent. (Right-wing books about the "homosexual agenda" are very much in this tradition, lingering lasciviously on descriptions of the most outré and scatological of sexual practices.)

Protestant hostility to Catholicism has certainly not disappeared. In Tim LaHaye and Jerry Jenkins's *Left Behind* novels, there's a Catholic cardinal among the Antichrist's inner circle, "all robed and hatted and vested in velvet and piping."[15] Many evangelical colleges bar Catholics and Jews from their faculty. Bob Jones University continues to call Catholicism a "cult," sparking a minor media firestorm after George Bush visited the school during the 2000 Republican primary campaign.

Still, the last few decades have seen a remarkable alliance between evangelicals and conservative Catholics based on sexual politics, especially shared opposition to abortion and gay marriage. Today, several of the leading lights of the Christian right, including William Bennett and Alan Keyes, are Catholic. Born-again Protestants made a hit of *The Passion of the Christ*, the sanguinary vision of right-wing Catholic Mel Gibson. When the hard-line Cardinal Ratzinger became pope in 2005, evangelicals hailed him as an ally.

Racism, too, has been a crucial ingredient in American right-wing movements, and it obviously remains strong in many places. In 2004, Alabama disgraced itself by voting against removing segregationist language from its state constitution. In 2001, the Family Research Council's Tony Perkins addressed the Louisiana chapter of the Council of Conservative Citizens, a leading white supremacist organization.[16] A 2004 survey by the American Mosaic Project at the University of Minnesota found that 48.3 percent of white conservative Christians said they would disapprove if their child wanted to marry a black person, compared with 21.8 percent of white Americans as a whole.

Nevertheless, racial prejudice is increasingly taboo among the religious right, and in many places evangelical culture is remarkably integrated. Megachurches are more conservative than older, more established congregations, but they're also statistically more diverse. The crowd at World Harvest was about 40 percent African-American, with dozens of interracial couples and biracial kids. At one point, a singer called out, "Do we have any black folks in the house this morning?" prompting happy shouts and cheers.

White evangelical leaders have worked hard to shed their movement's racist past, and their attacks on gay marriage are often coupled with denunciation of antimiscegenation laws. In the 1990s, the Traditional Values Coalition and Jeremiah Films made a video called *Gay Rights, Special Rights*, which portrayed the gay rights movement as a threatening co-option of the noble civil rights struggle. (One of the video's talking heads was Trent Lott, who in 2002 was forced to resign as Senate majority leader after saying that America should have elected segregationist Strom Thurmond in 1948.)

Black pastors are often featured prominently at antigay events. When I spoke to Kansas's Jerry Johnston, he was working to organize an April 2005 anti-gay-marriage rally in Kansas City. One of its themes, he said, would be "racial reconciliation."

Among the foremost figures in uniting people through homophobia is David Barton. Barton has helped make the Texas Republican party one of the most antigay in the country—its 2004 platform asserted that "the practice of sodomy tears at the fabric of society, con- tributes to the breakdown of the family unit, and leads to the spread of dangerous, communicable diseases. Homosexual behavior is contrary to the fundamental, unchanging truths that have been ordained by God, recognized by our country's founders, and shared by the majority of Texans."

Even as he attacks one group of citizens, Barton fashions himself as a new, nonracist style of reactionary by reaching out to black Christians (many of whom are probably unaware of his past ties to white power groups). He publishes an "African American History" newsletter, sells posters celebrating black history on his Web site, and has spoken at "unity rallies" with black pastors. In April 2004, he addressed five hundred people at an event organized by the Undoing Racism

Task Force in Lufkin, Texas, where several white pastors and ministry workers got on their knees and asked their black brethren for forgiveness for past injustices.[17]

In some states, anti-gay-marriage initiatives led to a slightly higher black vote for Bush in 2004. In Ohio, Bush won 16 percent of the African-American electorate, compared with 11 percent nationally, a result that Rod Parsley and others attributed to Issue 1.[18]

Like racism, overt anti-Semitism has also become unacceptable in most evangelical circles, supplanted by philo-Semitism and passionate Zionism. Partly, this is due to the right's identification with Israel's fight against Islamic terrorism, but more important is the enormous influence of premillenial dispensationalism, a major strain within American evangelical Christianity. Dispensationalists—a category that includes most prominent evangelical leaders—believe that the return of Jews to Israel and the restoration of Jewish sovereignty over the Temple Mount is a precondition for the rapture, the apocalypse, and the return of Christ.

That doesn't mean that anti-Jewish sentiment has disappeared from the Christian right. The dispensationalist scenario, after all, includes apocalyptic warfare in Israel and the violent death of most of the world's Jews. (In the *Left Behind* series, only those Jews who atone for the "specific national sin" of "[r]ejecting the messiahship of Jesus" are saved.[19]) Fundamentalist Christians will say that they're simply proclaiming the frightful truth, but much of their literature dwells on the details of Jewish torment with disquieting relish.

In addition, the language that the right uses to describe its enemies echoes all the tropes of classic anti-Semitism. The day after the 2004 election, the right-wing magazine *Human Events* posted a pseudosatirical piece on its Web site called "Declaration of Expulsion: A Modest Proposal." In it, the writer suggested excising several of the blue states from the union, saying,

As a class, liberals no longer are merely the vigorous opponents of the Right; they are spiteful enemies of civilization's core decency and traditions. Defamation, never envisioned by our Founding Fathers as being protected by the First Amendment, flourishes and passes today for acceptable political discourse. Movies, magazines, newspapers, radio/TV programs, plays, concerts, public schools, colleges, and most other public vehicles openly traffic in slander and libel. . . . When they tire of showering conservative victims with ideological mud, liberals promote the only other subjects with which they feel conversationally comfortable: Obscenity and sexual perversion. It's as if the genes of liberals have rendered them immune to all forms of filth.

Compare that to "The 'Decent' Jew," a 1937 missive by the Nazi Hanns Oberlindober. In it, Oberlindober describes the Jewish (and gay) sexual researcher Magnus Hirschfeld as

one of a legion of Jewish corrupters of the youth, sexual criminals, pseudo-scientists, playwrights and novelists, painters and sculptors, theater and cabaret directors, publishers and distributors of pornographic literature. They competed with each other to produce their filth, surpassing each other in obscenity, making easier the work of their racial comrades seeking to dominate an unnerved and powerless people rendered susceptible by such "art." The absence of moral rules was called freedom, and unrestrained drives were proclaimed to be the right of the young.

Oberlindober also wrote about how Jews "cold-heartedly preached and encouraged the murder of the unborn children of our people through abortion."[20]

Plenty of people on the right still think like Oberlindober. More often, though, the qualities the Nazis projected onto Jews are now ascribed to liberals and especially to homosexuals. Christian nationalists hate them as weak degenerates even as they fear their secret subversive networks, whose terrifying power is invoked to justify whatever is done in opposition.

At the Potters House church in Columbus on a Saturday evening before the 2004 election, pastor Tim Oldfield began his sermon by launching into a jeremiad against homosexuality. "We're living in a time that a lifestyle that at one time was on the list of mental disorders, called sodomy, is now called an alternative lifestyle," he said. "The Bible calls it abomination. Abomination is something *disgusting*." An old woman in the audience nodded and said, "*Very* disgusting."

A huge new building that looks like a roadside rest stop with a steeple, Potters House was one of three churches clustered at the dead end of a subdivision full of Bush/Cheney signs. A stack of voter registration forms sat on a counter in the lobby.

One of the first people I met at the Potters House was Rob Meyers, a church member who was active in the anti-gay-marriage fight. Meyers was also part of group called Minutemen United, headed by Dave Daubenmire, a local football coach turned evangelist. In 2004, Daubenmire ran for Ohio's State Board of Education in order to "defend our children against the ungodly, humanist indoctrination of the government schools," as he said on the Minutemen United Web site. During the Issue 1 campaign, Meyers, Daubenmire, and a handful of other Minutemen staged an impromptu protest at Ohio State University, demanding that the school's president, Karen Holbrook, be fired for her opposition to the measure. "Holbrook believes that candidates who live in same-sex relationships are the type of model professors the great Ohio State University wants to attract," said a Minutemen statement.

Meyers was confident that Issue 1 would galvanize the Christian vote. "I think this will drive them to the polls," he said. In the past, he said, about a fifth of his fellow congregants had been politically active. Gay marriage had awakened the rest.

Because Meyers seemed like a decent, personable man, I wondered what he would say if he met Julie Reeves and Leigh Mamlin and heard how worried they were about losing their kids' health insurance. Mamlin had fantasized about what would happen if she brought her kids to one of the local antigay churches. "Do you have the courage to look into my child's eyes and tell him, 'You don't deserve the financial security that the kids next door have?'" she imagined asking. "Hate me, but not my son."

When I brought Mamlin's family up, Meyers said, "I have nothing against them. . . ."

"God's word is against them," interjected his wife, a blond with frosty pink lipstick who'd been watching us warily as we spoke.

A few minutes later, the service began. The chapel looked like a high school gymnasium—it even had basketball nets on two sides. Flags of the world lined the walls, with American and Israeli flags flanking the stage. The Meyerses stood right at the front with their arms around each other.

A rock band played behind a worship singer who sounded very much like the 1980s pop balladeer Richard Marx. He was backed up by three gospel singers. Because it was Saturday night, not Sunday morning, the crowd was sparse—only a few dozen people. Few were dressed up. One woman wearing a faded pink sweatshirt was there alone. Even before the service started, she was crying with her head in her hands.

When Pastor Oldfield walked on stage and stood behind the Lucite pulpit, he immediately started talking about the election. "You need to pray and see the face of God about who you vote for," he said. "In the next few weeks, we're going to try to stimulate you to be part of the process. You need to vote!"

He announced an upcoming speech at the church by David Barton. "This is going to be a political . . . I shouldn't say political . . . a patriotic celebration!" he said.

And then he started talking about gays. "Ungodliness and perversion has come into the center focus of society," he said, his voice loud and staccato. "There are a lot of people who sit in the pews of churches, who have come to look on homosexuality as no longer exceedingly sinful. . . . We've come to a time when they've called us hatemongers, they call us homophobic." In the face of this onslaught, he said, Christians need the backbone to say that homosexuality "is an abomination before God and it is wrong and it demands repentance in our land!"

In the congregation, an old woman with a fluffy nimbus of hair shook her fist in agreement, then started applauding above her head. Shouts of "Amen" and "Oh Jesus" echoed around the room.

Despite their rhetoric of perversion and abomination, most fundamentalist Christians insist they don't hate gay people and, like Pastor Oldfield, they consider it a slur to be called homophobic. They hate sin, they'll say, not the sinners. Crucial to this belief system is the conviction that homosexuality can be cured. To that end, evangelicals have erected a massive network of counseling centers, inpatient programs, self-help books, and seminars devoted to turning gay people straight through so-called reparative therapy. They've even invented a holiday, National Coming Out of Homosexuality Day, to mirror the pro-gay National Coming Out Day.

Many Christian conservatives are personally as well as ideologically invested in the hope that people can "come out" of homosexuality. Plenty of them, like Phyllis Schlafly and Alan Keyes, have gay kids. Some gay people born into evangelical communities want desperately to belong. They're horrified by the idea of exile in some coastal metropolis, and cling to reparative therapy for the hope it offers of making them the people their families want them to be.

In 2000, I attended the national conference of Exodus International, an umbrella group for more than 150 ex-gay ministries. Held in August, it brought over 1000 ex-gays, would-be ex-gays, and their families to San Diego. Kids with bleach jobs and baggy jeans who wouldn't have looked out of place at a Limp Bizkit show milled about. Many wore T-shirts advertising Christian rock bands or proclaiming attitudinal slogans like "Satan Is a Punk." Everyone had a heartrending story about lacerating guilt and self-hatred. One twenty-year-old from the southern California city of Fontana recalled a night months before when a married man he'd just slept with dismissively dropped him off on a lonely street in West Hollywood. He said he lay down on the pavement, sobbing and saying, "Jesus, either you take my homosexuality away from me or I'm going to take my life away from you." The conference, he said, was the happiest five days he could remember. He was filled with hope that his life was about to change.

He was probably being set up for a cruel disappointment, since there's no evidence that reparative therapy can succeed in anything but getting gay people to abstain from sex. Frank Worthen, a former gay activist and one of the founders of the ex-gay movement, runs New Hope, a live-in reparative therapy program in San Rafael, California, where men stay for a year and work to escape their sexual attractions. When I met him in 2000, he admitted that 50 percent of the people who come to him go back to being gay, and many of those who don't simply become celibate. The workbook that he wrote for New Hope residents says, "Our primary goal is not to make heterosexuals out of homosexual people. God alone determines whether a former homosexual person is to marry and rear a family, or if he (or she) is to remain celibate, serving the Lord with his whole heart."

Among the ex-gay movement's dropouts are two of the founders of Exodus International, Michael Bussee and Garry Cooper, who left their wives for each other in 1979. John Paulk, a star of the movement lauded in books and videos about the homosexual agenda, was photographed in a Washington, D.C., gay bar in 2000. He claimed he had just stepped in to use the bathroom. One British ex-gay organization, Courage, later became an ex-ex-gay organization, renouncing the idea that homosexuality can be cured. In 2003, its founder, Jeremy Marks, wrote that he'd seen some ex-gays become "deeply depressed and hopeless, even suicidal," while those who found committed gay relationships often found happiness.

Marks's observations echo the findings of the American Psychiatric Association, which said in a 1998 statement, "psychiatric literature strongly demonstrates that treatment attempts to change sexual orientation are ineffective. However, the potential risks are great, including depression, anxiety and self-destructive behavior."

The right can't admit this; to do so would undermine the idea that homosexuality is a choice, which is key to arguments against gay rights. Instead, conservative evangelicals imagine themselves as proud bearers of spiritual samizdat that their enemies would suppress. "Focus on the Family is promoting the truth that homosexuality is preventable and treatable—a message routinely silenced today," says the Web site for Love Won Out, a series of one-day seminars that the group organizes all over the country.

This is a pattern that repeats itself again and again in the culture wars. When experts discredit some bit of fundamentalist orthodoxy, it's taken as further proof of the experts' bias. When religious conservatives are proven wrong, their faith in their righteousness only grows, along with their hatred of the conspiracy they see arrayed against them.

It was a Friday evening in Columbus during the presidential campaign, and Bush was in town for a rally with Arnold Schwarzenegger at the Nationwide Arena. The muscle-bound California governor is a social liberal, but the crowd left the event pumped with sour fury. As they streamed out, Lisa Dupler, a thirty-three-year-old from Columbus, stood near about a dozen anti-Bush protesters, holding up a rainbow-striped John Kerry sign. A thickset woman with very short, dark hair, Dupler barely flinched as people passing her hissed "faggot." An old lady looked at her and said, "You people are sick!" A kid who looked to be about ten or eleven affected a limp wrist and mincing voice and said, "Oh, I'm gay." Rather than scold him, his squat mother guffawed, then turned to Dupler and sneered, "Why don't you go marry your girl-friend?" Encouraged, her son yelled, "We don't want faggots in the White House!"

"Jesus! Jesus!" screamed twenty-six-year-old Joe Robles, pointing to his Bush-Cheney sign. "The man stands for God," he said of the presi-dent. "We want somebody who stands for Jesus. I always vote my Christian morals." Robles, a student at Ohio State University, told me that Kerry's daughter was lesbian. I said I thought that was Dick Cheney's daughter, but he shook his head no with confidence.

Robles said that Kerry would make it illegal for preachers to say that marriage should only be between a man and a woman. In California, he informed me gravely, such preaching had been deemed a hate crime, and pastors who indulge in it are fined $25,000, which "goes to lesbians."

Where had he heard this? From his pastor at World Harvest Church, he said. From Rod Parsley.

CHAPTER 3

Lord of the Laboratory:
Intelligent Design and the
War on the Enlightenment

Totalitarian propaganda can outrageously insult common sense only where common sense has lost its validity.
—Hannah Arendt, *The Origins of Totalitarianism*

It was an ordinary spring school board meeting in the small bedroom community of Dover, Pennsylvania. The high school needed new biology textbooks, and the science department had recommended Kenneth Miller and Joseph Levine's widely used *Biology*. But Bill Buckingham, a new board member who'd recently become chair of the curriculum committee, had an objection. *Biology*, he said, was "laced with Darwinism." He wanted a book that balanced theories of evolution with Christian creationism, and he was willing to turn his town into a cultural battlefield to get it.

"This country wasn't founded on Muslim beliefs or evolution," said Buckingham, a stocky, gray-haired man who wears a red, white, and blue crucifix pin on his lapel. "This country was founded on Christianity and our students should be taught as such."[1]

Carol "Casey" Brown, a fifty-seven-year-old board member and self-described Goldwater Republican, was stunned. So was her husband, fellow board member Jeff Brown. "I was picturing the headlines," Jeff told me later. "And we got them," added Casey.

As 2004 ended, journalists from around the country and the world had visited the Browns' little corner of Pennsylvania to report on the latest outbreak of America's chronic war over evolution. By then, Buckingham had succeeded in making Dover the first school district in the country to mandate that students be introduced to "intelligent design"—an updated version of creationism. In so doing, he ushered in a legal challenge from outraged parents and the ACLU that threatened to turn into a twenty-first century version of the infamous Scopes monkey trial.

The Dover case was part of a renewed revolt against evolution that's gathered force in America for the last few years, a symptom of the same religious fervor that helped propel George Bush to victory. Since 2001, the National Center for Science Education, a group formed to defend the teaching of evolution, has tallied battles over Darwin in forty-three states, and as of 2005 they were getting more frequent.

With the development of intelligent design, Darwin's foes have grown savvier—evolution, they now argue, is not just religiously but *scientifically* untenable. Biochemistry and mathematics, they say, have shown that the structure of proteins and amino acids in cells—the building blocks of life—is too complex to have been choreographed by anything short of a supernatural force. Ultimately, though, the partisans of creationism and intelligent design are not fighting over empirical data. What's going on in states and school districts nationwide is a struggle over the very nature of reality. The question is whether knowledge of the world is possible without reference to God as the creator, and whether science education should be permitted to contradict the Christian worldview. Across America, communities are answering no.

The same month Bush was reelected, the rural Grantsburg, Wisconsin, school district revised its curriculum to allow the teaching of creationism and intelligent design. After a community outcry—including a letter of protest from two hundred Wisconsin clergy members—the district revised the policy, but continued to mandate that students be taught "the scientific strengths and weaknesses of evolutionary theory," a common creationist tactic that fosters the illusion of scientific controversy over evolution.

Other anti-evolution initiatives affect entire states. In the November election, creationists took over the Kansas Board of Education. The last time they had a majority, in 1999, they voted to erase any mention of evolution from the state curriculum. The state became a laughingstock and the anti-evolutionists were defeated in the next Republican primary, leading to the policy's reversal. Newly victorious in 2004, the anti-evolutionists not only planned to introduce the teaching of intelligent design—they set about changing the state's official definition of science itself to include supernatural as well as natural explanations for the world's phenomena.

In December 2004, *The New York Times* reported that Missouri legislators were crafting a bill that would require state biology textbooks to include at least one chapter dealing with "alternative theories to evolution." Speaking to the *Times*, State Representative Cynthia Davis compared Darwinists to Al Qaeda. "It's like when the hijackers took over those four planes on Sept. 11 and took people to a place where they didn't want to go," she said. "I think a lot of people feel that liberals have taken our country somewhere we don't want to go. I think a lot more people realize this is our country and we're going to take it back."[2]

Right-wingers in Congress, on talk radio, and on cable TV stoked the anti-evolution rebellion, ranting that academic freedom meant the freedom to teach creationism. Having shown their strength in the election, cultural conservatives weren't in the mood to compromise. America is a democracy, and they had the numbers. They saw no reason that the principles of science shouldn't be up for popular vote.*

Seeking to avoid such controversy, many schools have decided not

---

* George Bush evidently agreed. In August 2005 the president—who previously said that the "jury is still out" on evolution—told a group of Texas journalists that schools should teach both evolution *and* intelligent design.

to teach evolution at all.* Fearing protests from pious patrons, some science museums have backed away from Darwin, refusing to show Imax movies like *Volcanoes of the Sea Deep* that contradict Genesis.

The Wedge Strategy

The latest eruptions in America's perennial war over origins haven't happened spontaneously. People like Bill Buckingham may have started their hometown crusades independently, but the Center for Science and Culture (CSC), the Seattle headquarters of the intelligent design movement, laid the groundwork for them years before.

Intelligent design is the heir to creation science, which attempted to cloak theological objections to evolution in scientific legitimacy. Its proponents use language that sounds secular and scholarly. They attack Darwin with arguments about cell structure and mathematical probabilities that are difficult for a layperson to evaluate and insist that their challenges to evolution are driven by fact, not ideology. "During the past decade," the CSC's Web site says, "new research and discoveries in such fields as physics, cosmology, biochemistry, genetics, and paleontology have caused a growing number of scientists and science theorists to question neo-Darwinism and propose design as the best explanation for the existence of specified complexity in the natural world."

But while CSC calls itself a secular organization, the impetus behind intelligent design is unmistakably religious—something its own fellows freely admit to sympathetic Christian audiences. The Center for Science and Culture operates out of the Discovery Institute, a Seattle think tank that's funded in part by savings and loan heir Howard Ahmanson, a leading patron of Christian nationalism. Ahmanson spent twenty years on the board of R. J. Rushdoony's Chalcedon Foundation,

---

* As *The New York Times* reported on February 1, 2005, "In districts around the country, even when evolution is in the curriculum it may not be in the classroom, according to researchers who follow the issue. Teaching guides and textbooks may meet the approval of biologists, but superintendents or principals discourage teachers from discussing it. Or teachers themselves avoid the topic, fearing protests from fundamentalists in their communities."

which advocates the replacement of American civil law with biblical law. "Chalcedon does not appeal to modern liberalized generic Christendom any more than it appeals to theological liberalism itself," it says on its Web site. "Rather, we appeal to those devout, rock-ribbed saints who believe that if the Bible is good enough for the church, it is good enough for the school and state; who believe that if Jesus Christ is Lord of the family, he is also Lord of the laboratory and the board room; who recognize that if Christianity is good enough for them, it is good enough for their great-great grandchildren."

The Center for Science and Culture also aims, in a far more elliptical way, to put God at the center of civic life. Originally called the Center for the Renewal of Science and Culture, CSC speaks in two languages—one for the general public, and one for the faithful. Talking to the latter, it's been candid about its true, grandiose goal of undermining the secular legacy of the Enlightenment and rebuilding society on religious foundations. As it said in a 1999 fund-raising proposal that was later leaked online, "Discovery Institute's Center for the Renewal of Science and Culture seeks nothing less than the overthrow of materialism and its cultural legacies."

The proposal, titled "The Wedge Strategy," began:

The proposition that human beings are created in the image of God is one of the bedrock principles on which Western civilization was built. . . . Yet a little over a century ago, this cardinal idea came under wholesale attack by intellectuals drawing on the discoveries of modern science. Debunking the traditional conceptions of both God and man, thinkers such as Charles Darwin, Karl Marx, and Sigmund Freud portrayed humans not as moral and spiritual beings, but as animals or machines who inhabited a universe ruled by purely impersonal forces and whose behavior and very thoughts were dictated by the unbending forces of biology, chemistry, and environment. This materialistic conception of reality eventually infected virtually every area of our culture, from politics and economics to literature and art.

As "The Wedge Strategy" suggests, many CSC fellows are troubled more by the philosophical consequences of evolution than by the fact that it contradicts a literal reading of the Bible. Most of them—though not all—are too scientifically sophisticated to insist that the world is a mere six thousand years old, the position taken by today's most doctrinaire creationists. In mainstream forums, CSC fellows eschew sectarian religious language. They don't want to be associated with the medieval persecutors of Copernicus and Galileo. Instead, they try to present themselves as heirs to those very visionaries, insisting that dogmatic secularists desperate to deny God are thwarting their open-minded quest for truth.

Most CSC fellows even accept evolution *within* species. What they dispute, in general, is the idea that random mutation and natural selection led to the evolution of higher life-forms from lower ones. Such a process seems to them incompatible with the belief that man was created in the image of God, and that God takes a special interest in him.

Several CSC fellows have impressive credentials from prestigious universities, and they know how to argue in mainstream forums. Phillip Johnson, one of the fathers of the movement, is a law professor at UC Berkeley. Jonathan Wells, author of the influential intelligent design book *Icons of Evolution*, has a Ph.D. in molecular and cell biology from Berkeley and another in religious studies from Yale. A member of the Unification Church whose education was bankrolled by Reverend Sun Myung Moon, he's written that he sought his degrees specifically to fight evolution. As he put it in an article posted on the Moonie Web site True Parents, "Father's words, my studies, and my prayers convinced me that I should devote my life to destroying Darwinism, just as many of my fellow Unificationists had already devoted their lives to destroying Marxism. When Father chose me (along with about a dozen other seminary graduates) to enter a Ph.D. program in 1978, I welcomed the opportunity to prepare myself for battle."[3]

Academic degrees let intelligent design proponents present their theory as something more respectable than creationism in drag. But as Wells's comments show, this isn't a skirmish about competing scientific analyses. It's a holy war.

One can believe in both God and evolution, of course, but intelligent design supporters think that evolution leads, at best, to an apprehension of God as distant and indifferent, as a kind of nebulous imminence. "A mere concept of God in the human mind is no help at all," wrote Phillip Johnson in his *The Wedge of Truth*, "because a God created by human philosophy is just another idol."[4]

Intelligent design strives to make science compatible with a God who is intimately involved with human beings, who issues commandments and demands obedience—a God who provides society's organizing principle. "What we need is for God himself to speak, to give us a secure foundation on which we can build," Johnson wrote. But what is the word of God? To Johnson, the answer is obvious. "When we have reached that point in our questioning, we will inevitably encounter the person of Jesus Christ," he wrote.[5]

Johnson wants Jesus to supplant materialism and naturalism as the foundation of scientific reality. Intelligent design is a tool to do that. According to "The Wedge Strategy," "Design theory promises to reverse the stifling dominance of the materialist worldview, and to replace it with a science consonant with Christian and theistic convictions."

To that end, "The Wedge Strategy" proposed an ambitious five-year plan to lay siege to the scientific and educational establishment. It envisioned ten states rectifying "ideological imbalance" in their science curricula by including intelligent design, design movements sprouting internationally, and legal reformers basing "legislative proposals on design theory"—in other words, on the perceived will of God. The plan, then, is to undermine the Enlightenment conception of the physical world as a prelude to undermining the Enlightenment's social legacies. What the authors of "The Wedge Strategy" want to discredit isn't just Charles Darwin—it's the very idea that truth can be ascertained without reference to the divine. Religious law makes much more sense when religion is seen as the foundation of reality.

The authors of "The Wedge Strategy" wrote that the second phase of their program "is to prepare the popular reception of our ideas" by cultivating opinion makers and "our natural constituency, namely, Christians." Armed with degrees and the credibility they bring, CSC fellows have secured invitations to testify before state boards of education. They've published op-eds in mainstream newspapers and are regularly consulted for "balance" in stories about evolution controversies.

The reframing of evolution, a theory undisputed among scientific experts, as one side of a public "debate" is an enormous victory for the Christian right. The right has helped create an atmosphere in which our understanding of empirical reality is subject to political pressure, in which the findings of science are trumped by ideology. It has succeeded where leftist postmodernists failed in subverting the authority of the rational.

When truth loses its meaning, all manner of deceptions can be fostered. How do we know the founding fathers *didn't* intend a theocracy? Who's to say there *weren't* weapons of mass destruction in Iraq? Can anyone prove there *isn't* a homosexual conspiracy? Was John Kerry a war hero, or did he shoot *himself*? There are two sides to every story, right? Who are you going to believe, your pastor or the liberal media?

This kind of psychological climate—at once utterly credulous and sullenly cynical—gives totalitarian movements space to grow. As Hannah Arendt wrote in *The Origins of Totalitarianism*, "Before mass leaders seize the power to fit reality to their lies, their propaganda is marked by its extreme contempt for facts as such, for in their opinion fact depends entirely on the power of man who can fabricate it."[6]

"The Wedge Strategy" wouldn't be progressing as effectively as it is without important allies in the Republican party, especially Pennsylvania senator Rick Santorum. During Bush's first term, Santorum tried to attach an amendment to the No Child Left Behind Act that would encourage the teaching of intelligent design. It said, "[W]here topics are taught that may generate controversy (such as biological evolution), the curriculum should help students to understand the full range of scientific views that exist, why such topics may generate controversy, and how scientific discoveries can profoundly affect society." The statement was eventually adopted as part of the "conference report" on the law, which means it has advisory power only.

The language sounds anodyne, but Santorum's intent was to give evolution's opponents the government's backing. In 2002, Ohio debated adding intelligent design to its statewide science standards. In a *Washington Times* op-ed supporting the change, Santorum quoted his amendment and then wrote, "If the Education Board of Ohio does not include intelligent design in the new teaching standards, many students will be denied a first-rate science education. Many will be left behind."[7]

Santorum, not surprisingly, came out in favor of Dover's policy. The school board, in turn, distributed copies of one of Santorum's pro-intelligent-design op-eds along with the agenda at their first public meeting in 2005.

Although Bill Buckingham first argued for teaching creationism in Dover, he soon adopted the phrase "intelligent design" instead. The change in language was significant, because intelligent design was crafted to circumvent the Supreme Court ruling that made it illegal for public schools to teach creationism. Masquerading as science, intelligent design is meant to neutralize First Amendment objections to teaching religious doctrine in public schools. Intelligent design's promoters hope to convince the public that evolution is a theory under fire within the scientific community, and thus doesn't deserve its preeminent place in biology curricula.

At Dover's June 14, 2004, school board meeting, Buckingham said he wanted the board to consider adopting the intelligent design textbook *Of Pandas and People: The Central Question of Biological Origin*. First published in 1989, *Of Pandas and People* contains one of the first uses of the phrase "intelligent design." It was a strategic response to the

Supreme Court's 1987 ruling in *Edwards v. Aguillard*, which overturned a Louisiana law mandating that "creation science" be taught alongside evolution. Since the court ruled that "creation science" is a religious doctrine, savvy opponents of evolution sought to recast the central tenets of creationism in a way that hid their religious inspiration. Thus intelligent design was born.

Percival Davis, one of *Of Pandas and People*'s authors, also cowrote the creationist text *A Case for Creation*. An online ad for *Pandas* on the Web site for Answers in Genesis—a major creationist group—describes it as a "superbly written" book for public schools that "has no Biblical content, yet contains creationists' interpretations and refutations for evidences [*sic*] usually found in standard textbooks supporting evolution!"

Of Pandas and People's copyright is held by the Foundation for Thought and Ethics, a Texas-based nonprofit headed by Jon Buell, an ordained minister and former staffer of the Campus Crusade for Christ. The foundation's articles of incorporation describe its mission as "proclaiming, publishing, preaching [and] teaching . . . the Christian Gospel and understanding of the Bible and the light it sheds on the academic and social issues of the day." The foundation publishes two other textbooks—an abstinence-only text called *Sex and Character* and *Never Before in History*, a book about "the decisive role that Christianity played in America's founding."

Not surprisingly, the Discovery Institute's Center for Science and Culture has close links with the Foundation for Thought and Ethics. The foundation's academic editor is William Dembski, a senior fellow at CSC, and it publishes books by CSC program director Stephen C. Meyer and program advisor Phillip Johnson.

In keeping with the agenda of the people who produced it, *Of Pandas and People* doesn't read much like a high school biology book at all—rather, it's a sustained attack on Darwinism:

> In creating a new organism, as in building a new house, the
> blueprint comes first. We cannot build a palace by tinkering

with a tool shed and adding bits of marble piecemeal here and there. We have to begin by devising a plan for the palace that coordinates all the parts into an integrated whole.

Darwinian evolution locates the origin of new organisms in material causes, the accumulation of individual traits. That is akin to saying the origin of a palace is in the bits of marble added to the tool shed.[8]

A statuesque woman with a strawberry blonde bob and crisply proper diction, Casey Brown isn't a scientist, but she prides herself on being well read, and after ten years on the school board, she knows what a good biology textbook looks like. When she saw *Of Pandas and People*, she was appalled. "It's poor science and worse theology," she lamented.

According to Brown, by the Dover school board's August meeting, Buckingham had given up on the idea of using *Pandas* as the main text, but he insisted that the board buy it as a supplement. Otherwise, he said, he wouldn't approve the purchase of *Biology*. One of Buckingham's supporters on the board was out sick that night, and without her, the vote deadlocked, 4–4. Finally, worried that the school would have to start the year without textbooks, one member switched her vote, and *Biology* was approved. The town's little drama seemed to be at an end.

But shortly after the motion to buy *Of Pandas and People* was defeated, Buckingham raised $850 from members of his church to buy the books privately. He gave the funds to another board member's father, who then anonymously donated sixty copies of the text to the school district.[9] When the books arrived, Buckingham and his allies denied any knowledge of who sent them. Then they set about figuring out how to integrate *Of Pandas and People* into the curriculum.

On October 18, 2004, the board voted on a resolution written by Buckingham and his supporters. It said, "Students will be made aware of gaps/problems in Darwin's theory and of other theories of evolution including, but not limited to, intelligent design. Note: Origins of Life is not taught." The *Pandas* books were to be kept in the science classroom, and teachers were instructed to read a statement referring students to them.

Casey and Jeff argued against it. "We kept maintaining this is going to get us into legal trouble. It was a clear violation," Casey said. As an alternative, she proposed offering a comparative world religions elective, which would teach the creation myths of various faiths.

But Buckingham was determined, and he challenged his opponents' "literacy, knowledge of American history and patriotism," as the local newspaper reported.[10]

Finally, the board voted. The mandate to teach intelligent design passed 6–3. Casey and Jeff Brown quit in protest. The other dissenter, Noel Wenrich, turned to Buckingham and said, "We lost two good people because of you."

"And Mr. Buckingham said, with profanity, good riddance to bad rubbish," Casey recalled. "And he called Mr. Wenrich every name in the book."

Not surprisingly, a handful of Dover parents soon joined with the ACLU to sue the school district, further increasing the town's rancor. They announced the lawsuit on December 14, 2004, at a press conference in the rotunda of Pennsylvania's Capitol building in Harrisburg. Reporters and cameramen crowded around the microphone as a succession of Dover parents, lawyers, liberal clergymen, and scientists spoke.

The Reverend Barry Lynn, executive director of Americans United for Separation of Church and State, had come from D.C. for the event. "We've been battling this from Hawaii to California to New Hampshire to Cobb County," he said, referring to the suburban Atlanta school district that had recently put warning stickers on its biology textbooks calling evolution "a theory, not a fact."

As the cameras rolled, a few protesters tried to edge their way into the frame. A man named Carl Jarboe, in a purple sport coat and a fur hat, stood near the parents holding a fluorescent green sign saying "ACLU Censors Truth." His wife, wearing a kerchief on her head and small round glasses, held a similar sign saying "Evolution: Unscientific and Untrue. Why Does the ACLU Oppose Schools Giving All the Evidence?"

The parents ignored them. Most were somewhat hesitant in front of all the cameras. They weren't culture warriors, and they didn't speak in ideological terms. Instead, they talked about what Buckingham and the other creationists were doing to their school and their community.

"We don't believe that intelligent design is science, and we have faith in ourselves as parents that we can do a good job teaching our children about religion," Christy Rehm, a thirty-one-year-old mother of four, said after the conference. "We have faith in our pastor, we have faith in our community that our children are going to be raised to be decent people. So we don't feel that it's the school board's job to make that decision for our children."

Jarboe, who introduced himself to me as a former assistant professor of chemistry at Messiah College, a nearby Christian school, was convinced that the parents were being used to further a sinister agenda. Like a great many members of the Christian right, he sees the ACLU as a subversive, possibly demonic institution. "I maintain it's a Communist front," he said.

He then pressed a flyer into my hand from a two-day creation seminar he'd attended at the Faith Baptist Church in the nearby town of Lebanon. It was run by Dr. Kent Hovind, a creationist who argues that, as the flyer said, "it has been proven that man lived at the same time as dinosaurs." To underline this point, Hovind runs Dinosaur Adventure Land, a theme park in Pensacola, Florida, with rides and exhibits about the not-so-long-ago days when humans and dinosaurs roamed the planet together.

Jarboe also suggested I read the work of Ken Ham, founder of the Kentucky-based creationist ministry Answers in Genesis, and Duane Gish, a professor at the Institute for Creation Research, which has a creationist graduate school in San Diego. (The institute publishes *The Grand Canyon: A Different View*, which attributes the chasm to Noah's flood. Since 2003, it's been sold at the Grand Canyon's government-run bookstore, despite the protests of many National Park Service employees.)

Gish and Ham are as respected in evangelical circles as mainstream science writers like Stephen Jay Gould and Richard Dawkins are in secular society. At Dover school board meetings, people who supported Buckingham quoted them to prove that creation science (or intelligent design, phrases they used interchangeably) is, in fact, science. With no agreement on the most basic of facts or sources of authority, discussions between today's creationists and evolutionists seem particularly futile. Dialogue is impossible without some shared sense of reality.

William Jennings Bryan's Revenge

Experts accept evolution as something very close to fact, but Americans never have. In a November 2004 CBS News/*New York Times* poll about evolution, 55 percent of people said that God created humans in their present form. Twenty-seven percent believed in the evolution of mankind guided by God, and 13 percent believed in evolution without God.

So it should come as no surprise that the majority of Americans—65 percent, according to the poll cited above—favor teaching creationism alongside evolution in public schools. Creationism is a perfect culture war issue, because it inevitably pits majorities in local communities against interloping lawyers and scientists. In a country gripped by right-wing populism, it's not hard to stoke resentment against scientists who have the gall to think that they know more than everybody else.

Thus the anti-Darwin cause is stubborn, and its rhetoric varies little. Indeed, many historians date the start of our current culture wars to 1925, the year of the famous Scopes monkey trial in Dayton, Tennessee.

In the 1920s the battle over evolution had been raging throughout the country, and it came to a head when twenty-four-year-old teacher John Scopes challenged his state's anti-evolution law. His persecution set the stage for a legendary courtroom showdown that pitted Chicago defense attorney Clarence Darrow against William Jennings Bryan, the crusading populist, fundamentalist, and three-time presidential candidate.

Bryan, the nation's leading anti-evolutionist, made his case in democratic terms. In his book *The Creationists*, historian Ronald Numbers wrote, "Throughout his political career, Bryan had placed his faith in the common people, and he resented the attempt of a few thousand elitist scientists 'to establish an oligarchy over the forty million American Christians' to dictate what should be taught in the schools."[11]

Bryan and his fellow Scopes prosecutors won their trial, but the national mockery that followed it did much to alienate conservative Christians from secular society, setting the stage for the cultural conflicts of later decades. In the wake of their Pyrrhic victory in Tennessee, many fundamentalists—a term that first entered the American lexicon during the trial—turned their back on mainstream schools and media and built their own counterculture instead.[12]

All of this happened underground, invisible to outsiders. In the cities and on the coasts, it seemed that creationism had been decisively and universally discredited. By midcentury, Cold War competition with the Soviet Union increased the country's concern for sound science education, and the National Science Foundation oversaw the creation of new biology textbooks that emphasized evolution. The 1960 movie *Inherit the Wind*, based on the Broadway play, portrayed Bryan as a treacherous demagogue and the opponents of evolution as savagely stupid hicks. It was nominated for four Oscars.

Meanwhile, though, the fundamentalist counterculture was nurturing new generations of creationists. Decades later, when they were strong enough, it provided them a base from which to attempt a takeover of the American mainstream.

In the years since Scopes, there have been repeated attempts to introduce creationism into public schools, with proponents often echoing Bryan's populist arguments. The 1987 *Edwards* case, however, seemed to shut off the creationists' legal avenues.

Many fundamentalists retreated into private schools or homeschooling, where the teaching of creationism thrives. Christian bookstores and textbook fairs abound in creationist texts and DVDs for all ages. There are radio shows, frequent seminars, and conferences for both teachers and students. Those who can afford it can join creationist tours of the

Grand Canyon and the Galápagos Islands. According to the Institute for Creation Research, creation science is taught at 188 evangelical colleges. There's a Center for Creation Studies at Jerry Falwell's Liberty University. In 2004, it awarded an honorary doctorate to Ken Ham.

A former science teacher from Australia, Ham has built one of the powerhouses of the creationist movement. Answers in Genesis has a staff of one hundred, and churns out massive numbers of creationist books, videos, DVDs, and teachers guides. Right now, Ham is overseeing construction of a $25 million, 50,000-square-foot creationist museum and planetarium near Cincinnati, which is set to open in 2007. He spends his life traveling around the country and the world, delivering the message that the Bible is the literal world of God, the Earth is but a few thousand years old, and that dinosaurs were really dragons who lived in the Garden of Eden before the fall of man.

I met Ham in February 2005 at an Answers in Genesis conference held at D. James Kennedy's ten-thousand-member Coral Ridge Presbyterian Church in Ft. Lauderdale, Florida. A few hundred people, many of them homeschooling parents, had come to the three-day event. The entire ninth grade class—about one hundred students—from Kennedy's private Christian school attended several lectures.

Coral Ridge's narrow white spire shoots up from the flat concrete dullness of North Federal Highway like a mirage; silhouetted against a pastel Florida sunset, it seems a space-age version of a medieval cathedral. Inside, the church has a vaulting white chapel streaked with colored light refracting through small stained-glass windows.

There's a mahogany lectern at the front of the room, and at the Answers in Genesis conference, speaker after speaker stood before it and offered detailed biblical exegeses and scientific-sounding "proof" that, for example, carbon dating is inaccurate. At one point Kennedy told the audience that evolution—"the most destructive idea that has ever entered the mind of man"—inspired communism, and is thus responsible for 135 million deaths.

Ham was the most dynamic of the speakers at Coral Ridge. With his hollow cheeks and shaggy gray beard, he has a vaguely antediluvian look, like an Amish patriarch or street-corner prophet. But as he paced in front of his listeners, speaking rapidly and then stopping suddenly for emphasis, asking the audience questions and cracking jokes, he seemed a very modern showman.

"I make no apology for the fact that I start with the revealed word of God as the basis of my thinking," Ham told the audience. "That's my starting point, my axiom. . . . But if you go to the public schools, where they deny God has anything to do with reality, then it's man who determines truth." Talking about science without reference to God is inherently anti-Christian, he said. "You're either for Christ or against him."

Everyone, said Ham, views reality through a pair of metaphorical glasses. "You've either got on God's word glasses, or man's word," he said. There's no way to take the glasses off, to achieve objectivity. The question becomes which lens you're going to trust. "The Bible gives us an account of history to enable us to have the right presuppositions to know the right way of thinking in every area," he said. "Ain't it exciting being a Christian? We have the history to explain the universe!"

In the hall outside, tables were piled high with creationist books for toddlers, graduate students, and everyone in between. Most of the children's books dealt with dinosaurs in the Garden of Eden, with Noah's Ark, or both. *D Is for Dinosaur*, a rhyming alphabet book by Ham and his wife, Mally, contains this passage:

K is for Knowledge, which made Noah sad;
The world would be judged, because people were bad!
God warned He would send a terrible flood
That would cover the world with water and mud.

When I spoke to Ham, he was confident that his ideas were migrating into the mainstream. "Because of all the information we pump out—the books, the DVDs and so on—AIG is like a big reservoir and we have all these conduits," he said. "People are getting materials, and they share it with their friends and others. It's like a spiderweb. It grows. When you look across the country and you see all the battles in regard to creation and evolution in the science classroom, I think a lot of the people who are involved in those have been influenced by the creation materials."

For all the highly publicized cases like Dover, Pennsylvania, Ham said, there are other, usually rural public schools that are teaching creationism under the media's radar. "I know of public school teachers who tell me that they teach creation to their students, or they teach them the problems of evolution and don't have a problem," he said. "It's only when some liberal atheist family gets involved and calls the ACLU in that there might be a problem."

But evolution's opponents are getting tired of hiding. As the creationist counterculture has grown, so has its desire for mainstream recognition and acceptance. Ham predicts we'll see many more public school battles in the years to come. "People are starting to do something, starting to take a stand," he said. Intelligent design is a tool to do that. "I think a lot of the people involved in trying to get intelligent design in the classroom don't necessarily understand what the intelligent design movement stands for," Ham said. They just know that it's a way to strike at Darwin.

Indeed, although many of the conservatives storming the barricades of science education use the rhetoric of intelligent design, the substance of their arguments differs little from those made by William Jennings Bryan in Dayton, Tennessee, eighty years ago.

On December 15, 2004, Pat Buchanan guest-hosted a debate about the Dover school board's decision on MSNBC's *Scarborough Country*. It was stacked four to one in favor of the board—besides Buchanan, the guests were Christian music star Natalie Grant, Al Mohler, president of Southern Baptist Theological Seminary, Republican strategist Jack Burkman and, for balance, Dave Silverman, a spokesman for American Atheists. Apparently, there was no need to invite a biologist.

Just as Bryan had, Burkman framed the issue in terms of populist democracy. "Why should the state and the federal government have a monopoly on defining what constitutes science?" he asked. "I see no problem with presenting a creationist view in the schools, given that 70 percent of Americans want that. The law should reflect democratic desires. It should reflect public desires."

In Dover, most of the public seemed to desire schools that teach creationism, although many balked at the cost of a lawsuit.

An area of quaint farms being colonized by new subdivisions, Dover is transforming into an exurban American nowhere, a place of highways and strip malls and SUVs adorned with patriotic magnets. It's a town so Republican that local elections are usually decided entirely in the primaries. Settled by Germans and traditionally dominated by Lutherans, it's also home to a number of increasingly assertive evangelical churches.

According to Jeff and Casey Brown, Dover has always had a laissez-faire ethos, but in the last few years there have been telling signs of a growing religious militancy. For twenty years, a painting depicting the descent of man—a gift from an alumnus—hung in the Dover high school science wing. Not long before the textbook fight, a town employee deemed it indecent, and while working on renovations at the school, he took it outside and burned it.

During Dover's debate over intelligent design, one of the school board members shocked Casey by asking whether she'd been born again. Shortly after they quit the board in protest, the Browns met with Anna Badkhen, a *San Francisco Chronicle* reporter, at the town diner. As they left, Badkhen later wrote, a waitress in her thirties slipped her a note. "Beware," it read. "God wrote over 2,000 years ago that there would be false prophets and teachers. If you would like to know the truth read the Bible."[13]

"I would say ten years ago that wouldn't have happened," Casey told me a few weeks later. She was sitting at the kitchen table in her family's rambling house on Dover's pretty rural edge, alternately knitting and smoking Montclair cigarettes. Jeff, an electrician with silver mutton-chops and a tweed newsboy hat, paced around behind her. Voluble and ironic, he's lived in the area his whole life and seems to relish his role as the town's freethinker. On the table was a copy of *Evolution: A Theory in Crisis*, by Michael Denton, a former senior fellow at the Discovery Institute. A stranger had sent it with a note arguing that students needed to be made aware of flaws in Darwin's theory.

Many of the Dover residents who disagreed with the school board's decision were motivated by worries over the cost of a lawsuit rather than a belief in evolution. "I would say that people who are against what the school board is doing in principle are a minority, a great minority," said Dover native Noel Wenrich, who had recently quit the school board after moving to another district. "However, when it comes to spending money on it, it's a whole other issue."

Even with money at stake, the board's popular backing was strong. According to a January 2005 poll by Susquehanna Polling and Research, most Dover voters believed that intelligent design was synonymous with creationism, but they still supported the board's policy by a 54–36 margin, with 10 percent either undecided or indifferent. Forty percent "strongly" supported teaching intelligent design, compared with 29 percent who were strongly opposed.

Talking to Wenrich, it was clear how little credibility Darwin had in Dover. A thirty-six-year-old Army veteran and father of two, Wenrich himself didn't believe in evolution, and spoke in much the same way as intelligent design's most ardent proponents. "It is going full circle now from the religious community ruling what can be thought, that's what they tried to do in the Middle Ages," he said. "We've come down to the scientific community trying to tell us what we can think. Basically what the scientific community currently is doing is saying, 'You'll have no god before mine. Mine happens to be Darwin.' Any other thought will not be tolerated."

When Buckingham tried to challenge Darwin, though, Wenrich felt honor-bound to put his duty to the school above his personal politics. "If it were my money I'd have no problem," he said. "I'd go out and fight it. But to use the public's money that's supposed to be educating our kids is absolutely irresponsible. They're already looking at putting off buying textbooks, not buying library books, not updating computer equipment. When we're looking at those budget cuts, it's irresponsible to go out and pick a fight with the Supreme Court."

The school board didn't need to worry about most of its legal fees. It was being represented pro bono by the Thomas More Law Center, a right-wing Catholic firm that describes itself as "the sword and shield for people of faith." (Rick Santorum was on its advisory board.) Wenrich told me that Thomas More lawyers had been advising Buckingham for months before the ACLU filed its lawsuit.

Despite the law firm's help, the suit would be financially devastating to the district, the second poorest in the county. Dover would have to pay for lost wages of people called to testify, and it would have to provide outside counsel for some witness, like the Browns, who didn't want Thomas More representing them. Jeff Brown guessed that depositions alone would cost the district $30,000. Then, if Dover were to lose, federal civil rights law would make it liable for the ACLU's legal fees. "It won't be cheap," Witold Walczak, the ACLU's Pennsylvania legal director, said at the December 2004 press conference at the state Capitol.

"It will kill us," said Casey Brown. Dover was already broke. The board had just been forced to cut its library budget almost in half, from $68,000 to $38,000, and to eliminate all field trips.

With money, religion, and education all on the line, relationships in the close-knit town were fraying. As 2004 ended, people stopped speaking and crossed one another off their Christmas card lists. "We were friends," Casey said about the other board members. Only one of them, Angie Yingling, was still talking to her. Yingling, meanwhile, was feuding with the rest of the board because, although she'd initially voted with Buckingham, she changed her mind when she realized how much it might cost. She later claimed that the rest of the board had bullied her by saying she wouldn't be a Christian if she voted against them. By December, she was accusing her colleagues of trying to foist their "fundamentalist Christian holy-rolling cult beliefs" onto public education.

Despite Yingling's defection, the school board became even more militant as the controversy raged. After the Browns and Wenrich resigned, the remaining members got to appoint their replacements.

Among their choices were Edward Rowand, a pastor at a local evangelical church, and Eric Riddle, who homeschools his children because he doesn't believe the public schools are sufficiently Christian.

Surprisingly, the Center for Science and Culture didn't back the Dover school board. On December 14, 2004, it put out a statement calling Dover's policy "misguided" and saying it should be "withdrawn and rewritten." The statement quoted CSC Associate Director John West arguing that while discussion of intelligent design shouldn't be prohibited, nor should it be required. "What should be required is full disclosure of the scientific evidence for and against Darwin's theory," said West, "which is the approach supported by the overwhelming majority of the public."

This was a departure from the plan laid out in "The Wedge Strategy," which declared, "We will also pursue possible legal assistance in response to resistance to the integration of design theory into public school science curricula."

Why the change? Nick Matzke, a spokesman for the National Center for Science Education, was convinced that the CSC wanted to wait for a better test case and a friendlier Supreme Court, which they'll get if Bush is able to nominate a few new justices. The Dover policy, Matzke said, probably couldn't survive a court challenge right now, and if it were to be overturned, the precedent would be a setback for the missionaries of intelligent design.

"Their current strategy is not to have an intelligent design policy passed," Matzke said. "They just want a policy that says students should analyze the strengths and weakness of evolution."

To that end, CSC is supporting initiatives like the one in Cobb County, Georgia. The sticker the county put on its biology textbooks said, "This textbook contains material on evolution. Evolution is a theory, not a fact, regarding the origin of living things. This material should be approached with an open mind, studied carefully, and critically considered."

The idea behind such rhetoric is to weaken belief in evolution before proposing an alternative. As "The Wedge Strategy" says, "If we view the predominant materialistic science as a giant tree, our strategy is intended to function as a 'wedge' that, while relatively small, can split the trunk when applied to its weakest points." The tree needs to be felled before a new one can be planted.

The Postmodern Right

There's a tremendous irony in the way conservatives have adopted their position on evolution. After all, the right has been complaining about relativism—the idea that there is no absolute truth—for years. Now, challenging the conclusions of science in the name of cultural tolerance, conservatives have created their own version of radical deconstructionism. Aping the French academicians they once excoriated, they're undermining the very idea of empirical reality, dismissing inconvenient facts as the product of an oppressive ideology.

In the 1990s, the right released a flood of books challenging postmodernism, poststructuralism, and deconstructionism—related schools of thought that saw truth as a function of power and reality as a social construct. Conservatives anathematized postmodern philosopher Michel Foucault. In her 1996 book *Telling the Truth*, an attack on academic leftism, Lynne Cheney, wife of future vice president Dick Cheney, called Foucault's work "nothing less than an assault on Western Civilization. In rejecting an independent reality, an externally verifiable truth, and even reason itself, he was rejecting the foundational principles of the West."

Cheney's book abounds in examples of the havoc postmodern ideas have wrought in American life. At the outset, she wrote of how the "author of a textbook for future teachers urges skepticism for the idea that the people now known as American Indians came to this hemisphere across the Bering land bridge. Indian myths do not tell this story, she writes. Moreover, she observes, the scientific account has nothing 'except logic' to recommend it."

It would be hard to make up a better analogy to the intelligent design movement. Like the guilt-ridden lefties they revile, conservatives

are demanding official skepticism for an idea ac
majority of scientists because it conflicts with
attacking those who would uphold traditio
Christian bigots. This pattern doesn't just appl
the Christian nationalists' entire relationship
host of pet pseudoscientific theories that buttress it.
They include reparative therapy to "cure" homosexuality; a mythical
link between abortion and breast cancer; "post-abortion syndrome," a
psychiatric disorder that exists almost exclusively in pro-life lore; and
the efficacy of abstinence-only education, an entire cottage industry of
scientific distortion.

Of course, not all right-wing hostility to science is ideological. Some
of it is merely mercenary. Although many fundamentalists have doctri-
nal objections to environmentalism, the Bush administration's refusal
to acknowledge global warming has much more to do with its ties to
the energy industry than with its religion.

But the right's subversion of science works the same whether
motivated by God or mammon. Conservatives have created parallel
research institutions, replete with scholarly sounding journals, which
produce studies to serve as "evidence" in public policy debates. On
the economic right, the Competitive Enterprise Institute and Citizens for a Sound Economy manufacture articles, papers, and expert
commentary challenging environmental regulation. On the cultural
right, the Center for Science and Culture has its analogues in the

---

* On a very few occasions, the cultural right has even acknowledged its debt to
postmodernism. A striking example is found in an essay from *Three Views on Creation and Evolution*, a 1999 book edited by Discovery Institute fellows John Mark
Reynolds and J. P. Moreland. The essay is a defense of young earth creationism—
the doctrine that the universe is only around six thousand years old—co-written by
Reynolds and Discovery fellow Paul Nelson. Like many fundamentalist arguments,
it starts with the literal word of the Bible and reasons backward. Reynolds and Nelson are honest enough to admit that the evidence from natural science is against
them, but they don't accept the primacy of natural science over scripture. For them,
an old earth has nothing except logic to recommend it. "In a postmodern world, we
see no reason for traditional Christians to give up on an idea that intrigues them,"
they write.

...ased Medical Institute for Sexual Health, which promotes
...ence education, and the National Association for Research and
...erapy of Homosexuality in Encino, California, the "scientific"
wing of the ex-gay movement.

Cowed by charges of liberal bias, the mainstream media turns to
these outfits for balance—and thus creates the perception that there's
scientific controversy over issues like global warming or evolution,
when in fact there's remarkable consensus.

Such spurious fairness is the enemy of accuracy. It also fails to insu-
late the media from bias charges, since bias has become the key to an
entire right-wing worldview. Without bias, it would be impossible for
Christian nationalists to reconcile the facts reported on TV and in
newspapers with the rhetoric coming from President Bush and a thousand pulpits. The conviction that conspiratorial forces are hiding the
truth, and that only members of the movement are undeceived, justifies
a refusal to acknowledge otherwise glaring realities.

It also makes constructive discussion nearly impossible, as I learned
talking to creationists in Dover. Some of them were smart and articu-
late, well versed in the arguments they were making, but there was no
common ground to appeal to. I could quote *National Geographic* or
Stephen Jay Gould, but those sources had no validity in their eyes.
They, in turn, would refer to the Institute for Creation Research, Ken
Ham, or the Old Testament.

"The intelligent design model is adhered to by approximately one-
third of world-class scientists," Michael Johnson, a local Baptist
preacher, assured me after one school board meeting, citing the Institute for Creation Research.

I replied that most experts I'd read and spoken to insist that there's
a consensus among almost all mainstream scientists in support of evolution, but Johnson argued that these experts were liars. "There are a lot
of smoke screens," he said. "They take numbers and figures and abuse
them and misrepresent the reality." He offered to e-mail me leads about
"world-class scientists" who could enlighten me. "Dr. Phillip Johnson,
maybe you've come across him," Johnson said. "He's on the lecture cir-

cuit at major universities. A lot of these guys are accepting him. He's regarded as an authority in the science field."

A tall, light-haired man with a small mustache, Johnson, who ministers to a flock of several hundred, was genial and easygoing. His wife, Shirley, a soft-spoken woman who wore a black coat and scarf, no makeup and wire-rim glasses, looked more like an independent bookstore owner than a Baptist preacher's wife. She was genuinely upset about the social consequences she attributed to evolution. "I think genocide comes from that—survival of the fittest," she said. She also blamed Darwinism for creating existential despair. If evolution is true, life has no meaning, she said. "Where's this universe heading? What's the purpose of it all? There's no standard, no guidelines."

But neither Shirley nor Michael Johnson had any doubt that evolution isn't true. I asked why they thought mainstream scientists were misrepresenting the research. "Once truth leaks out, its powerful," Johnson said. "So you've got to cloud, you've got to make sure there's a lot of layers of lies and cover-ups in order to keep confusion reigning and misrepresentation occurring."

Why would scientists want to be so duplicitous? Johnson answered with an analogy. "You see this principle worked out at times, like with the Iraq war." Adopting a whiny, mock-outraged voice, he said, "'There's all these people dying every day! My gosh, we've got to get out of there!'"

His voice returning to normal, he said that, in fact, "there's been the least amount of casualties in the history of warfare. This is world-war terrorism, they're shipping people in from all over the place, insurgents they're called, to go against the coalition of armies—and there's another thing, some of the politicians will try to convince people we're going this war alone, that this is unilateral war. No. We have about thirty-three, thirty-four countries that have joined us. . . . Why do people play with figures like that?

"It's because they have something to protect," he concluded. "They don't like the idea that America is setting up democracy and becoming more powerful in the world."

You can't argue with that kind of logic.

CHAPTER 4

The Faith-Based Gravy Train

R ecovery begins at the cross.

That's the motto of Set Free Indeed, a publicly funded faith-based drug rehab center in Baton Rouge, Louisiana. Founded by Tonja Myles, a former crack addict who says she was redeemed by Christ, and her husband, Darren, Set Free Indeed calls itself a "ministry" and puts scripture reading at the center of its program. Several crosses hang on the lobby walls of its new outpatient clinic, along with two framed color pictures of Myles with George W. Bush, who has touted her work as a model of the kind of faith-based charity his administration is pouring money into.

Before Bush, Set Free Indeed was a private Christian support group for recovering addicts, run first out of the Myles's home and later from the Healing Place, a local megachurch. The name comes from John 8:36: "Whom the Son sets free is free indeed." Tonja Myles claims that, after being born again, her cravings for drugs disappeared, and the people who come to her Friday night gatherings seek similar deliverance.

Recently, the ministry has gotten a lot bigger. Louisiana helped Set Free Indeed fund an outpatient clinic, "Free Indeed," which opened at the end of 2004. On staff are licensed counselors, a doctor, and a nurse. Through a system of vouchers, the federal government pays for addicts to be treated there. Some clients are under court order to stick with it.

According to Myles, there are about 135 people in the program. For five months, the recovering addicts attend Free Indeed three times a week. At each session, they choose a passage from the Bible and discuss in small groups how the scripture relates to their struggles. Counselors pray with them, seeking supernatural intervention to fight their addictions.

The Friday night support group has moved into permanent quarters at the Center of Hope, a building owned by another megachurch, which will soon also house an anti-abortion crisis pregnancy center and other faith-based social services. People in the outpatient program are required to attend support group meetings regularly, although they can substitute AA if they like. In the field abutting the Center of Hope, three white crosses taller than telephone poles soar into the sky.

Christianity pervades every aspect of Set Free Indeed. "We rely solely on the foundation of the Word of God to break the bands of addiction," says its Web site, setfreeindeedministries.com. "We believe that through practicing the Word of God and practical living skills, people struggling with addiction can reestablish their lives. Once a person admits that they have a problem and recognizes that God can set them free, the rebuilding process can begin."

In the faith-based regime that's coming to supplant the New Deal, conversion is a key to recovery.

The diversion of billions of taxpayer dollars from secular social service organizations to such sectarian religious outfits has been one of the most underreported stories of the Bush presidency. Bush's faith-based initiatives have become a spoils system for evangelical ministries, which are now involved in everything from prison programs and job training to teenage pregnancy prevention, supplanting the safety net that was supposed to catch all Americans. As a result of faith-based grants, a growing number of government-funded social service jobs explicitly refuse to hire Jews, gay people, and other undesirables; such discrimination is defended by the administration and its surrogates in the name of religious freedom. Bringing the dispossessed to Jesus Christ has become something very close to a domestic policy goal of the United

States government. And all this has happened with far less notice or public debate than attended the removal of Terri Schaivo's feeding tube or the halftime baring of Janet Jackson's breast.

In March 2005, Bush proudly told a conference of religious leaders that the federal government gave $2 billion in grants to faith-based groups the year before.[1] In 2003, it distributed $1.17 billion. Some of that money went to longtime government contractors like Catholic Charities and Lutheran Social Services, which have established separate, secular agencies to provide state-funded social services. But much of it went to small religious organizations that put evangelism at the center of their work.

Metro Atlanta Youth for Christ, for example, received an annual federal grant of $363,936 for three years, doubling its budget. The group used the money to hire three "abstinence educators." These educators aren't required to have any specific credentials in public health. They do, however, have to be Christian, because Metro Atlanta Youth for Christ won't employ people who aren't. After all, its raison d'être is proselytizing. According to its Web site, "The mission of Youth for Christ is to participate in the body of Christ in responsible evangelism of youth, presenting them with the person, work and teachings of Christ and discipling them into the local church."

Other federal grantees include Bethany Christian Services—listed on the Department of Health and Human Services Web site as Bethany Crisis Pregnancy Services—which bills itself as a "not-for-profit, pro-life, Christian adoption and family services agency," and Pat Robertson's Operation Blessing, which won a grant for $1.5 million over three years.

While religious initiatives are being fattened with federal funding, secular social service agencies are being starved.* Surveying the results

---

* In 2004, the *Detroit News* undertook a six-month investigation of the consequences of Bush's tax cuts. Its findings: "The Bush administration and Congress have scaled back programs that aid the poor to help pay for $600 billion in tax breaks that went primarily to those who earn more than $288,800 a year. . . . The affected programs—job training, housing, higher education and an array of social services—provide safety nets for the poor. Many programs are critical elements in welfare-to-work initiatives and were already badly underfunded."

of the faith-based initiative in a 2004 *Washington Monthly* article, Amy Sullivan, a writer often quite sympathetic to religion, stated, "The policy of funding the work of faith-based organizations has, in the face of slashed social service budgets, devolved into a small pork-barrel program that offers token grants to the religious constituencies in Karl Rove's electoral plan for 2004 while making almost no effort to monitor their effectiveness."[2]

A similar pattern reveals itself on the state level across the country. More than half of state governments have established their own faith-based offices to distribute funds to religious groups. One of the leaders is Jeb Bush's Florida, home to Lawtey Correctional Institution, the nation's first faith-based prison. Lawtey is ostensibly open to all religions, but in practice almost all the volunteers, both clergy and laymen, are evangelical Christians.[3]

Identifying Sinners

Christian nationalist thinkers have long dreamt of replacing welfare with private, church-based charity that would be dispensed at the discretion of the godly. In his 1996 book *Renewing American Compassion*, Marvin Olasky, one of the chief theorists behind Bush's faith-based initiative, argued, "It is time now, however, to talk not about reforming the welfare system—which often means scraping off a bit of mold—but about replacing it with a truly compassionate approach based in private and religious charity. Such a system was effective in the nineteenth century and will be even more effective in the twenty-first, with the decentralization that new technology makes possible, if we make the right changes in personal goals and public policy."[4]

Olasky's dream of restoring the moral glory of the Gilded Age will probably remain unfulfilled for the foreseeable future. But his ideas have helped shape an ascendant movement that is challenging not just church/state separation, but the whole notion of secular civil society and social services based on empirical research rather than supernatural intervention. While Olasky and other supporters of faith-based funding make gestures toward ecumenicism, they're driven by the conviction that the poor and addicted are sinners who need to be redeemed by Jesus Christ. That's a perfectly valid approach for a church to take. When America adopts it, it stops being the country many of us thought we knew.

Most politically aware people have heard George Bush's phrase "compassionate conservatism," but few realize what it really means. During the 2000 presidential campaign, the media largely interpreted it as either a code for moderation or an empty catchphrase akin to Bush père's vision of a "kinder, gentler" America. This suited Republicans fine, since it allowed them to communicate on two levels, with a vague, anodyne message for most Americans, and a much more precise, coded one for the evangelical right.

The latter could recognize compassionate conservatism as a specific doctrine rooted in right-wing Christianity. *Compassionate Conservatism* is the title of another of Olasky's books. George W. Bush wrote its introduction, calling Olasky "compassionate conservatism's leading thinker." Olasky stood beside Bush during one of the first policy speeches of his 2000 presidential campaign, when Bush laid out his plan to shift $8 billion in federal funds to faith-based agencies.

Olasky's work thus serves as a valuable guide to the kind of society that Bush and his Christian nationalist backers are striving to create. His vision is a deeply radical one, heavily influenced by Christian Reconstructionism. He yearns for the days before the New Deal, when sinners could be denied aid until they repented. "An emphasis on freedom also should include a willingness to step away for a time and let those who have dug their own hole 'suffer the consequences of their misconduct,' " Olasky wrote in *The Tragedy of American Compassion*. "The early Calvinists knew that time spent in the pit could be what was needed to save a life from permanent debauch (and a soul from hell)."[5]

A gawky, bearded scarecrow of a man, Olasky seems to be drawn to totalitarian ideologies. Born into a Russian Jewish family in Massachusetts, as a young man he was a militant Communist, joining the party in 1972, well after Stalin's crimes had been revealed and most leftist intellectuals had become disillusioned with the Soviet Union. But while writing his Ph.D. thesis about the persecution of Communists in Holly-wood, Olasky was beset by doubts. As he later wrote in an essay about his conversion, "One day near the end of 1973 I was reading Lenin's famous essay, 'Socialism and Religion,' in which he wrote, 'We must combat religion—this is the ABC of all materialism, and consequently Marxism.' At that point God changed my worldview not through thun-der or a whirlwind, but by means of a small whisper that became a repeated, resounding question in my brain: 'What if Lenin is wrong? What if there is a God?' "[6]

That question persisted and, in 1976, influenced by the writings of Francis Schaeffer, Olasky became a Christian. He also remarried, his first marriage having fallen apart in the early 1970s. Just as he'd gravi-tated toward the most extreme faction of the left, he and his new wife, Susan, now searched out the furthest reaches of the right. She told *The New York Times* that in looking for a church, "We asked ourselves which denomination represented the extreme opposite of the hard left," even-tually joining a conservative Baptist congregation.[7] Later, when Olasky became a journalism professor at the University of Texas at Austin, they joined Redeemer Presbyterian Church, part of the same breakaway Presbyterian denomination as D. James Kennedy's Coral Ridge Min-istries. Today Olasky is a church elder.

Olasky got to know George Grant, the former executive director of Coral Ridge Ministries, eventually hiring him as an editor and book reviewer at *World*. (Grant, remember, is an unabashed theocrat who has called for Christian "world conquest.") Reconstructionism has clearly influenced Olasky—his books approvingly cite R. J. Rushdoony and others like him. Howard Ahmanson, the California millionaire who sat on the board of the Chalcedon Foundation and who funds the Center for Science and Culture at the Discovery Institute, has been one of Olasky's patrons, providing grants to write several of his books and paying him to edit the sixteen-volume series *Turning Point: A Christ-ian Worldview*.

Olasky has authored more than a dozen books, including several concerning media bias and abortion. His fame on the right, though, stems from his 1992 *The Tragedy of American Compassion*, a revisionist history of United States social policy that presents the twentieth century as a long decline from the moral heights of the 1800s, when the poor were well served by religious benevolence instead of government bureaucracy.

Like much Christian nationalist mythology, Olasky identifies two primary enemies as responsible for the country's fall—religious liberalism and "political socialism," which he blames for jettisoning a one-on-one, salvation-minded approach to the poor.

"[T]hroughout the nineteenth century, the rock on which compassion stood was undergoing erosion," he wrote. "The chief erosion was theological: the belief that sinful man, left to himself, would return to wilderness, seemed harshly pessimistic. . . . The erosion for a time did not seem crucial, but the long-term effect was severe enough to make the twentieth century not the Christian century, as celebrants in 1900 predicted, but the century of wilderness returning."[8]

The Tragedy of American Compassion didn't receive much mainstream notice when it was first published, but it developed a following on the right. As *The New York Times Magazine* reported in a 1999 profile of Olasky, "Former Secretary of Education William Bennett hailed it as the 'most important book on welfare and social policy in a decade' and handed a copy to the new Republican Speaker, Newt Gingrich. Gingrich read it from cover to cover and liked it so much, he had it distributed to all the incoming freshmen. In his first address to the nation, Gingrich declared: 'Our models are Alexis de Tocqueville and Marvin Olasky. We are going to redefine compassion and take it back.'"[9]

When the book was brought to the attention of professional historians, it was promptly ripped it to shreds. In a review published in a scholarly journal and widely circulated online, Case Western Reserve University historian David C. Hammack called *The Tragedy of American Compassion* "a political tract that makes no effort to be a convincing history: it ignores other historians, defines questions narrowly and arbitrarily, and picks facts from here and there to support a preconceived thesis." Toward the end of his review, he wrote, "Marvin Olasky is engaged in a campaign for control of Americans' view of their past, with the aim of shaping their actions in the future."[10]

Not surprisingly, views like Hammack's did almost nothing to curb Olasky's influence. The theory of liberal bias had already thoroughly discredited most of academia in the eyes of the right, inoculating its thinkers from professional criticism. Cultural conservatives rejected the past presented to them by most mainstream historians. Olasky, like David Barton, gave them one more to their liking, and his vision has come to undergird the thinking of many of the people now running our country.

First as Texas governor and then as president, George W. Bush has made Olasky's ideas his own. When Bush ran for president, he adopted "compassionate conservatism" as the heart of his domestic policy, making Olasky the head of his campaign's policy subcommittee on religion. In speeches, Bush spoke of mustering "armies of compassion," language lifted right out of Olasky's oeuvre. Accepting Jesus had helped *him* quit drinking, and that experience seemed to be all the evidence Bush needed that Olasky's theories would work for the entire nation.

The two met briefly in 1993, then again two years later during Texas's showdown over a local branch of Teen Challenge, a faith-based drug treatment program with around 130 semi-autonomous centers nationwide. In 1995, the Texas Commission on Alcohol and Drug Abuse found the San Antonio branch of Teen Challenge to be in violation of state regulations. One of the problems it cited was Teen Challenge employees' lack of training in substance abuse treatment, and the commission threatened to close the program unless it hired licensed counselors. That was unacceptable to Teen Challenge, which mustered evangelical support to fight the state, including grateful graduates of the program who testified that it had saved their lives.

During the controversy, Bush sought out Olasky for advice and, under his guidance, sided with Teen Challenge. In 1997, he pushed through legislation exempting faith-based facilities from some of the regulations applying to their secular counterparts. Religious drug treatment counselors wouldn't be forced to undergo training or to obtain regular state licenses. The state established a separate, Christian organization, the Texas Association of Christian Child Care Agencies, to accredit faith-based programs like Teen Challenge. Its six-member board included representatives from the facilities it was overseeing.

Some of the results were brutal. As Texas journalists Molly Ivins and Lou Dubose wrote in their book *Bushwhacked*, "Four years after Governor Dubya Bush freed Christian residential child-care facilities from state supervision, an emergency-room physician examined an eighteen-year-old boy rescued from a South Texas boys' home by his mother. The doctor told her her son had been 'tortured.'"

The boy had been at Roloff's Anchor Homes, named for Lester Roloff, described by Ivins and Dubose as a "self-made hellfire-and-brimstone come-to-Jesus preacher." Two weeks after the abuse was reported, Roloff's Anchor Homes was reapproved by The Texas Association of Christian Child Care Agencies. But the allegations were true, and in 2001, Roloff's headmaster was found guilty of abuse in a criminal trial. His wife, Ivins and Dubose wrote, was permanently banned from working in Texas child-care facilities because of her treatment of a girl at another faith-based facility, Rebekah Home: "The girl, DeAnne Dawsey, was bound with duct tape, kicked in the ribs, and locked in solitary for thirty-two straight hours of taped Roloff sermons."[11]

It needs to be said that Roloff's Anchor Homes isn't typical of faith-based facilities. As the protests in favor of Teen Challenge show, many who choose to go through religious rehab become ardent supporters of the programs, which they insist helped them where secular alternatives failed. Still, when the government removes regulation and decrees that religious faith can substitute for professional training, abuse is inevitable.

The potential for abuse is just one of many dangers inherent in faith-based initiatives. The larger threat is less immediate but more insidious—the institutionalization of religious sectarianism in public life. Rarely before in the United States have public resources been doled out on a confessional basis. Under the faith-based regime, the most that religious minorities and secularists can hope for are separate-but-equal alternatives to the government programs run by evangelical Christians. So far, they haven't even gotten that.

One of the first things Bush did when he became president was to create a White House Office of Faith-Based and Community Initiatives. He went on to set up similar offices in major government departments—Justice, Labor, Health and Human Services, Housing and Urban Development, Education, Agriculture, Commerce, Veterans Affairs, the U.S. Agency of International Development, and the Small Business Administration. Some of the staff at these offices were recruited from the cadres of the Christian right. David Kuo, former deputy director of the Office of Faith-Based and Community Initiatives, used to work at the Christian Coalition. Deanna Carlson, the associate director of the faith-based office at the Department of Health and Human Services, was formerly director of community outreach for the Family Research Council. Christian nationalists in the administration have the opportunity to channel grants to their friends in the movement.*

Indeed, much of the faith-based funding is structured to help *build* the movement. Because many small churches and grassroots ministries don't know how to write grant proposals or work with the government, the Bush administration has established the Compassion Capital Fund. Large, experienced organizations like Pat Robertson's Operation Blessing get Compassion Capital grants to teach smaller organizations how

---

* One way of doing this is by packing the panels that review grant applications with movement supporters. The journalist Esther Kaplan, author of *With God on Their Side: How Christian Fundamentalists Trampled Science, Policy, and Democracy in George W. Bush's White House*, filed a Freedom of Information Act request to learn the names of the outside experts tapped to review applicants for abstinence-only funding from the Department of Health and Human Services. Among them were David Noebel, president of Summit Ministries (a Christian worldview training center in Colorado), along with two representations from Focus on the Family, three from the Family Research Council, and three from Concerned Women for America.

to apply for funds themselves. Compassion Capital recipients also distribute a percentage of their federal money to smaller sub-grantees. Thus Robertson's organization gets to hand out taxpayer dollars to faith-based programs of its choosing, enlarging its network and political clout in the process.

This two-way transfer of money and power between Republicans and the religious right has caused much of our political culture to mutate into something barely recognizable. With public policy flowing from a congeries of authoritarian theologies, government gatherings have often come to resemble revivals. Senators call on Jesus to heal the sick. Government contractors justify their work with scripture instead of studies. The cover of a four-color Department of Labor brochure, written to help religious groups apply for federal grants, features a drawing of a fiery shrub like the one Moses saw in Exodus and the words, "Not everyone has a burning bush to tell them their life's calling."

Early in Bush's first term, an event promoted by the Reverend Sun Myung Moon, head of the Unification Church, offered a particularly vivid glimpse of what was to become the strange new status quo in Washington. On April 25, 2001, the top tier of Republican congressional leadership—including Trent Lott, Dennis Hastert, and Rick Santorum—assembled for a lunchtime "faith-based summit" in the Great Hall of the Library of Congress. John DiIulio, then the head of Bush's Office of Faith-Based and Community Initiatives, was also there. Dozens of religious leaders were invited to the meeting. Hundreds more gathered at more than fifty local conferences held across the country, where they watched the event in D.C. via a Moon-funded satellite broadcast.

In the vaulted and gilded hall on Capitol Hill, politicians and preachers took their turn at the podium, disparaging the notion of church/state separation and celebrating the intercessory power of Christ. "For those struggling, and for those who are trying to help those who are struggling, I look to the Bible," said Texas senator Kay Bailey Hutchison. "In James Chapter 1, verses 2–4: 'Consider it pure joy, my brothers, whenever you face trials of many kinds, because you

know that the testing of your faith develops perseverance, perseverance must finish its work so that you may be mature and complete,
not lacking anything.'"

Robert L. Woodson Sr., a black conservative and Olasky ally who
heads the National Center for Neighborhood Enterprise, gave a speech
that seemed to argue that the testimony of the Bible is all the empirical
data needed to prove the efficacy of faith-based initiatives. "[T]hose
who question whether or not faith-based grassroots leadership works
. . . they say where's the evidence," he said. "No one ever asks the secular
programs for their success, but all of the sudden they want the data.
Well, I tell you the data that I use is the experience that the blind man
had in the book of Matthew, when he was healed by Jesus of his blind-
ness." Woodson's group went on to receive over $1.8 million from the
Compassion Capital Fund.

The conference ended with a performance by a white gospel singer
in a black button-up shirt and white tie. Several of the clergymen in
attendance joined him on the podium, along with Senator Santorum
and Reverend Moon. They swayed back and forth as the singer crooned
about hastening to the lord's call.

"The Separation Between Religion and Politics Is What Satan Likes Most"

A few hundred miles away, Bob Wineburg, a professor of social work at
the University of North Carolina at Greensboro, was watching these
events with horrified amazement.

Wineburg has done extensive research on faith-based social services, and a local minister he sometimes collaborates with had invited
him to one of the satellite conferences in Raleigh, at North Carolina
State University. Under the impression that the conference was a government event, Wineburg was shocked when he was given a handbook
that contained, along with the conference agenda, excerpts from
Moonie tracts that proclaimed God's concern with man's "internal
character" and bemoaned American individualism.

Three attendees were chosen to read the passages out loud. "A great

revolution is necessary if we are to unify the world, and it will be a revolution of human character," one of the tracts declared. Another said,
"This American nation is founded upon Judeo-Christian principles, yet
Americans have become very individualistic. Was Jesus an individualistic person? How did Americans come to be so egoistic and individualistic when Jesus had nothing of an individualistic nature?"

Those who've watched the career of Moon, the South Korean cult
leader, felon, billionaire, and self-described messiah, would find this
rhetoric familiar. Moon envisions a worldwide theocracy under his
dominion. He has said that "individualism is what God hates most" and
praises totalitarianism for inculcating obedience—an obedience he
expects will one day be transferred to him.

After the readings in the North Carolina auditorium, attendees were
instructed to form small groups and discuss the passages' relevance to
their own work. "I was so stunned, I couldn't believe all this was going
on," said Wineburg, who gave me a copy of the handbook. "It was
bizarre. I felt like I was from another planet."

Like most Americans, Wineburg had been unaware of the power
Moon holds in our nation's politics. The reverend, who once served
eleven months in prison for income tax fraud, is best known for marry-
ing thousands of strangers in mass weddings. Those events earned him
a public reputation as a spectacle-mad eccentric, but that obscures his
role as a significant D.C. power broker. In fact, Moon is an important
patron of the Republican party and of the conservative movement.
Through his various front groups he's been a major proponent and
minor recipient of Bush's faith-based funding.

The relationship between Moon and the Christian nationalists
seems odd, since Moon sees himself as Jesus's successor, not his servant.
But the would-be messiah has long recognized the need to co-opt the
religious right. "My dream is to organize a Christian political party,
including the Protestant denominations and Catholics, and all the
other religious sects," he said in a 1973 speech. In the same speech, he
called for an "automatic theocracy to rule the world."[12]

Moon's own religious following is small, but his resources are vast.

As of 1997, *The Washington Post* reported, his movement controlled more than $300 million in "commercial, political, and cultural enterprises" in Washington, D.C., alone. He spends his money freely to subsidize the right. (George W. Bush's parents have been especial beneficiaries of Unificationist largesse, collecting an estimated million dollars in speaking fees to appear at Moon conferences abroad.)[13] In the late 1980s, Moon bought the *Washington Times*, a conservative daily newspaper that provides a home to many prominent right-wing pundits even as it loses millions of dollars every year.

In 1995, Moon spent $3.5 million to bail out Falwell's near bankrupt Liberty University. The next year, Moon's News World Communications lent Liberty an additional $400,000.[14]

Recently, Moon has put his resources behind the faith-based cause. In the weeks before the April 2001 conference at the Library of Congress, Moon barnstormed across the country, giving a series of speeches plugging Bush's faith-based proposal. He invited local ministers and gave many who attended gold Christian Bernard watches, each valued at several thousand dollars, as a symbol of his "unchanging love."[15]

As John Gorenfeld reported in *Salon*, the next year Moon held a three-day God and World Peace conference where he gathered several important political figures, including senators and congressmen, to call for support of Bush's faith-based initiatives. At one session Jim Towey, who replaced DiIulio as the White House's faith-based czar, gave the opening remarks. Gorenfeld wrote,

> Moon followed, and called for all religions to come together in support of the Bush plan for faith-based initiatives. Coming from Moon that made perfect sense, because he already believes all religions will come together—under him. "The separation between religion and politics," he has observed on many occasions, "is what Satan likes most." His gospel: Jesus failed because he never attained worldly power. Moon will succeed, he says, by purifying our sex-corrupted culture, and that includes cleaning up gays ("dung-eating dogs," as he calls them) and American

women ("a line of prostitutes"). Jews had better repent, too.
(Moon claims that the Holocaust was payback for the crucifixion
of Christ: "Through the principle of indemnity, Hitler killed 6
million Jews.") His solution is a world theocracy that will enforce
proper sexual habits in order to bring about heaven on earth.[16]

As part of the faith-based initiative, millions of federal dollars have
been appropriated to enforce proper sexual habits through abstinence
education, some of which has gone to organizations connected to
Moon. As Gorenfeld reported, Free Teens USA, a Unificationist-run
afterschool celibacy club, received $475,280 in federal money in 2002.
Moon operatives have also garnered faith-based money under Bush's
Healthy Marriage Initiative. Meanwhile David Caprara, a speaker at the
April 2001 conference whom the *San Francisco Chronicle* describes as a
"longtime political operative in Moon front groups," now directs the
faith-based office in the federal government's Corporation for National
and Community Service.[17]

The fact that Moonies are getting money might suggest an ecumenical aspect to the faith-based initiative, but that's misleading. While
a fraction of the billions of dollars the government has doled out has
gone to the Unification Church as well as to a small handful of Jewish
and Muslim groups, the overwhelming majority of the funding is being
pumped into churches and Christian ministries.

Exact percentages are nearly impossible to come by, because the
faith-based initiative is structured in a way that makes it incredibly difficult to track where all the funds are going. There are multiple pots of
money administered by several government agencies and distributed in
different ways. Some grants go to the states, which then funnel them to
local faith-based groups. Millions more go, via the Compassion Capital
Fund, to intermediary groups like Pat Robertson's who then pass it on
to operations of their choosing. And some money goes directly to operations like Metro Atlanta Youth for Christ. Nonreligious groups often
get government grants from the same pots of money, further clouding
the situation.

The most comprehensive analysis of the distribution of faith-based funds was done by the Associated Press in 2005.[18] AP looked at grants handed out in 2003 by five federal departments—Health and Human Services, Housing and Urban Development, Education, Labor, and Justice. Money given to the states for distribution wasn't included. Besides analyzing the figures, AP reporters conducted 150 interviews with recipients in thirty states. It then published a state-by-state list of grant recipients. Out of more than 1600 grantees, around 50 were Jewish, 5 were Muslim, and 1 was Buddhist. One could argue that there's some justice in this—Jews, Muslims, and Buddhists constitute a very small fraction of the population. In practice, however, the fact that a Zen Buddhist temple in California received $5500 does nothing to help the Buddhists in Maryland, Pennsylvania, or New York. In most states *all* the faith-based grants went to Christian groups, and some of those groups are devoted first and foremost to religious conversion. Small grants to non-Christian groups allow Bush and his supporters to speak of faith-based initiatives in pluralistic terms, but they don't change the essentially sectarian nature of "compassionate conservatism."

Amazingly, the administration seems to have no central tally of how much federal money is going to religious groups, or what's being done with it. "They want to do everything they can to avoid particular, number-crunching evaluation," Billy Terry, a consultant who has sat on several of the federal panels that review faith-based grant applicants, told me. "They couldn't evaluate what they've done if they wanted to. There's no data. There's no structure."

Even DiIulio, the first head of the faith-based office, eventually concluded that the program was meant to help the Bush base, not the poor. "There is no precedent in any modern White House for what is going on in this one: a complete lack of a policy apparatus," he famously told *Esquire* reporter Ron Suskind. "What you've got is everything—and I mean everything—being run by the political arm. It's the reign of the Mayberry Machiavellis."[19]

DuIulio, a conservative Democratic social scientist, is a true believer in the power of inner-city churches to heal their communities, and he wanted to channel money to them to do social work—not to prosely-tize. In order to build consensus with Democrats, he was willing to bar the use of government funds for explicitly religious purposes. That brought him into conflict with Christian nationalists like Olasky.

DiIulio thought he could defy the religious right and still work for the White House. According to Suskind's *Esquire* article, when Karl Rove pressed DiIulio to stop feuding with Christian conservatives "and start fighting the guys who are against us," DiIulio told him, "I'm not taking any shit off of Jerry Falwell."

He underestimated Falwell's clout, and that of others like him. Suskind wrote,

> On his primary mission—push forward ideas and policies to partner government with faith-based institutions—DiIulio says that he saw the beginning of what was to become a pattern: The White House "winked at the most far-right House Republicans, who, in turn, drafted a so-called faith bill that (or so they thought) satisfied certain fundamentalist leaders and Beltway libertarians but bore few marks of compassionate conservatism and was, as anybody could tell, an absolute political nonstarter. It could pass the House only on a virtual party-line vote, and it could never pass the Senate."[20]

No bill was ever passed, and DiIulio was forced out. Bush instituted his faith-based agenda through executive order—an audacious move that, by fiat, radically changed the relationship between church and state. There was little new money for social programs, but money that had already been appropriated was now channeled in new directions. Millions went toward programs that seek to instill conservative social values like abstinence education and marriage promotion.

In 2004, Bush introduced Access to Recovery, opening the door to federally funded faith-based drug treatment like that offered at Free Indeed. The initiative provided $100 million to fourteen states and the California Rural Indian Health Board, a tribal organization, to implement voucher-based drug treatment. More states are expected to be added to the program in coming years.

Vouchers are key to the right-wing plan for sectarian social services. Legally, programs funded with vouchers allow for much more evangelizing than other kinds of government grants, because it's the individual addict, not the government, who's choosing where the money goes. (The same principle applies to school vouchers, which is one reason they're so crucial to the Christian right's program). In *Compassionate Conservatism*, Olasky cites Carl Esbeck, a prominent Christian nationalist lawyer who would later become head of the faith-based initiatives office in the Department of Justice, arguing that vouchers free users from the restraints of the First Amendment.

Louisiana, one of the Access to Recovery states, received $22.8 million to fund voucher-based drug treatment. The state contracted with Tonja Myles to train other faith-based providers to obtain state licenses and use the vouchers. The voucher system meant that the government would now pay to put people through Free Indeed, the state-funded outpatient clinic Myles had just opened.

Addiction and Redemption

Housed in a single-story building near the interstate that serves as Baton Rouge's main artery, Free Indeed is freshly painted, light, and welcoming. Except for the religious touches—the evangelical magazines in the rack and Bible quotes on the walls—it feels like a suburban doctor's office. According to Thomas Coyne, a veteran social worker from New York hired by Louisiana to consult on the state's drug treatment programs, it was one of the more impressive facilities he'd encountered. "Quite honestly, I'd rather be treated in a Free Indeed" than a secular program, he told me. Compared to clinics he's seen in hospitals, "it's much nicer, cleaner. The staff is friendly, not punitive, not suspicious."

Tonja Myles is clearly proud to offer the people who come to her a dignified environment. "We see people from the curbside to the country club, because addiction does not care who you are," she told me. "I wanted a place that I would feel at home. So what if the person is homeless—who says they have to come to a place for service and it's substandard?"

Myles, a forty-one-year-old black woman, was crisply dressed in white capri pants, a white denim jacket, and a red and white striped shirt. She describes herself as very socially conservative, but she's not strident, and she exudes easygoing charisma. "We're real here," she said. "We're raw." She's against abortion, but having seen how the justice system in the South works against black people, she's also opposed to the death penalty. She believes homosexuality is a sin and said that Set Free Indeed has helped some people "get out of that lifestyle," but she said she welcomes gay people who want to get off drugs without trying to get straight. "I just want to see them clean," she insisted.

When I met her, Myles was still in training to become a certified substance abuse counselor. Her authority derived from hard experience, not education. There's a Pentecostal tradition of recounting the depths to which one sunk before being lifted up by Jesus, and Myles's story fits into it perfectly. The daughter of an alcoholic, she told me she was molested as a little girl and was sexually active by the time she was ten. Soon she was snorting coke and smoking crack, and by her late teens she was an addict. She prostituted herself to buy drugs, was raped, had two abortions, and ended up in the hospital after she tried to commit suicide.

And then, when she was nineteen or twenty—she said she doesn't remember—she was saved. It happened suddenly, after her grandmother prayed over her. "I tell people I died that day—I died a spiritual death. The old Tonja died and the new one was resurrected."

After that day, she said, she never relapsed. "I took God at his word: He who the son sets free is free indeed. I believe that. I didn't look back."

That was the story she told me. The one she's told to the evangelical press begins even more luridly, making her redemption all the more glorious. After Bush praised Myles during the 2003 State of the Union address—which she watched from the First Lady's box—the evangelical magazine *Charisma* wrote a profile of her. It described Myles as not only a former drug addict and prostitute, but also an ex-Satanist.[21] This last detail would have been meaningful for *Charisma* readers, since the evangelical subculture is rife with stories about Satan's activities on Earth.

The second time I met Myles, at Set Free Indeed's Friday night support group, I asked her about this. She told me she'd worshipped Satan since childhood. And what did this worship entail? "Rituals, a lot of S&M, a lot of orgies, a lot of Wicca, Ouija board, the Satanic Bible. All that junk."

She continued, "I've seen people sacrifice animals. . . . They get together and they do it in the park or whatever."

What kind of animals? "Cats, dogs, pigs, horses," she said. "Horses?" I asked. Yes, she said, horses.

Horses are expensive, and I found it unlikely that drug addicts would sacrifice them. It also seemed doubtful that if such bloody rituals had taken place in public parks, leaving behind ritually mutilated carcasses, they wouldn't have been discovered. But for some evangelicals, Myles's tale would have seemed like confirmation of their deepest suspicions about the roots of social breakdown. In her milieu, it was all perfectly consistent.

And here is the difficult thing for a secularist: some people are healed in this milieu. I was skeptical about some of Myles's stories, but I had little doubt that she really was helping many of the suffering people who came to her. At the Friday night support group, I looked around the diverse crowd praying under the low fluorescent lights. There were white-haired women with spun-sugar bouffants who probably felt more comfortable in the churchlike setting than they would have at AA. There were clean-cut frat boy types in button-down shirts, and young mothers with their restless kids who told me harrowing stories about the men who abused or betrayed them. Set Free Indeed had helped some of them find the courage to leave their dangerous relationships.

All these hurting people came together, and Myles offered them the promise of relief. Unlike AA, which says the demon of addiction will be with you forever, Set Free Indeed says you can wipe the slate clean. You can be reborn.

"My name is Tonja," Myles told me, "and I am *not* an addict."

I left thinking that it's a good thing that Set Free Indeed exists. But the issue isn't whether the program will continue. The Friday night support group takes place in a donated space and doesn't rely on government money, and the outpatient clinic should be able to find benefactors among the nation's many wealthy megachurches, some of which have invited Myles to speak.

The issue is whether, at a time when social services budgets are being slashed and waiting lists at other programs are long, public money should be going to a program that's geared exclusively toward evangelical Christians. After all, there can be positive social benefits to a whole host of religious practices—but that doesn't mean the government funds them. Even if Set Free Indeed works, when it gets taxpayer money, it means we're becoming a country in which people literally have to pray for public help.

Besides, although I was impressed by some of what I saw at Set Free Indeed, there's no evidence that it or any other religious drug treatment works as well as or better than secular alternatives. Myles is eager to start collecting such evidence, because she's convinced it will bolster the faith-based case. In the Bush administration, though, there's an astonishing indifference to measuring the results of faith-based programs, despite the billions being spent on them. As Amy Sullivan wrote in the *Washington Monthly*, "Unfortunately, in the midst of all of the instructions included in the various executive orders, it turns out that the Bush administration forgot to require evaluation of organizations that receive government grants. . . . The accountability president has chosen not to direct any money toward figuring out whether faith-based approaches really work."[22]

Against Reason

This lacuna is partly a result of administration indifference, but there's something else operating. Evidence doesn't mean the same thing for the Christian nationalists as it does for others. After all, they've already rejected materialistic naturalism—they've already rejected *science*—as the basis for knowledge. The kind of results they're after can't be quantified.

In February 2005, I went to a conference on faith-based social services sponsored by the Federalist Society, a conservative legal group, and held in D.C.'s Cannon House Office Building. Among the speakers were Carl Esbeck, the lawyer Olasky cited to argue for vouchers, and Jim Towey, director of the administration's Office of Faith-Based and Community Initiatives.

During a presentation on the effectiveness of faith-based providers, Gerard Bradley, a professor at Notre Dame Law School who chaired the Federalist Society's Religious Liberties Practice Group, seemed to concede that what data exists doesn't particularly help their case. "It seems to me that when we're talking about what works, what's effective, what are the numbers, we're talking about objective or even secular outcomes," Bradley said. Then he added, "It may turn out that the numbers are a wash."

Instead, he argued for a different kind of measurement, one that considered the benefits of conversion. "God does work in the world," he said, and people "who welcome Jesus into their hearts" will be better off. Most research can't measure that, he said, because most social scientists don't entertain the idea that "grace makes the difference," not "some secular variable."

To the Christian nationalists, then, publicly funded religious social services auger nothing less than an epistemological revolution. They allow knowledge derived from the Bible to trump knowledge derived from studying the world. No longer would American domestic policy and American civic life be based on facts available to all of us, on the kind of rationality that looks at "objective or even secular outcomes."

It would be based on faith.

There is one ill that faith-based programs are proven to ameliorate—unemployment among Christian evangelicals. The Christianization of the safety net has created a kind of affirmative action for the born again. That's because the Bush administration decreed faith-based groups exempt from a 1965 executive order that bars religious discrimination in federally funded hiring. As a result, Jews, Hindus, Muslims, gay people, secularists, and others can't compete for a growing number of social service jobs.

Religious organizations were already exempt from the 1964 Civil Rights Act barring hiring discrimination. Churches are free to prefer Christian employees, synagogues can favor Jews, and mosques can hire only Muslims. In the past, however, the federal government held that such exemptions don't apply to publicly funded positions—if a salary is paid for by tax dollars, the job has to be open to all.

No more. Now, government money can and does go to social service agencies that hire only Christians. Last year in Bradford, Pennsylvania, a publicly funded group, Firm Foundation, which provides job training to prison inmates, posted a help wanted ad for a site manager. The applicant, it said, must be "a believer in Christ and Christian Life today, sharing these ideals when opportunity arises."

Conservative Republicans are trying to codify the right of places like Firm Foundation to discriminate. In March 2005, the House of Representatives passed the Job Training Improvement Act, which would explicitly allow federally funded faith-based job training programs to hire and fire people based on their religion. Six months later, they passed a measure giving the same latitude to Head Start early-childhood programs run by religious groups.

The New Missionaries

This new era of taxpayer-financed discrimination threatens to reshape established faith-based organizations that have long maintained secular wings. In New York City, for example, the Salvation Army brought in a consultant to Christianize the social services division, which receives more than $50 million in public money to operate a range of services in the city, including foster care, HIV counseling, and group homes. The consultant requested a list of gay employees, discouraged the hiring of non-Christians, and demanded that all staffers fill out forms detailing their church attendance. Anne Lown, the Jewish former associate director of the Social Services for Children program, was one of several employees driven out for refusing to cooperate.

I met with Lown at a Starbucks in her neighborhood in West Harlem, near the Columbia University campus. A tall, thin woman with brown bobbed hair, who looked younger than her fifty-six years, Lown is the daughter of the renowned cardiologist Dr. Bernard Lown, who fled Nazism in Lithuania and, in 1985, received the Nobel Peace Prize for his work with International Physicians for the Prevention of Nuclear War. She speaks in a somewhat dispassionate, even voice, but it's obvious that she's still amazed by what she went through, and by the fact that it hardly made a ripple in the media. She and seventeen other current and former employees, represented by the New York Civil Liberties Union, are now suing the Salvation Army and the city, state, and federal government. The Justice Department, ostensibly the government agency charged with protecting civil rights, has sided against them. As the *Los Angeles Times* reported, "The department's position in the case—that religious groups should be able to hire or fire people based on their religious views, even when administering publicly funded programs—is a cornerstone of President Bush's faith-based initiative."[23]

Indeed, it seems likely that the Salvation Army received tacit permission from the administration to discriminate in exchange for supporting Bush's domestic agenda. During the summer of 2001, when the administration was still trying to push its faith-based legislation through Congress, *The Washington Post* revealed that the Bush team was in secret talks with the Salvation Army. Citing an internal Salvation

Army document, reporter Dana Milbank wrote, "The White House has made a 'firm commitment' to the Salvation Army to issue a regulation protecting such [faith-based] charities from state and city efforts to prevent discrimination against gays in hiring and domestic-partner benefits, according to the Salvation Army report. The Salvation Army, in turn, has agreed to use its clout to promote the administration's 'faith-based' social services initiative, which seeks to direct more government funds to religious charities."[24]

Originally called the East London Christian Mission, the Salvation Army was founded in London 1865 by the Methodist minister William Booth. From the beginning, it strove to evangelize the poor through good works. Booth developed a quasi-military structure that remains in place, giving his missionaries military ranks. (He was the general). The Salvation Army makes a distinction between soldiers, who sign a declaration of evangelical belief called a "soldier's covenant," and employees, who are outside the Army's military hierarchy and spiritual reach.

Lown, who had been an employee at the Salvation Army for twenty-four years and oversaw 800 workers, said religion had never had anything to do with her job. As long as she'd been there, the New York social services division had been independent from the evangelical side of the organization. Her office ran more public programs than any Salvation Army division in the United States, most of them for children. Almost all of the money came from the state and local government, and Lown assumed that it would be illegal to infuse taxpayer-funded services with Christianity. Her division had gay, Jewish, Muslim, and Hindu employees, reflecting the city it served.

At some point, the Salvation Army hierarchy decided this pluralism was no longer acceptable. In spring 2003, the New York Division of the Salvation Army brought in Salvationist Colonel Paul Kelly as a consultant to heighten the agency's evangelical aspect. He drafted a reorganization plan that encouraged efforts to recruit more Salvationists and questioned the hiring of a human resources employee who "represents an Eastern religion." He wrote, "The Army's 'Christian perspective' is rarely emphasized."[25]

According to the complaint filed by the NYCLU, Kelly asked the human resources director at Salvation Army headquarters, Maureen Schmidt, whether one of the human resource staffers at the social services division, Margaret Geissman, was Jewish, because she had a "Jewish sounding name."

Schmidt told him she was not. Geissman, who described herself to me as a conservative Catholic, told me that Schmidt then starting asking her to point out gay and non-Christian employees at the division. She refused to answer, but day after day Schmidt kept pushing. "She said Kelly wanted to know and that eventually they were going to find out about everyone," Geissman told me. "She said the new vision for the Salvation Army was to have Christians and Salvationists and not to have homosexuals."

Shortly after Colonel Kelly arrived on the scene, a management reorganization was undertaken. Lown's boss, a twenty-seven-year veteran of the Salvation Army, was fired for reasons Lown still doesn't know. About five days later, the newly promoted head of social services, Alfred Peck, told Lown that he needed her, and everyone under her, to fill out a new form. When he gave it to her, she was dumbfounded.

The form, marked "confidential," asks employees to list their "Present Church," "Minister of the Church," and "Other Churches attended regularly during the past ten years." It also asks them to sign a statement authorizing the churches "to give to the Salvation Army any information they may have regarding my character and fitness for work with children." It claims that any "false information or statements are punishable under the laws relating to perjury."

Lown told Peck that she wouldn't fill out the form, and that she wouldn't ask anyone else to, either. That's when she contacted the New York Civil Liberties Union. Eventually, eighteen employees, including Geissman, joined the lawsuit against the Salvation Army. Several of the plaintiffs had worked for the agency for over a decade.

While this was happening, the push to Christianize the agency kept moving forward. According to the NYCLU complaint, "On September 16, 2003, the Salvation Army rescinded a policy statement that had

guaranteed 'equal employment without unlawful discrimination as to
. . . creed.' The revised Employee Manual, dated January 1, 2004, inter-
poses a new religious exception, providing for 'equal opportunity for
employment [. . .] except where prohibition on discrimination is incon-
sistent with the religious principles of the Salvation Army.' "

Lown finally quit in February 2004, saying the work environment
had become intolerably hostile. "There was a sense of real fear," she
said about that time. "When people heard that the HR director was
asked to name all the homosexuals in the agency, people got really
scared. What did they want that for? What were they going to do with
the information?"

Employees also worried about what the new emphasis on evangelism would mean for the Salvation Army's clients. "Foster care is not a
voluntary setup," said Lown. "It's coercive. You don't have a choice
about it, and a birth parent doesn't really have the power to say I don't
want my child going to that agency because I don't want my children
raised as Christians. That worried all of us."

As of this writing, the lawsuit was slowly making its way through
the courts. Lown took a position similar to her old one with Catholic
Charities. She was anxious about joining another religious agency, but
she needed a job and, since faith-based groups dominate the field of
child welfare in New York, she didn't see much of a choice.

Lown still can't believe that what the Salvation Army did didn't
cause more of an uproar. "I'm very concerned about the lack of strong
voices that are protesting this," she said. "My father is an immigrant
who came from Eastern Europe in the 1930s, from Lithuania, and I've
lost a lot of family in the Holocaust. Religious freedom and not being
discriminated against are very important."

Christian nationalists talk a lot about religious freedom as well, but
to them it means something quite different. In 2003, the White House
put out a paper explaining why government-funded religious charities
should be allowed to discriminate. It was called "Protecting the Civil
Rights and Religious Liberty of Faith Based Organizations: Why Reli-

gious Hiring Rights Must Be Protected." A "key principle" of the president's approach, it said, is that when religious groups "receive Federal funds, they should retain their right to hire those individuals who are best able to further their organizations' goals and mission." Religious freedom has come to mean the freedom not to employ people of the wrong religion, and few in America have even noticed the difference.

CHAPTER 5

AIDS Is Not the Enemy:
Sin, Redemption, and the Abstinence Industry

Every year for the past twelve years, D. James Kennedy has hosted the Reclaiming America for Christ conference, usually at his Coral Ridge Presbyterian Church in Ft. Lauderdale. The events bring together hundreds of committed Christian nationalists for two days of lectures, seminars, and devotions that, as the 2001 conference Web site puts it, chart "the path for believers to 'take back the land' in America." Speakers have included Roy Moore, David Barton, and Rick Scarborough, as well as the occasional GOP operative like Clinton prosecutor Kenneth Starr.

Former vice president Dan Quayle delivered a speech at the first Reclaiming America for Christ conference in 1994. In his book *Eternal Hostility*, Frederick Clarkson described the scene: "Quayle's speech was unremarkable, except for his presence during the recitation of the pledge of allegiance—to the 'Christian flag,' which preceded his remarks. The Christian flag, white with a gold cross on a blue field in the upper left corner, flies outside Kennedy headquarters. The assemblage recited together: 'I pledge allegiance to the Christian flag, and to the Savior, for whose Kingdom it stands. One Savior, crucified, risen and coming again, with life and liberty for all who believe.'"[1]

For all who believe. Reclaiming America for Christ is a place where the Christian nationalist movement drops its democratic pretenses and indulges its theocratic dreams. So at the 2003 conference, when the abstinence educator Pam Stenzel spoke, she knew she didn't have to justify her objection to sex education with prosaic arguments about health and public policy. She could be frank about the real reason society must not condone premarital sex—because it is, as she shouted during one particularly impassioned moment, "stinking, filthy, dirty, rotten sin!"

A pretty, zaftig brunette from Minnesota with a degree in psychology from Jerry Falwell's Liberty University, Stenzel makes a living telling kids not to have sex. Rather, she makes a living trying to scare kids out of having sex—as she says in her video *No Screwin' Around*, if you have sex outside of marriage "to a partner who has only been with you . . . *then you will pay.*" A big part of her mission is puncturing students' beliefs that condoms can protect them. She says she addresses half a million kids each year, and millions more have received her message via video.

Thanks to George W. Bush, abstinence education has become a thriving industry, and Stenzel has been at its forefront. Bush appointed her to a twelve-person task force at the Department of Health and Human Services to help implement abstinence education guidelines. She's been a guest at the White House and a speaker at the United Nations. Her nonprofit company, Enlightenment Communications, which puts on abstinence talks and seminars in public schools, typically grossed several hundred thousand dollars a year during the first Bush term.

At Reclaiming America for Christ, Stenzel told her audience about a conversation she'd had with a skeptical businessman on an airplane. The man had asked about abstinence education's success rate—a question she regarded as risible. "What he's asking," she said, "is does it work. You know what? Doesn't matter. Cause guess what. My job is not to keep teenagers from having sex. The public schools' job should not be to keep teens from having sex."

Then her voice rose and turned angry as she shouted, "Our job should be to tell kids the truth!"

"People of God," she cried, "can I beg you, to commit yourself to truth, not what works! To truth! I don't care if it works, because at the end of the day I'm not answering to you, I'm answering to God!"

Later in the same talk, she explained further why what "works" isn't what's important—and gave some insight into what she means by "truth." "Let me tell you something, people of God, that is radical, and I can only say it here," she said. "AIDS is not the enemy. HPV and a hysterectomy at twenty is not the enemy. An unplanned pregnancy is not the enemy. My child believing that they can shake their fist in the face of a holy God and sin without consequence, and my child spending eternity separated from God, *is* the enemy. I will *not* teach my child that they can sin safely."

The crowd applauded.

Of course, Stenzel isn't just teaching her child.

Publicly funded abstinence programs were introduced to the United States in 1981, when $11 million was appropriated under the Adolescent and Family Life Act. It wasn't enough money to make much of an impact, though, and the law was soon tied up in a court challenge brought by the ACLU. Significant funds didn't start flowing into abstinence until 1996, when a provision of the welfare reform law—added at the last minute with little notice and no debate—allocated $250 million for abstinence education to be distributed over five years. States accepting the funds were required to match every four federal dollars with three of their own.

It was a lot of money, but it wasn't always used as conservatives intended. The funds were channeled through state health officials who sometimes didn't believe in abstinence education; Hawaii used its money to fund afterschool tutoring and extracurricular activities, Massachusetts spent the grant on public-service advertisements, and California simply turned the money down.[2]

Under Bush, the abstinence movement has come into its own, receiving lavish federal funding and developing the infrastructure to implement it. The president's 2006 budget asked for $206 million for abstinence education, an increase of $39 million from the year before. By the end of Bush's first term, the government had spent almost a billion dollars on chastity programs, and 30 percent of schools with sex-ed programs taught abstinence only.[3] By law, federally funded abstinence programs aren't allowed to discuss contraception except to mention failure rates. The programs must teach "that abstinence from sexual activity is the only certain way to avoid out-of-wedlock pregnancy, sexually transmitted diseases, and other associated health problems" and "that sexual activity outside of the context of marriage is likely to have harmful psychological and physical effects."

Most research shows that abstinence programs don't do much to stop teens from having sex. Some do succeed in helping kids delay losing their virginity, which almost all adults regard as a positive thing. Any health benefits, however, are negated by the abstinence movement's relentless anticondom message, which seems to dissuade teens from bothering with protection when they do have sex. According to research by sociologists Peter Bearman and Hannah Brückner, teens who take virginity pledges—a key component of many abstinence programs—have sex an average of eighteen months later than those who don't. But Bearman and Brückner also found that in the interim they're more likely to have oral or anal sex, and that when they do lose their virginity, they're less likely to use condoms and to seek treatment if they contract STDs.[4]

In 2005, Texas sponsored a study of the abstinence programs Bush pioneered in the state and later made a model for the nation. High school students, it emerged, were *more* sexually active after taking chastity lessons, although researchers attributed this to the fact that they were getting older rather than to abstinence education itself, which seems to have little effect one way or the other.[5]

So if the aim is to prevent teen pregnancy and sexually transmitted diseases, abstinence programs don't work. As Pam Stenzel's comments make clear, though, the abstinence industry has always been more concerned with public morals than public health.

Comprehensive sex education has long been a target of the right. In the 1960s, groups like the John Birch Society and the Christian Crusade linked it to a diabolical conspiracy against American moral values. A 1968 Christian Crusade booklet titled *Is the School House the Proper Place to Teach Raw Sex?* warned that if "the new morality is affirmed, our children will become easy targets for Marxism and other amoral, nihilistic philosophies—as well as V.D.!"[6]

The essential arguments haven't changed, although secular humanism now replaces Marxism in most anti-sex-ed screeds. Yet the right's broader approach to the problem has advanced significantly, and in almost exactly the same way as have its challenges to evolution. Originally, conservative Christian activists just wanted to keep Darwin and sex education out of schools. When that didn't work, they developed an alternative, quasi-scientific infrastructure that would legitimate their religious beliefs in secular terms, and which they hoped to use to replace the doctrines they objected to.

Abstinence funding pumps federal dollars into this network. The money gets distributed in different ways. Some goes directly to abstinence educators and the creators of abstinence textbooks. Some goes to schools, which can use it to buy curricula or bring in speakers like Stenzel, who charges between $3500 and $5000 for each appearance. In a particularly egregious instance, more than $1 million went to the Silver Ring Thing, an outfit that, as the ACLU alleged in a 2005 lawsuit, stages three-hour revivals in which kids are urged to accept Jesus Christ as their personal savior.* (The Silver Ring Thing's newsletter has described its "mission" as "offering a personal relationship with Jesus Christ as the best way to live a sexually pure life.")

And, according to figures from the Sexuality Information and Edu-

---

* Three months after the ACLU filed suit, the Department of Health and Human Services acknowledged that Silver Ring Thing "includes both secular and religious components that are not adequately safeguarded." The administration ordered Silver Ring Thing to submit to a "corrective action plan" before receiving additional

cation Council of the United States (SIECUS), by 2005 $130 million in abstinence funds went to anti-abortion crisis pregnancy centers, the birthplace of organized abstinence education and a crucial part of the pro-life movement's infrastructure. Crisis pregnancy centers, or CPCs, have long, well-documented records of lying to women about their sexual health, but that hasn't stopped Bush from essentially putting them on the federal payroll.

Divine Deception

CPCs mimic ordinary women's health clinics, but they exist almost solely to dissuade women from getting abortions. They originated even before *Roe v. Wade* in states that had liberalized their abortion laws, but they really caught on in the 1980s, and today there are upward of four thousand CPCs in the United States. Usually advertised under neutral-sounding names like "Women's Resource Center" or "Pregnancy Help Center," CPCs lure clients with offers of free pregnancy tests. Some have even set up shop in the same buildings as abortion clinics, imitating the clinics' signs in order to trick women into visiting them.

The Pearson Foundation, a now defunct St. Louis–based group that once ran dozens of CPCs nationwide, recommended this tactic in a manual titled *How to Start and Operate Your Own Pro-Life Outreach Crisis Pregnancy Center*. "[I]f the girl who would be going to the abortion chamber sees your office first with a similar name, she will probably come into your center," it said.

Once at a CPC, women are sometimes made to watch gory videos about abortion before they're allowed to see their pregnancy test results. They're usually given false or exaggerated information about abortion's health risks, sometimes delivered by an activist wearing a white coat to look like a medical professional. Increasingly, CPCs are purchasing ultrasound equipment in the hopes that women who see images of their fetuses will be less likely to abort. According to an

---

grant money. See Ceci Connolly, "Federal Funds for Abstinence Group Withheld," *The Washington Post*, August 23, 2005.

account posted on the Planned Parenthood Web site, a woman who accidentally wandered into a CPC located in the same building as a Brooklyn Planned Parenthood clinic was shown her ultrasound results with the words "Hi Mommy!" typed underneath.[7]

Crisis pregnancy centers do some good—helping pregnant women with baby clothes and medical expenses, for example. But their deceptive practices have led to a number of lawsuits and government investigations. In 1991, Oregon senator Ron Wyden—then a congressman— held hearings about crisis pregnancy centers and concluded that they "hold out that they are health clinics, but when the women get there, there are no medical professionals. A very strident, very aggressive anti-abortion campaign is what they get." In 2002, New York attorney general Eliot Spitzer launched a major investigation of several CPCs, which was settled when they agreed to be more forthright with their clients about which services they do and do not offer.

Of course, some women who take pregnancy tests at CPCs are not actually pregnant. Sexually active and usually unprepared for motherhood, these women often need help avoiding unwanted pregnancies in the future. But many CPCs are ideologically opposed to birth control. As the Pearson manual instructed, "[N]ever counsel for contraception or refer to agencies making contraceptives available." Such counseling "is not only inaccurate but unacceptable and against the general pro-life philosophy, and Christian principles."

Needing an alternative line of counseling, crisis pregnancy centers pioneered abstinence education. They encouraged their clients to stop having sex and to embrace "secondary virginity." Before long, some CPC workers started taking this message into the wider community, delivering presentations at schools, churches, and community centers. Many went on to become leaders in the abstinence movement. Stenzel was one of them. A dedicated pro-life activist who often speaks of how she was conceived when her mother was raped at fifteen, Stenzel got her start in abstinence counseling working as director of the Alpha Women's Center, a CPC in Minnesota.

When government grants for abstinence education became available, veterans of CPCs parlayed their experience into taxpayer funding. In Austin, for example, an abstinence program called LifeGuard Character and Sexuality Education is run by Austin LifeCare Pregnancy Services, a CPC founded by Susan Olasky, Marvin Olasky's wife. In 2004, LifeGuard received more than $50,000 in federal abstinence money to put on classroom presentations about the dangers of premarital sex and to conduct informational meetings with parents.[8]

Abstinence programs, in turn, sometimes lionize the work of crisis pregnancy centers. The teachers' guide for *WAIT Training*, a popular abstinence-only curriculum, offers suggested subjects for student reports including "The Crisis Pregnancy Helpers."[9] *Sex and Character*, a textbook which is published by the same company that puts out *Of Pandas and People*, has a section on the meaning of "compassion" that offers the example of "when people volunteer at crisis pregnancy centers and open their homes to pregnant girls who need a place to stay."[10]

Ms. Purity

The Abstinence Clearinghouse, which serves as the headquarters of the abstinence movement, is located in a single-story building in Sioux Falls, South Dakota, that used to be occupied by a CPC called the Alpha Center. Both were founded by Leslee Unruh, the doyenne of the chastity industry and a frequent visitor to the White House.

Like many abstinence educators, Unruh developed her message at her CPC, which she opened in 1984. The desperate women who sought help there inspired her to start giving presentations about sexual purity in schools and churches. By 1993, she was part of a group called the Alliance of Chastity Educators. "As speakers, ACE members were bombarded by requests for trusted abstinence resources," the Abstinence Clearinghouse Web site explains. "It was obvious to all of them that a central location was needed where abstinence-until-marriage materials could be easily evaluated, accessed and the numerous requests be handled."

To serve that need, Unruh founded the Abstinence Clearinghouse in 1997. Its advisory board includes Pam Stenzel as well as leading Christian nationalists like D. James Kennedy and Beverly LaHaye. In 2002, the clearinghouse received a $2.7 million contract with the Department of Health and Human Services to develop official standards for abstinence programs.

Unruh is a fifty-one-year-old mother of five. When I met her in the summer of 2005, her hair was dyed blonde, which made her look uncannily like the actress Melanie Griffith. She has none of Pam Stenzel's abrasiveness—she's ebullient and big sisterly, the kind of woman other women like to confide in. Unruh is as ardently opposed to condoms and premarital sex as Stenzel is, but she presents abstinence as a tool of female empowerment and as a way to restore the chivalry to which she believes women are entitled. She speaks angrily of the plight of the women she met at the Alpha Center, and how she believes traditional sex educators failed them.

"I'm a feminist," she told me. "And I'm happy to be a feminist. And I believe that many of our feminist friends have let women down. And I'm really sick of it.

"A girl would come in, she'd be back in a month," Unruh said. The girls spoke the language of the sexual revolution—"You know, do what you want, go out and have all the sex you want, be sexually gratified." But they weren't being gratified, sexually or emotionally. "They were hurting," she said. "Their hearts were being broken, they were pregnant, or they had a sexually transmitted disease. I used to look at them and say, 'Why are you settling for this? Isn't there something better than this?'"

Unruh's own history told her there was. Earlier in her life she had an abortion that she came to regret. The pregnancy, she told me, resulted from being raped by her abusive first husband. Through her work, she wants to help other women put similar experiences behind them. "It's a great feeling to see people do well in life, for me to meet a young woman who's had an abortion, or had multiple abortions, and to say, 'Hey, don't let anybody tell you that just because you've had an abortion, or you picked the wrong guy, that you can't pick a decent guy down the road. That you can't be happy. You can.'"

Perhaps unintentionally, the Abstinence Clearinghouse building reflects Unruh's passage between sin and redemption, misery and satisfaction. Behind it lies a little flower-filled garden with a koi pond that serves as a sanctuary for women who want a place to grieve over past abortions. Some come there in the evening and leave toys or other small mementos. A wall serves as a "memorial for the unborn," with small commemorative metal plates attached to a marble slab. The messages on them are heartrending in their guilt and remorse. "Baby Carlsen. 1963. Who were you to be?" says one. "Baby Always. 1985. My most selfish act," says another. Nearby is a small statue of a crying child angel.

The garden is a sad and plaintive place, but inside the office, the mood is cheerful and bustling. The receptionist answers the phone brightly, "It's a great day at the Abstinence Clearinghouse!" There are framed photos everywhere, including several of Unruh with Bush and one of her and her second husband, Alan, with James Dobson and Summit Ministries' David Noebel, author of numerous books about the Christian worldview.

Next to the reception area is a room housing a little shop called the Sex Love and Relationship Store, which sells "purity" merchandise. The vibe is girlishly romantic, with purple walls decorated with the word "love" painted along the top in red and gold and in many languages. When I visited, Pachelbel's Canon was playing softly in the background. In addition to books about abstinence, modesty, and Christian relationships, the store sells purity rings, including one with a cultured pearl and small diamonds that costs $199, for parents to give to their virgin daughters. There are laminated "Virginity Vouchers" ("Redeemable on Wedding Day") and a doll-size duchess satin wedding dress called Ms. Purity, which, according to its tag, "represents a keepsake of sacred transition to finer womanhood."

The abstinence movement is obsessed with the paraphernalia of weddings; it offers the same soft-focus vision of married bliss found in glossy brides' magazines. The *WAIT Training* curriculum tells teachers to stage mock wedding ceremonies with the class—"use hand-me-down wedding dresses, bridesmaid dresses, prom dresses, cocktail dresses, hand-me-down tuxedos, jackets, suit coats, sports jackets, flowers, cake, and ring to make the ceremony a real event." A student worksheet called "The Wedding of My Dreams" instructs, "Imagine that you had all the money you needed to plan the ultimate wedding. What plans would you make?"[11]

Part of this is a calculated attempt to restore the cultural cachet of marriage, but it also represents deeper longings. People like Unruh are in rebellion against the soulless, mechanized sex they see proliferating in our porn-saturated culture. They want to remystify love, to restore the promise of fairy tales and fireworks. They want to eliminate the very real anxiety that the prospect of divorce creates in many people, and they think they can do it by refashioning sex as a kind of emotional superglue that will hold two people together eternally.

Couples who wait until marriage to have sex, Unruh told me, routinely have simultaneous orgasms. "The hormonal symphony between the two, you can have it right away," she said. "It's reaching it together. It's the fireworks. It's a bonding. It's intimacy."

But that bonding can elude those who sleep with more than one person. "The secretions from one person are different from the next person," she said. Apparently that impedes the synchronization required for the hormonal symphony. People who have sex with more than one person "mess up their body processes." (Although, she said, in time those who choose secondary virginity can restore their equilibrium).

Unruh's physiology seemed dubious, but it was easy to see the power of her romantic vision. "These couples who are married all these years, they can just look in each other's eyes" to feel sexual passion, she said. She told me about meeting a woman whose husband had been paralyzed from the neck down in an accident. "She said, 'All those orgasms that I had with him before the accident, now, he looks at me, we look into each other's eyes for an hour and we get that tingly feeling. It's there. I have that through my emotions, in my heart.'"

To give a sexually active woman birth control, in Unruh's thinking, is to treat her as incapable of such transcendence. If a girl plans to abstain but has sex anyway, "I'm going to believe in her that she can start over again," Unruh said. "I don't care if she starts over seven times, or twenty times. I'm going to believe in her each time she comes back, because that's what important. I don't say, 'No, you know what, you look kind of sexy, and you look like you're sexual, and I don't think you're going to abstain, so let's give you a female condom, let's give you another kind of condom, let's put you on the patch, let's give all these chemicals to you.' "

Critics may scoff at the idea of secondary virginity, she said, "but isn't it important to give somebody a second chance and say you can start over, and don't worry about the past, just talk about the future?"

But what, I asked her, about a woman who doesn't want to start over? What would she tell a young woman who listened to her presentation but said she was going to continue having sex regardless? "I'm not going to give them a condom," she said. "No. Never. Cause they're going to come back to me, and they're going to say it didn't work."

The abstinence industry is implacably, doctrinally anticondom for two reasons. As Unruh indicates, many purity advocates insist that condoms don't work, so teaching about them is dangerous. Behind the scientific argument, however, lies a philosophical objection to the very idea of safe sex. These two beliefs often run together, so that attempts at sex without profound repercussions seem like doomed exercises in hubris.

It is this refusal to discuss safe sex or birth control—except to emphasize their failure rates—that makes abstinence-only programs controversial. Christian nationalists usually believe that their enemies want to see kids have sex as early and as often as possible. James Dobson has blamed opposition to abstinence education on the mercenary motives of Planned Parenthood and greedy abortionists who profit from knocked-up kids. Unruh has even darker suspicions, telling me that the sex education world is full of pedophiles who want access to children and others who are trying to introduce bestiality into public school classes. "There's a lot of perversion out there, wacko weird sexual stuff," she said.

Actually, there is broad agreement among children's health advocates that the longer teenagers wait to have sex, the better. Most of the sex educators that people like Unruh and Dobson abhor actually promote abstinence as the best option, but they also say that teenagers who are going to have sex, as some always are, need to be encouraged to use condoms. Unruh may say she doesn't care if a girl has to start over seven times or twenty, but without a condom, the odds are much higher that the girl will get a disease that makes starting over impossible.

One fundamental difference between sex ed and abstinence education, then, is whether the emphasis is on saving kids' bodies or saving their souls. Most abstinence textbooks and programs seem designed to guide students, implicitly or explicitly, toward a conservative religious morality. Occasionally the proselytization is obvious. Teenagers who participated in Silver Ring Thing events were given Silver Ring Thing Sexual Abstinence Study Bibles, which instruct, "If you have accepted God's wonderful gift of salvation through his Son, Jesus Christ, your name will be found in the Book of Life, and you will spend eternity in heaven with God. If you have chosen to reject Christ, then your final destination will be the lake of fire. No arguments. Case closed."[12]

Usually the message is subtler. Abstinence textbooks often contain references to evangelical self-help authors like James Dobson. They repeat evangelical lore as fact: *Sex Respect* teaches that abortion increases the risk of breast cancer, a frequent contention of anti-abortion activists that's disputed by almost all mainstream scientists. *Sex and Character* implies that homosexuality is a choice, telling the story of "Jerry," who "was tired of his homosexual lifestyle. With the threat of AIDS he decided to make a change. But he was too late. He was already infected . . ."[13]

The evangelical critique of America's slide into decadence saturates abstinence curricula. The student manual for *Facing Reality* features a cartoon of two teenage girls talking about the proliferation of STDs and AIDS:

"I wonder if mother nature's trying to tell us something about sex," says one.

"Mr. McDonald says it's like a ballgame. If you play by the rules, you're ok," the other responds.

"Mr. Egan says it's more like a war."

"What's that mean?"

"He says the sexual revolution is over . . . all we're doing now is taking care of the dead and wounded."[14]

The narrative of a fallen society in need of redemption drives the abstinence movement. Although often unspoken, it can lead to a condescending and punitive attitude toward those who refuse to see the light, even from seemingly empathetic people like Unruh.

Unruh doesn't just want to see her values respected; she wants to see them enforced. "Did you ever think the day would come when there would be people not smoking on airlines? " she asked me. "I remember feeling sick the whole time I was on a flight." Now, she said, she smiles when she sees smokers confined to the grimy little rooms—she calls them cages—set aside for them at airport terminals. "You know what I think of? I think of those people having sex"—sex outside of marriage—"in those little cages." She wants to restore a taboo, and she wants the government to help.

Unruh does not believe that people can live healthily and happily unless they adopt her sexual standards. Speaking of those who reject abstinence in their own lives, she said, "They're so busy with their worldview, believing there must be a pill, a powder, a potion that will keep me so I don't have to control myself. There is nothing. You've got to control yourself. You've got to learn what 'wait' means. You've got to learn what 'not now' means. We want instant gratification in everything—'I should be able to do this if I want to do this.' Well then, there are going to be consequences to it."

Nothing infuriates abstinence advocates more than the notion of "safe sex." During her talk at Reclaiming America for Christ, Stenzel announced, "There is no way statistically that you can have sex with someone who is not a virgin and not get a disease." *Choosing the Best*, one of the most widely used abstinence-only curriculum, compares sex with a condom to Russian roulette and says, "there is a greater risk of a condom failure than the bullet being in the chamber."[15]

The Number One Weapon

Part of the abstinence industry's anticondom line is based on distortions of scientific data, but there is one truth at the center of it—condoms offer little protection against HPV, or human papillomavirus, the most common sexually transmitted disease in America. HPV has thus become key to the abstinence movement—Unruh has called it "the number one weapon we have."[16]

According to the Centers for Disease Control and Prevention (CDC), 50 to 75 percent of sexually active men and women acquire genital HPV infection at some point in their lives. Because the disease can be spread through contact with parts of the genitals not covered by condoms, there is no reliable way, short of abstinence, to avoid the disease. (According to the CDC, "[T]he effect of condoms in preventing HPV infection is unknown.")

There are more than thirty different types of sexually transmitted HPV viruses, and most of them are harmless. "Most people who become infected with HPV will not have any symptoms and will clear the infection on their own," the CDC says. However, it says, ten types of HPV "can lead, in rare cases, to development of cervical cancer."

While the effect of condoms in preventing HPV infection is unclear, condom use has actually been associated with lower rates of cervical cancer. Yet the abstinence industry is correct that, when it comes to HPV, there is no such thing as safe sex. HPV is a serious problem that all women need to be educated about, and the abstinence industry deserves credit for raising its profile.

But almost all abstinence materials leave out a crucial fact. Even for women with dangerous strains of HPV, cervical cancer is usually preventable with routine Pap testing.* Imparting this information could save lives by encouraging women to get checkups, but it's rarely

---

* "Regular Pap testing and careful medical follow-up, with treatment if necessary, can help ensure that pre-cancerous changes in the cervix caused by HPV infection do not develop into life threatening cervical cancer," the CDC says. "Most women who develop invasive cervical cancer have not had regular cervical cancer screening."

included in abstinence textbooks, perhaps because it would lessen HPV's effectiveness as a rhetorical weapon.

The truth is that the abstinence industry needs HPV to be dangerous. That's why, when a vaccine arose in 2005, several leading abstinence advocates—the very people who have spent years warning of the disease's horrors—could scarcely hide their dismay.

Having completed successful trials of HPV vaccines, the pharmaceutical companies GlaxoSmithKline and Merck will soon file for regulatory approval to start marketing them. But as the British magazine *New Scientist* reported in April 2005, American religious groups "are gearing up to oppose vaccination."

"Abstinence is the best way to prevent HPV," the Family Research Council's Bridget Maher told *New Scientist*. "Giving the HPV vaccine to young women could be potentially harmful, because they may see it as a licence to engage in premarital sex."[17]

"I'm very concerned about the HPV vaccine," Unruh told me. "You know, here we go again." To her, the vaccine, like condoms, is just another way for people to avoid living as they should. She also suggested that it would benefit child molesters, since it would cover up the viral evidence of their crimes. "Have you read any of the NAMBLA stuff on the HPV vaccine?" she asked darkly, invoking the North American Man-Boy Love Association, a pro-pedophile fringe group. "You need to read that."

Establishing Legitimacy

There is no way to know if right-wing evangelicals will interfere with the vaccine's Food and Drug Administration approval, or with nationwide vaccination campaigns. Under Bush, though, the FDA, like other scientific bodies, has been heavily politicized. Bush has stacked committees with people drawn from the Christian nationalist movement, and they have often succeeded in bending policy to suit their ideology. Thus it's slightly alarming to note that one of the president's appointees to the 15-member panel that will advise the government on the HPV vaccine is Reginald Finger, a former medical analyst for Focus on the Family. In October 2005, Finger spoke to *The Washington Post* about the vaccine, saying, "There are people who sense that it could cause people to feel like sexual behaviors are safer if they are vaccinated and may lead to more sexual behavior because they feel safe." (He then disassociated himself from that position, saying he was withholding judgment on the vaccine pending a formal review).[18]

The Bush administration's cavalier approach to empirical facts has been widely documented, perhaps most damningly by the Union of Concerned Scientists. In February 2004 the group released a statement signed by over sixty prominent scientists—including twenty Nobel laureates—charging the Bush administration with unprecedented political manipulation of science. One of the ways the administration did this, it said, was "by placing people who are professionally unqualified or who have clear conflicts of interest in official posts and on scientific advisory committees."

An example, according to the statement, was the appointment of W. David Hager to the FDA's Reproductive Health Advisory Committee. It described Hager as an "obstetrician-gynecologist with scant credentials and highly partisan political views," and noted that he is "best known for co-authoring a book"—*As Jesus Cared for Women*—"that recommends particular scripture readings as a treatment for premenstrual syndrome."

Hager, who is close to James Dobson, comes from the Christian nationalist counterintelligentsia that works to give the movement's theories a gloss of scientific legitimacy. He's a member of the advisory board of the Medical Institute for Sexual Health, the Austin-based think tank that is to sex education what the Discovery Institute is to the teaching of evolution. Founded in 1992 by Joe McIlhaney, an evangelical gynecologist close to George W. Bush, the medical institute translates the Christian worldview of sex into scientific language, publishing professional-seeming reports designed to discredit mainstream scientific findings about condom effectiveness and to promote abstinence education.*

In 1995, the Texas Department of Health wrote a letter to McIlhaney's

---

* McIlhaney also wrote the foreword to the abstinence textbook *Sex and Character*.

institute criticizing a slide presentation he'd been showing throughout the state. It included a detailed slide-by-slide critique, prepared by two doctors, a registered nurse, and the director of the state's HIV/STD Epidemiology Division, that pointed out a number of distorted, downright false, and "ridiculous" statements in McIlhaney's lesson. "Some of the data presented suffers from investigator bias," the letter said. "Dr. McIlhaney's presentation tended to report the outlier data as 'proof' that condoms don't work rather than present those reports in the context of the entire data set. The only data that was reported in the presentation are those which supported his bias on the topics he addressed. Intellectual honesty demands that he present all the data."

These days, the Medical Institute for Sexual Health gets much more respect from the government. Thanks to Bush, it received at least $1.5 million in federal contracts related to abstinence education and STD research. Bush put McIlhaney on the Presidential Advisory Council on HIV/AIDS and on the advisory committee to the director of the Centers for Disease Control and Prevention. Important administration officials from the Department of Health and Human Services attend the institute's annual conferences.

Now the medical institute and its allies bring the country's health officials into line, not vice versa. As the Union of Concerned Scientists documented, the Bush administration had a CDC fact sheet on proper condom use replaced with a document emphasizing condom failure rates and the effectiveness of abstinence. More important, Hager succeeded in blocking over-the-counter access to emergency contraception—the so-called morning-after pill—despite widespread consensus on its safety.

Because the morning-after pill is only effective if taken within seventy-two hours of unprotected sex, women's health advocates have lobbied to make the pill available without a prescription, and in 2003, the panel Hager was on voted 23–4 to do just that. In a highly unusual move, however, the FDA rejected the panel's advice. It did so after receiving a memo from Hager, one of the four minority voters, who argued that greater access to emergency contraception would increase "risky" behavior among young adolescents.[19] The FDA already had a host of independent studies denying that canard. Nevertheless, after receiving Hager's memo, it rejected the panel's advice and refused to allow emergency contraception to be sold over the counter. (In August 2005, Susan Wood, chief of women's health at the Food and Drug Administration, resigned over the FDA's continuing refusal to make the pill available without a prescription. "I can no longer serve as staff when scientific and clinical evidence, fully evaluated and recommended by the professional staff here, has been overruled," she wrote in an e-mail to her colleagues.[20])

A bald, hawk-nosed man with a thin grey mustache, Hager has boasted about his role in keeping the pill prescription-only. Delivering a sermon in the campus chapel of Kentucky's evangelical Asbury College in October 2004, he said, "I was asked to write a minority opinion that was sent to the commissioner of the FDA. For only the second time in five decades, the FDA did not abide by its advisory committee opinion, and the measure was rejected.

"I argued from a scientific perspective, and God took that information, and he used it through this minority report to influence the decision," Hager said. "Once again, what Satan meant for evil, God turned into good."[21]

But Hager almost certainly wasn't arguing from a scientific perspective. He was using scientific language to rationalize an evangelical Christian position. He was doing exactly what Ned Ryun teaches his charges at Generation Joshua: taking "a firm, solid biblical worldview" and translating it into "terms that the other side accepts."

People like Ryun have a perfect right to use this rhetorical strategy, disturbing as it may be to those who don't share their agenda. Yet when the United States government works this way, it turns all nonevangelical Americans into "the other side." The nonreligious are no longer even part of the debate, because the arguments and rationales presented in public are a sham. Only believers are privy to the real reasons that the administration does what it does. The Department of Health and Human Services operates like a giant crisis pregnancy center, deceiving in the name of some higher good.

The Bush administration's elevation of the Medical Institute for Social Health into a new scientific establishment has echoes in Hannah Arendt's *Origins of Totalitarianism*. She wrote of how totalitarian movements created "paraprofessional" associations of teachers, doctors, lawyers, and the like, which mimicked ordinary professional groups in order to erode their legitimacy and eventually replace them. As she noted,

> None of these institutions had more professional value than the imitation of the army represented by the stormtroopers, but together they created a perfect world of appearances in which every reality in the nontotalitarian world was slavishly duplicated in the form of humbug.
>
> The technique of duplication, certainly useless for the direct overthrow of government, proved extremely fruitful in the work of undermining actively existing institutions and in the "decomposition of the status quo," which totalitarian organizations invariably prefer to an open show of force. If it is the task of movements to "bore their way like polyps into all positions of power," then they must be ready for any specific social and political position.[22]

The American status quo—a system that worked, imperfectly but consistently, according to certain rational rules and respect for certain empirical realities—is decomposing. The individual lies or small curtailments of freedom that we've seen so far are not as troubling as the larger phenomenon of a government run according to ideological fictions. If the Christian nationalists have their way, after all, it won't just be the Department of Health and Human Services that works this way. The movement's leaders have much bigger prizes in mind.

CHAPTER 6

No Man, No Problem:
The War on the Courts

According to David Gibbs, the attorney for Terri Schiavo's parents, Terri sobbed in her mother's arms after the courts condemned her to death. "Terri Schiavo was as alive as any person sitting here," he told a banquet of leading Christian nationalists in April 2005. "Anything you saw on the videos, multiply times two hundred. I mean completely animated, completely responsive, *desperately* trying to talk." Schiavo, said Gibbs, would struggle to repeat the word "love" after her mother, and managed to get out something like "loooo."

It was the first day of the Confronting the Judicial War on Faith conference in Washington, D.C., the inaugural event of a recently formed group called the Judeo-Christian Council for Constitutional Restoration. Around two hundred committed right-wing activists had converged on the Washington Marriott from twenty-five states to hear from movement leaders like Phyllis Schlafly, Roy Moore, and Tony Perkins. Schiavo, the brain-dead Florida woman whose husband had removed her feeding tube in the face of protests by her parents, Congress, and the Christian right, had died the week before. Some at the banquet had been in Florida, keeping vigil outside Schiavo's hospice. Emotions were still raw, the sense of emergency was still acute, and many cried as they listened.

"America needs a healing," said Gibbs, a trim man in his midthirties with glasses and shellacked black hair. The crowd murmured its assent. "We're sitting here, desperately as a nation needing to adopt the heart of God. . . . We're on the eve of a real major decision. Are we going to do it God's way, or are we going to head down the path of whatever these judges think is best? Terri was alive. The courts killed her. The courts killed her in a barbaric fashion. Others are already facing and will face a similar fate if we don't do something."

Those at the conference were there to figure out what that something should be. The executive committee of the Judeo-Christian Council for Constitutional Restoration included influential right-wing figures like Schlafly, Jerry Falwell, and Michael Farris. Rick Scarborough, the Baptist preacher organizing nationwide networks of "patriot pastors," was the council's acting chairman and the conference's master of ceremonies. A flyer introducing the group said, "We have come to perceive activist judges as the greatest threat to life and liberty. When the courts abandon their legitimate role as impartial arbiters and seek to impose their will on a nation, a free people must respond."

Having won control of two branches of the federal government, Christian nationalists view the courts as the last intolerable obstacle to their palingenetic dream. Believing America to be a Christian nation, they see any ruling that contradicts their theology as de facto unconstitutional, and its enforcement tyrannical. They're convinced that they must destroy the judiciary's power to liberate themselves. A series of outrages—the *Lawrence v. Texas* decision, Terri Schiavo's death, the filibuster of Bush's judicial nominees—has stoked their sense of crisis.

The entire Christian nationalist agenda ultimately hinges on conquering the courts. A remade judiciary could let state governments criminalize abortion and gay sex. It could sanction the reinstitution of school prayer and the teaching of creationism and permit the ever greater Christianization of the country's social services. It could intervene on the right's behalf in situations like the Schiavo case. It could intrude into the most intimate corners of Americans' private lives.

To take just one example, if the Supreme Court overturned *Roe v. Wade*, it would undermine the ruling Roe was based on, *Griswold v. Connecticut*. That 1965 decision, which struck down bans on birth control for married women (extended to unmarried women in 1972's *Eisenstadt v. Baird*), was the first to infer a right to privacy from the constitution. If the court ruled that no constitutional right to privacy exists, states would again have the latitude to make contraception illegal.

Without *Griswold*, some states might ban birth control pills, which many evangelicals consider abortifacients, since they can interfere with the implementation of a fertilized egg. That prospect would have been far-fetched just a few years ago, but recently contraception has been under attack nationwide. A rash of Christian pharmacists have refused to fill prescriptions for both the morning-after pill and for ordinary oral contraceptives—180 such incidents were reported in one six-month period in 2004.[1] Some pharmacists turned women away because they were unmarried, and a few refused to transfer their prescriptions to other pharmacies that *would* fill them. In Denton, Texas, three pharmacists working at an Eckerd drug store refused to fill a rape victim's prescription for the morning-after pill. ("I went in the back room and briefly prayed about it," said one of them. "I actually called my pastor . . . and asked him what he thought about it.")[2] They were fired, but four states have "conscience clause" laws protecting such pharmacists, and at least eleven others—including Texas—are considering them.[3] (Ten states already have laws protecting doctors who refuse to prescribe contraception.)

"This is a very big issue that's just beginning to surface," the Christian Legal Society's Steven H. Aden told *The Washington Post*. "More and more pharmacists are becoming aware of their right to conscientiously refuse to pass objectionable medications across the counter. We are on the very front edge of a wave that's going to break not too far down the line."[4] If it does, it will be up to the courts to determine which liberties can be washed away.

Some Christian nationalists seem to hope that the end of *Griswold* would open the door to the criminalization of all kinds of biblically incorrect sex. In 2003, Rick Santorum told the Associated Press,

> [I]f the Supreme Court says that you have the right to consensual sex within your home, then you have the right to bigamy, you have the right to polygamy, you have the right to incest, you have the right to adultery. You have the right to anything. Does that undermine the fabric of our society? I would argue yes, it does. It all comes from, I would argue, this right to privacy that doesn't exist in my opinion in the United States Constitution, this right that was created, it was created in *Griswold*. . . . You say, well, it's my individual freedom. Yes, but it destroys the basic unit of our society because it condones behavior that's antithetical to strong, healthy families.[5]

Note what Santorum was objecting to. Not just abortion, or polygamy, or even adultery, but to the right *to consensual sex within your home*. If people do *not* have that right, then the potential for Christian nationalist intrusion into people's personal lives would be limitless.

Reconstructionists and Republicans

The fact that adults' access to contraception was suddenly subject to debate was evidence of how fevered the climate was in the spring of 2005. In such an atmosphere, few in the media seemed astonished when, at Confronting the Judicial War on Faith, congressmen and Senate staffers shared the stage with men who advocate the execution of sexual deviants and the replacement of democracy with the bloody strictures of the Old Testament. Even by the illiberal standards of the religious right, the conference was remarkable in bringing together lawmakers and Capitol Hill aides with unabashed theocrats, and the comity between the two groups was a sign that something had changed in America. In the fury and rancor over the judiciary, the bounds of acceptability had shifted even further to the right—almost as far as it is possible to go.

Michael Peroutka, a prominent militia supporter, member of the neo-Confederate League of the South, and presidential candidate of the far-right Constitution party, was a speaker. So was Tom Jipping, a counselor to Senator Orrin Hatch, and Manny Miranda, Senator Bill Frist's former chief counsel on judicial nominations. (Miranda had resigned the previous year in the midst of a probe into illegal GOP snooping into the computer files of Senate Democrats).

Then the House Majority Leader, Tom DeLay, a friend of Rick Scarborough, was supposed to give the keynote address, but a last-minute trip to the pope's funeral in Rome kept him away. (He delivered a laudatory greeting via video instead.) Filling in for DeLay was Texas congressman Lamar Smith. Missouri congressman Todd Akin also spoke, sharing the stage with Herb Titus and Howard Phillips, both prominent adherents of Christian Reconstructionism.

The doctrine devised by the late R. J. Rushdoony, Reconstructionism calls for federal democracy to be replaced by a network of small sovereign communities run by fundamentalist Christians. It is proudly opposed to secular law—as Rushdoony wrote in the Fall 1996 edition of *The Journal of Christian Reconstruction*, "The humanist West is our modern throne of iniquity, framing mischief by enacting laws. We must return to God's law. We must work towards a true Christendom. Thy kingdom come, O Lord!"[6]

Reconstructionists used to be politically radioactive, but that seemed to change in the wake of Terri Schiavo's death. Schiavo had become a mythical figure, martyred and quasi-divine, in the stories that percolated through the Christian nationalist subculture, and when she slipped away, she took some of the right's last measure of restraint with her. Those calling for the imposition of theocracy were still a small minority, but they were no longer beyond the pale. The right was boiling, its rhetorical radicalism increasing so quickly that comments that seemed outré one day appeared tame the next. Calls for the mass impeachment of judges were followed by demands that the courts themselves be abolished, then prayers to deliver judges to Satan, and finally coy hints about murdering them.

The lawyer David Gibbs, a graduate of Falwell's Liberty University, is a Baptist, not a Reconstructionist. But whether he knew it or not, Reconstructionism shaped his thinking, just as it shaped the thinking of the Christian nationalist movement as a whole. He had imbibed R. J. Rushdoony and David Barton's distorted views of history and with them an essentially theocratic vision of the law.

"You say, how can that happen in our country?" he asked at the banquet, as attendees drank coffee and nibbled on dry chocolate cake. "Clearly this case illustrates as strongly as any that we have eliminated all of the moral absolute standards out of our law. How many here understand we were founded as one nation under God?"

The crowd murmured yes.

"What does that mean?" he said. "Well, to our founding fathers, what that meant is they were going to take the word of God, and God has given us in the Bible his word, and they said this book will always be true, and if there is ever a close call in policy, in leadership, in law, in society, if there's ever a question, we want to look to the source of absolute truth. That's why the Ten Commandments are so important. They were the original source of American law. The Bible was understood to be authoritative. When the founding fathers said 'One Nation under God,' they made the decision that they would submit to what God had put forward in his law."

Circuit Court Judge George Greer, who decided the Schiavo case, had put that legacy aside. Gibbs quoted him saying, "You won't find a Ten Commandments hanging outside *my* door."

By the time Gibbs finished speaking, people all over the room were in tears. Scarborough, moved, invited the audience to get on their knees. Men and women in evening clothes dropped to the floor, heads bowed. Among them, a preacher started up:

"Father, we echo the words of the apostle Paul, because we know

Judge Greer claims to be a Christian. So as the apostle Paul said in First Corinthians 5, in the name of our Lord Jesus Christ, when you are gathered together, with the power of our Lord Jesus Christ, deliver such a one to Satan for the destruction of the flesh, that his spirit may be saved in the day of our Lord Jesus."

The next day, on a panel called "Remedies to Judicial Tyranny," constitutional lawyer Edwin Vieira discussed Justice Anthony Kennedy's majority opinion in *Lawrence v. Texas*, which struck down that state's antisodomy law. Vieira accused Kennedy of relying on "Marxist, Leninist, Satanic principles drawn from foreign law" in his jurisprudence.

What to do about Communist judges in thrall to the devil? Vieira said, "Here again I draw on the wisdom of Stalin. We're talking about the greatest political figure of the twentieth century. . . . He had a slogan, and it worked very well for him whenever he ran into difficulty. 'No man, no problem.'"

The audience laughed, and Vieira repeated, " 'No man, no problem.' This is not a structural problem we have. This is a problem of personnel."

The full Stalin quote is this: "Death solves all problems: no man, no problem."[7]

John Birch's Legacy

Right-wing loathing for the courts is nothing new; it dates back at least to desegregation. Enraged by a series of civil rights decisions, the John Birch Society led a campaign to impeach Earl Warren, chief justice of the United States Supreme Court. Birchers railed against judicial tyranny and proposed laws very much like Roy Moore's Constitution Restoration Act. A 1972 pamphlet by the prominent Bircher Dan Smoot described the Court's decision in *Brown v. Board of Education of Topeka* as the beginning of despotism: "From the time that decision was handed down until the time when the people of America demand that Congress correct the situation, we actually have no Constitution at all. We are at the mercy of the judicial oligarchy." That oligarchy went on to abolish "a most cherished and important right" in ruling against school prayer. The solution to these outrages, Smoot wrote, was for Congress to strip the Supreme Court of its jurisdiction over education, religion, and state elections.[8]

If that rhetoric sounds familiar, it's partly because much of the Christian nationalist movement has its roots in the John Birch Society. Rushdoony was a sympathizer; in *Institutes of Biblical Law*, he compared the group's cellular structure to the early Christian church.[9] Summit Ministries president and Christian worldview author David Noebel was a member, as was Tim LaHaye, who ran John Birch Society training seminars in California in the 1960s and 1970s.[10] Nelson Bunker Hunt, a member of the John Birch Society's national council, was influential in helping LaHaye form the Council for National Policy, which has counted a number of Birch veterans as members. "The JBS was with the CNP from the beginning," wrote investigative journalist Russ Bellant.[11]

Many current Christian nationalist fixations mirror the obsessions of the John Birch Society, especially a fearful loathing of secular liberals. Like today's Christian nationalists, the John Birch Society reached its zenith at a time of great international uncertainty, but its members believed America's most dangerous enemies were at home. "According to JBS theory," Chip Berlet and Matthew Lyons wrote in their book *Right-Wing Populism in America*, "liberals consciously encourage the gradual process of collectivism; therefore, JBS reasoning goes, many liberals and their allies must actually be secret traitors whose ultimate goal is to replace the nations of Western civilization with a one-world socialist government."[12]

The same assumptions undergird Christian nationalism; as Tim LaHaye and David Noebel wrote in their 2000 book *Mind Siege*, "[W]e are being ruled by a small but very influential cadre of committed humanists. These politicians are determined to turn America into an amoral, humanist country ripe for merger into a one-world, socialist state."[13]

Some John Birch campaigns have recurred almost unaltered in recent years. Birchers, for example, believed they had to save the retail traditions of Christmas from an assault by cosmopolitan secularists. In the late 1950s, they grew alarmed about an alleged plot to replace department store Christmas decorations with U.N. insignia. "The UN fanatics launched their assault on Christmas in 1958, but too late to get very far before the holy day was at hand," warned a 1959 Birch pamphlet titled *There Goes Christmas?!* "They are already busy, however, at this very moment, on efforts to poison the 1959 Christmas season with their high-pressure propaganda." As part of their devious scheme, the pamphlet said, partisans of the United Nations were selling UNICEF Christmas cards that "omit any reference to Christ."[14]

In 2004, the right once again grew frenzied about a so-called war on Christmas taking place in the nation's major department store chains. Christian nationalists were livid that Macy's and Bloomingdale's, both owned by Federated Department Stores, used the phrase "happy holidays" instead of "merry Christmas" in their displays. The substitution seemed to them to be part of a secular assault upon the Christian character of Christmas, and thus upon Christianity in general, and they mobilized to fight back.

The Committee to Save Merry Christmas launched in California. "A covert and deceptive war has been waged on Christmas to remove any mention of it from the public square during the Christmas season," its Web site said. "During the past several years, and with great effectiveness, we have observed a consistent and relentless move to culturally pressure merchants, businessmen and individuals to remove the words 'Merry Christmas' from their advertising, decorations and promotional materials."

There was one profound difference between these two episodes. The John Birch Society never had anywhere near the kind of power achieved by the Christian nationalists, and the mass media of the 1950s did not treat their campaign to save department store Christmas decorations as a matter of great national import.

In 2004, though, the Committee to Save Merry Christmas was trumpeted on cable TV and talk radio. *The O'Reilly Factor* on Fox News ran "Christmas Under Siege," a series of segments about a purported conspiracy against the holiday by "secular progressives." On his radio show, Bill O'Reilly told a caller, "Remember, more than 90 percent of

American homes celebrate Christmas. But, the small minority that is trying to impose its will on the majority is so vicious, so dishonest—and has to be dealt with."

The cries of yuletide persecution grew even louder in the run-up to the 2005 holiday season. Boycotts were launched against department stores accused of jettisoning the phrase "merry Christmas." The Alliance Defense Fund announced it had 800 lawyers standing by to defend the holy holiday against anyone who would try to keep Christmas hymns out of schools or crèches out of government buildings. Liberty Counsel, another Christian right legal outfit, claimed to have 750 lawyers mobilized for the same fight. Fox News anchor John Gibson published a book titled, *The War on Christmas: How the Liberal Plot to Ban the Sacred Christian Holiday Is Worse Than You Thought*, which concluded that said war is "really a war on Christianity."[15]

The mainstreaming of Bircher ideology isn't just a media phenomenon—it has affected the highest levels of government. In the 1960s, promoting John Birch Society propaganda could prove politically catastrophic. The 1961 revelation that Major General Edwin A. Walker was using Birch books and magazines to "indoctrinate" U.S. troops stationed in Europe was a national scandal; Walker was denounced on the Senate floor and relieved of his command.[16] *The New York Times* ran an article headlined, "Right-Wing Officers Worrying Pentagon," which cited civilian officials' concern about the spread of Birchite propaganda in the military. Birchers weren't even welcome as volunteers on Barry Goldwater's 1964 presidential campaign because they carried the stigma of extremism.[17]

Today there is no such restraint on Birch-style radicalism. A scandal similar to the Walker affair occurred in the summer of 2003 after Lieutenant General William G. Boykin, wearing his military dress uniform, told an evangelical group that Islamists hated America "because we're a Christian nation, because our foundation and our roots are Judeo-Christian . . . and the enemy is a guy named Satan."

Boykin gave at least twenty-three similar talks, almost always in uniform. At several of them, he showed photos from the capital of Somalia, where he had commanded Delta Forces during the 1993 battle there. In the pictures, there were black streaks in the sky, photographic evidence, he said, of a "demonic spirit over the city of Mogadishu." Speaking of a Somali warlord, he told one audience, "I knew my God was bigger than his. I knew that my God was a real God and his was an idol."

Under Bush, Boykin was promoted. In October 2003, he became the new deputy undersecretary of defense for intelligence and was given the job of tracking down Osama bin Laden.[18]

Drawing on John Birch Society theories, Reconstructionists laid much of the intellectual groundwork for the fight against the judiciary. In the same volume of *The Journal of Christian Reconstruction* in which Rushdoony attacked secular law, a Republican state representative from Oklahoma named William D. Graves published an essay called "The Case for Curbing the Federal Courts." Graves argued that the Supreme Court, by claiming the power to review the laws of Congress and to force the states to adhere to the Bill of Rights, was exercising "judicial tyranny" over the nation, and he recommended using Article III of the Constitution to strip the body of its jurisdiction over areas of the law including school prayer and abortion.[19]

In the last few years, as more conservatives joined the battle against judges, they drew on such Reconstructionist ideas. Suddenly, the theocrats had a seat at the table. This marked a shift on the right. Not long ago, mainstream Christian right activists thought it wise to distance themselves from Reconstructionism, lest they be tainted as totalitarians—in 1996, Ralph Reed denounced the creed as an "authoritarian ideology that threatens the most basic civil liberties of a free and democratic society."[20] Pat Robertson was less hesitant about flirting with Reconstructionism, but when he was seeking accreditation for his Regent University Law School in the early 1990s, he, too, tried to separate himself from the partisans of theocracy, forcing out the school's Reconstructionist dean, Herb Titus.[21]

With the rise of Christian nationalism, however, Reconstructionist thinkers started migrating toward the political mainstream—or, rather, the mainstream started migrating toward them. Especially after the 2004 elections, it grew ever harder to discern where the fringe ended and the new right-wing establishment began.

There is little appreciable distance, for example, between freshman Oklahoma senator Tom Coburn and Howard Phillips, both of whom have called for the execution of abortionists, a crucial plank in the Reconstructionist agenda. Coburn is just one senator of one hundred, of course, and America is a long way from putting gynecologists on death row. But with his victory in the 2004 election, the extreme and the government moved closer together.

Both Coburn and Senator Sam Brownback had been slated to speak at the Confronting the Judicial War on Faith conference, but canceled at the last minute. Nevertheless, Phillips told me he had no doubt where the two men's loyalties lay. "I know and admire Senator Coburn, and if anyone would feel comfortable here, it's Tom Coburn," he said. "Coburn and Brownback are totally in sync with the people here."

Throughout his career, Phillips has moved along the continuum linking conservative Republicans to the furthest edge of the right. A big, lumbering man with an avuncular manner, a boxer's flattened face, and unkempt gray eyebrows, he uses a cane to help support his wide-hipped bulk. His roots are in the mainstream—he was educated at Harvard, where he was elected student council president, and served as assistant to the chairman of the Republican National Committee and as the director of the U.S. Office of Economic Opportunity in the Nixon administration. He helped midwife the new right that has proved so effective in winning elections for Republicans, but despite that success, he doesn't really believe in democracy anymore. He believes in theonomy, or government according to biblical law.

As one of the conservative strategists who recruited Jerry Falwell to found the Moral Majority, Phillips was a pivotal figure in the birth of Christian nationalism, but like Marvin Olasky, he was raised Jewish.

His mother's first language was Yiddish, and as a child, Phillips was sent to Hebrew school and Zionist youth camp. He was still Jewish when he helped launch Falwell. His conversion, he told me, happened during the first Reagan administration on Yom Kippur, the Jewish day of atonement.

"It just suddenly hit me that the Old Testament is about blood covering our sins," he said. "And then I realized I could not atone for my own sins, and that the blood of Jesus Christ provided that covering for me." He now attends McLean Bible Church, a Virginia megachurch whose formerly Jewish pastor, Lon Solomon, is on the executive committee of Jews for Jesus. (In 2002, Solomon was appointed by Bush to serve on his Committee on Mental Retardation, much to the displeasure of mainstream Jewish groups.)

Phillips discovered Rushdoony through Frank Walton, the former head of the Heritage Foundation, who gave him a Rushdoony tract arguing that socialized medicine is unbiblical. He and Rushdoony later became friends, and Phillips embraced Reconstructionism. "Rushdoony had a tremendous impact on my thinking," he said. As time goes on, he said, his late mentor's influence is growing. "He had a lot to do with the founding of the homeschool movement. He was a brilliant man. The smartest man I've ever met."

The smartest man that Phillips ever met was very clear that, as he wrote in his *Institutes of Biblical Law*, "[a]ll enemies of Christ in this fallen world must be conquered." Rushdoony made no apologies for embracing every sanguinary decree in the Old Testament. About gay people, for example, he wrote, "Not arrested development or immaturity but deliberate and mature warfare against God marks the homosexual. God's penalty is death, and a godly order will enforce it."[22]

When I spoke to Phillips at Confronting the Judicial War on Faith, he tried to play down the harshness of Reconstructionist justice, arguing that just because something is a capital crime, the death penalty needn't be applied in every case. "It means it's an option," he said. Public humiliation can sometimes be used instead.

In keeping with the Reconstructionist abhorrence of public schools,

Phillips had his six children educated at home. (Today his eldest son, Doug, runs Vision Forum, a San Antonio company that sells books, tapes, and other materials to fundamentalist homeschoolers.)

While his peers Richard Viguerie and Paul Weyrich became part of the Republican elite, Phillips bolted the GOP and spent recent years haunting the right-wing fringe. He founded the ultra-right U.S. Taxpayers party in 1992, which later became the Constitution party. In 1996 he was the party's presidential candidate, getting James Dobson's endorsement but few others. He ran again in 2000, and got around 0.1% of the vote. By 2005, Phillips's party had dues-paying members in almost every state, but he'd been able to recruit only a motley assortment of white supremacists, Christian Reconstructionists, and militia types to run in state and city races, and the Constitution party's only victories were seats on local Oregon planning commissions.[23]

With the campaign against the judiciary, though, Phillips regained some of his former relevance. He was deeply involved in the battle over Roy Moore's monument, and he collaborated with Moore and Herb Titus on the Constitution Restoration Act. The act would do exactly what Graves suggested in *The Journal of Christian Reconstruction*, stripping the Supreme Court of its jurisdiction over matters of church/state separation. Most of the major Christian nationalist groups have championed it. At Confronting the Judicial War on Faith, Phillips announced that his "good friend" James Sensenbrenner, chairman of the House Judiciary Committee, had promised to hold congressional hearings on the act.

For Phillips, the fight over judges is ultimately a fight over the right to impose biblical law. As he said in a 2003 speech given at a rally for Roy Moore, "The overarching question we face today is: 'Who is America's sovereign?' and 'What is his law?' . . . The holy Bible makes clear that Jesus Christ is our sovereign. He is king of kings, lord of lords, the ruler of all nations. America's founding fathers understood and acted on this Biblical truth. . . . Clearly, if the words of the framers are honored, Congress has no authority to restrict the establishment of Biblical religion in the State of Alabama—neither has any federal judge such authority."

"The Focus of Evil": Weakening the Courts

Because their goal is theonomy, Christian nationalists were bound to come into collision with the courts, with or without Roy Moore or Terri Schiavo. The movement's leaders see judges, often correctly, as the only thing protecting American secularism. They know that if they can take the courts, they'll have the country.

To do that, they're pursuing two somewhat contradictory strategies. Christian nationalists are pressuring politicians to pack the bench with their ideological allies and training a new generation of homeschooled jurists who will approach the law with a Christian worldview. At the same time, they're trying to strip the courts of much of their current authority and railing against judges who override the popular will. They are simultaneously fighting a war for the judiciary and a war on it.

The first part of the Christian nationalists' judicial agenda was constantly in the news in 2005, as Democratic senators filibustered seven of Bush's most right-wing nominees to the federal bench. One of those held up was William Pryor, who, as attorney general of Alabama, filed a brief defending Texas's antisodomy law in *Lawrence v. Texas*. In it, he compared homosexuality to "prostitution, adultery, necrophilia, bestiality, possession of child pornography, and incest and pedophilia." Another nominee, Janice Rogers Brown, was quoted in a Connecticut newspaper telling a Catholic legal group that secularists were at "war" with religious believers. "It's not a shooting war," she said, "but it is a war."[24]

Such language might well call into question Brown's judicial neutrality, especially on First Amendment issues. To her strongest backers, however, the very idea that there can be contradictions between conservative theology and the legitimate law is preposterous, because they see their theology as the *source* of legitimate law. To them, the filibuster against Brown, Pryor, and the others was yet another sinister attempt to suppress America's Christian heritage. It represented bigotry against what they called "people of faith."

It also represented an opportunity for Christian nationalists to assert their dominion over the Republican party.

In the days before the Confronting the Judicial War on Faith conference, some right-wing congressmen hinted that "liberal" judges deserved violent reprisals. After Terri Schiavo's death, Tom DeLay declared, "The time will come for the men responsible for this to answer for their behavior." A few days later Texas senator John Cornyn suggested that a series of recent attacks on judges had been provoked by liberal rulings.* These remarks were widely denounced, leading Senate Majority Leader Bill Frist to try to distance himself from them. "I believe we have a fair and independent judiciary today," he told the Associated Press.[25] That comment, in turn, incited howls of derision at Confronting the Judicial War on Faith.

Frist, whose presidential ambitions are well-known, was torn between establishment civility and the livid passions of the GOP's base. He'd deviated from the movement line and had to make amends, so shortly after Confronting the Judicial War on Faith, Frist agreed to deliver a video message at Justice Sunday, the highly publicized and hugely controversial rally and telecast. The message: the filibuster of Bush's nominees represented discrimination against Christians.

Several thousand people attended Justice Sunday, which was held at Highview Baptist Church in Lexington, Kentucky. Hundreds of thousands more watched it via satellite broadcast at churches nationwide or at home on Christian TV.

As the evening rally began, the stage at Highview Baptist was bathed in violet light, and huge portraits of Bush's judicial nominees were arranged around the podium. Host Tony Perkins spoke, along with James Dobson, Al Mohler, president of the Southern Baptist Theological Seminary, Bill Donohue, president of the Catholic League for Religious and Civil Rights, and several others.

---

* Speaking on the Senate floor, Cornyn said, "[W]e seem to have run through a spate of courthouse violence recently that's been on the news and I wonder whether there may be some connection between the perception in some quarters on some occasions where judges are making political decisions yet are unaccountable to the public, that it builds up and builds up and builds up to the point where some people engage in—engage in violence."

Their language was bellicose. "Those people on the secular left, they say, 'We think you're a threat,' " Donohue bellowed at one point. "You know what? They're right." This brought laughter and cheers.

Dobson declared, "I think this is one of the most significant issues we've ever faced as a nation, because the future of democracy and ordered liberty actually depends on the outcome of this struggle." After all, the Supreme Court is responsible for "the biggest holocaust in world history"—the legalization of abortion. "For forty-four years, the Supreme Court has been on a campaign to limit religious freedom. It goes back to 1962 with Bible reading and '63, prayer in schools, both prohibited," Dobson reminded his audience. He continued, "*We do have a right* to participate in this great representative form of government."

The crowd shouted and applauded. Evidently, they believed that liberals were trying to disenfranchise them. Goaded by their leaders, they'd conflated the right to participate with the right to proselytize with public resources. They'd come to believe in a right to impose Christianity, the faith of the majority. Anything else seemed undemocratic.

Bill Frist's address consciously eschewed militant language. "All of us who are active in politics, whether Republican or Democrat, need to remember the lesson of Ronald Reagan, that we can disagree without being disagreeable," he said. He proceeded to repeat a litany of GOP talking points, saying nothing particularly inflammatory. His words, though, were less important than his presence. By appearing on Justice Sunday, he lent his authority and credibility as Senate Majority Leader to those who argued that opponents of Bush's judges were enemies of God.

In the end, Frist's performance wasn't enough to keep the Christian nationalists in his corner. During the summer of 2005, he tacked to the center, coming out in favor of federal funding for stem cell research. His shift delighted moderates but enraged his erstwhile allies. James Dobson excoriated him, and he wasn't invited to address Justice Sunday II, held August 14 at the Two Rivers Baptist Church in Nashville, Tennessee, Frist's home state. Tom DeLay appeared instead.

Lost in the fight over the filibuster of Bush's nominees was the fact that, even with a handful of his choices held up, Bush had *already* succeeded in transforming much of the judiciary into an arm of the conservative movement. Every president nominates judges who seem philosophically simpatico, but Bush went much further. He changed the judicial vetting procedure and put forward a slate of jurists far more radically partisan than any in American history.*

Ever since the Eisenhower administration, judicial nominees have been prescreened by the American Bar Association, the largest legal association in the country. Bush scrapped that tradition. Instead, he turned to the right's expansive legal infrastructure to find judges, seeking recommendations from the Federalist Society, the powerful conservative legal group whose members include John Ashcroft, Kenneth Starr, and Antonin Scalia. It was a step, one of many, toward subjugating every branch and function of government to ideology.

When he first became president, Bush included a few moderates among his judicial picks, renominating two circuit judges chosen by Clinton, Barrington Parker and Roger Gregory, both of whom were confirmed. (While Parker had issued rulings that angered abortion rights activists, Gregory is considered pro-choice). Since then, however, not a single one of Bush's appeals court nominees was pro-choice, and several were anti-abortion activists. The vast majority of them were confirmed.

Michael McConnell, whom Bush appointed to the Tenth Circuit, joined right-wing figures like Marvin Olasky and James Dobson (as well as evangelical progressive Jim Wallis) in signing a 1996 statement

---

* In their paper "The Decision-Making Ideology of George W. Bush's Judicial Appointees: An Update," Kenneth L. Manning of the University of Massachusetts–Dartmouth and Robert A. Carp of the University of Houston wrote, "Statistical analysis of the overall decision-making behavior of George W. Bush judicial appointees indicates that his judges are the most conservative on record," especially on social issues, where "Bush's jurists are significantly more conservative than any other president's appointees."

titled "The America We Seek: A Statement of Pro-Life Principle and Concern" which bemoaned the nation's "virtue deficit" and called for a constitutional amendment banning all abortion.

McConnell, it should be said, is seen by many of his colleagues, liberal and conservative, as thoughtful and intellectually honest. Robin Charlow, a pro-choice law professor at Hofstra University who knew McConnell's record well, told me, "He is not a crazy person. He's not going to go out of his way to distort the law, and he doesn't assume that everything he believes politically is the law."

Other Bush appointees have been at least as conservative as McConnell, and generally less distinguished. Lavinski Smith, for example, whom Bush put on the Eighth Circuit Court of Appeals, was little known outside far-right legal circles until his nomination. Smith was the executive director of the Arkansas branch of the Rutherford Institute, a Christian nationalist legal organization whose founding directors included R. J. Rushdoony and Howard Ahmanson. It was most famous for representing Paula Jones in her lawsuit against Bill Clinton.

James Leon Holmes, a former president of Arkansas Right to Life appointed by Bush to the U.S. District Court for the Eastern District of Arkansas, was notorious for penning articles denouncing birth control and female equality. A 1997 piece for an Arkansas Catholic publication that he co-wrote with his wife argued that, in marriage, "the wife is to subordinate herself to the husband" and that "the woman is to place herself under the authority of the man." It went on to decry feminism for ushering in "artificial contraception and abortion on demand, with recognition of homosexual liaisons soon to follow."[26]

If the Christian nationalists have their way, these judges offer just a taste of what's to come. Of course, the immediate goal is to get similar jurists on the Supreme Court, where they'll overturn *Roe v. Wade*. But many Christian nationalists are taking an even longer view and planning for more epochal changes. In order to place the law under the dominion of Christ, they're working to groom a new generation of legal activists from childhood. For them, after all, the Christian home-schooling movement is more than a rejection of the state. It is the incubator of a revolution.

"If we're going to stop judicial tyranny, I think we need to have a comprehensive plan," Michael Farris, president of Patrick Henry College, said on the second day of the Confronting the Judicial War on Faith Conference. He was speaking on the "Remedies to Judicial Tyranny" panel, along with Phyllis Schafly, former congressman Bill Dannemeyer, and the Stalin-quoting Edwin Vieira. "A comprehensive way of approaching the problem is, we've got to train the next generation."

Farris teaches constitutional law at Patrick Henry and, via the Internet, to thousands of homeschooled teenagers. "My purpose, when I teach kids constitutional law, is to make them mad," he said. "I want them to see what the truth is, and I want them to see what the Supreme Court and the Congress have done to them."

Once Farris's students learn about judicial tyranny, he said, they want to know what they can do about it. "And I say, 'You in the first row need to be appointed to the Supreme Court, and you in the second row need to be in the Senate to confirm him, and you in the third row need to be the president of the United States to nominate him.' That's frankly why I started Patrick Henry College, because I'm sick and tired of having to lobby people that I helped get elected. I want to train them from scratch to believe in the principles that this nation was founded on. If our leaders don't believe in the principles of freedom, how can we expect anything other than slavery?"

If people who think like Farris succeed in taking over the judiciary, Christian nationalists will lose interest in their campaign to weaken it. Until then, they've decided that if they can't control the courts, they'll castrate them. To do that, they're pushing a series of bills and initiatives that would strip courts of their jurisdiction over large areas of state and local law, abolish lower courts, and threaten uncooperative judges with impeachment. Increasingly, the religious right is asserting that the principle of judicial review, which allows judges to evaluate laws' constitutionality, is illegitimate, a position that essentially removes any check on the power of the president and Congress.

Article III of the Constitution gives Congress the power to establish federal courts below the Supreme Court. According to many at Confronting the Judicial War on Faith, this also implies Congress's right to abolish these courts. While the Constitution gives terms of office for members of Congress and the president, it says that judges shall hold their offices "during good behavior." Throughout American history, this has meant that judges were appointed for life, barring criminal or ethical violations. Christian nationalists would stretch the definition of "good behavior" to include hewing to conservative legal doctrines.

These strategies might sound obscure, but their impact would be profound. If judges could lose their jobs at the whim of Congress, judicial independence would become meaningless. Stripping courts of their jurisdiction would free states from complying with the Bill of Rights, since federal courts would be powerless to enforce it. The end of judicial review would mean the end of any real mechanism for upholding the Constitution.

Imagine, for example, if Congress passed Roy Moore's Constitution Restoration Act. Under the act, federal courts would lose their jurisdiction to rule on many matters of church/state separation, and judges whose rulings limited the government's power to pay heed to the Lord would be subject to impeachment. The court would no longer be able to hear cases involving prayer in school and Ten Commandments displays. Furthermore, by foreclosing challenges to the "acknowledgement of God as the sovereign source of law, liberty, or government," the act could be used to argue that biblical law supercedes civil law.

The current Supreme Court would probably rule the Constitution Restoration Act unconstitutional, but if they did, Christian nationalist lawmakers would almost certainly challenge the Court's authority. Invoking the act itself, they might start impeachment proceedings. That would plunge the country into legal limbo, with two branches of gov ernment locked in a fight for power and the law entirely subject to sheer political muscle.

Howard Phillips seems to relish this possibility. At the Confronting the Judicial War on Faith conference, he said, "This is one of the most important pieces of legislation ever put forward. And if this legislation is enacted, it could produce a constitutional crisis. Frankly, my friends, that's exactly what we need." Such a crisis, he hoped, would put the courts in their place.

If, somehow, the Constitution Restoration Act did stand, many First Amendment protections would no longer apply to the states. Some, like Alabama, might declare themselves officially Christian. Schools could institute prayer and Bible reading—parents who objected would have no recourse to the federal courts to challenge them. A judge could set off a constitutional crisis by even trying to hear such a case.

Roy Moore has effectively shown how the Constitution Restoration Act could be used to shut down challenges to the teaching of creationism. When a district court judge ruled the anti-evolution stickers put on textbooks in Cobb County, Georgia, unconstitutional, the county appealed, and Moore filed a supporting brief. In it, he wrote, "[B]anning God from the discussion of the creation of life directly contradicts a founding principle of this country: the belief—as the country's founding document, the Declaration of Independence, proclaims—that we 'are endowed by [our] Creator with certain unalienable rights.'" Again, a judge who ruled against the right of school districts to acknowledge God in science class could be impeached.

All this might sound far-fetched, but it's no longer unimaginable. The Constitution Restoration Act wouldn't have a hard time passing the House, where in the spring of 2005 it had thirty co-sponsors. It had eight co-sponsors in the Senate. Under the Senate rules that are in effect as I write this, there's little chance of its ever coming to a vote— Democrats, and a few Republicans, would block it. After the filibuster fight, though, it didn't seem improbable that those rules would be disregarded if they stood in the way of something the Christian nationalists considered important.

The Constitution Restoration Act is just one of a number of schemes the right has developed to enfeeble the courts. At the Confronting the Judicial War on Faith conference, many proposed abolishing overly liberal courts—especially the Ninth Circuit, which earned the wrath of the right by ruling the phrase "under God" in the Pledge of Allegiance unconstitutional. Meanwhile, Christian nationalist congressmen have created a "judicial activism working group," co-chaired by Tom DeLay, to explore further remedies. Speaking to the conference via video, DeLay apologized for missing the event and emphasized its importance. He accused the judiciary of having "run amok," and said that to rein it in, it would be necessary to "reassert Congress's constitutional authority over the court."

"Judicial unaccountability is not a political issue," he said. "It is a threat to self-government." Then he enumerated the measures Congress was taking. The House, he said, already passed an amendment to break up "that leftist Ninth Circuit that meets in San Francisco and told them they could go meet in Guam."

Using language that could have been lifted from a John Birch Society tract, Michael Schwartz, chief of staff to Oklahoma senator Tom Coburn, went further, attacking the principle of judicial review itself. "The Supreme Court is inherently an anti-majoritarian institution," Schwartz said. "As long as it purports to grade the papers of Congress, it is contrary to the very basis of this republic, which is not sovereignty of judges, but sovereignty of the people. And until we can restore sovereignty of the people, it is a sick and sad joke to claim that we have a constitution."

That statement—that courts lack authority to rule against the will of "the people"—is an invitation to mayhem. Constitutional protections mean nothing without judges who have the legitimacy to interpret and apply them. If the law's meaning rests with the passions of crowds, order falls apart. All would be at the mercy of populist demagogues claiming to be the voice of "the people." They'd amass far more power than any American judge has ever had. That's not conservatism. It's the beginning of fascism.

Like many Christian nationalists, Schwartz would be happy to see the solid institutions of American government smashed. He's a revolutionary—he said so himself. The journalist Max Blumenthal attended the conference dressed like a young conservative in slacks and a blazer. When he approached Schwartz outside the Marriott, Schwartz thought he was a sympathizer. Before Blumenthal said anything, Schwartz smiled at him and said, "I'm a radical! I'm a real extremist. I don't want to impeach judges. I want to impale them!"[27]

Such outbusts reveal the apocalyptic mind-set that has seized the GOP. In the conference's closing speech, former presidential aspirant and 2004 Republican senatorial candidate Alan Keyes drew enthusiastic applause with his comment, "I believe that in our country today the judiciary is the focus of evil." One doesn't defer to process when dealing with the devil. One fights by any means necessary.

This kind of thinking has led to a series of spasms of Republican antinomianism in recent years. Again and again, laws and rules that stood in the right's way were twisted or ignored as mere technicalities compared with the higher laws of scripture and national destiny.

Righteous subversion of the law was on lurid display during the campaign against Bill Clinton, who conservatives were determined to remove from his democratically elected office before anyone had ever heard of Monica Lewinsky.* Right-wing lawlessness resurfaced after the 2000 election, when rowdy Republican aides and activists in Miami physically stopped a vote recount by staging what one conservative

* As David Brock wrote in *Blinded by the Right*, his mea culpa memoir of his role in the anti-Clinton campaign, "Though it attracted little attention outside of our circle, the idea of impeaching the president had been gaining momentum for almost a year before Clinton became enmeshed in the scandal over his sexual relationship with White House intern Monica Lewinsky. After Clinton was resoundingly reelected in 1996, the political right, true to form, refused to recognize the legitimacy of the election. And even as it became clear to all but the most deluded anti-Clinton partisans that the Starr investigation had found no prosecutable crime in Whitewater or any of the other constantly shifting accusations in the Clinton scandals, the right pressured Congress to remove Clinton from office."

columnist approvingly called a "bourgeois riot."[28] It pervaded the 2003 redistricting battle in Texas, which began when Tom DeLay engineered the redrawing of the electoral map to bump up the number of House Republicans. (The map wasn't due for revision for another eight years, but, as DeLay said, "I'm the majority leader, and I want more seats." When Democrats in the Texas legislature fled to neighboring states to prevent a quorum and thus stop Republicans from eliminating a handful of Democratic districts, DeLay called on the Department of Homeland Security to track them down.)[29]

The rule of law eroded further in the Terri Schiavo case. Christian nationalists demanded that Florida Governor Jeb Bush ignore the courts and seize the woman by force. Alarmingly, his administration tried. As the *Miami Herald* reported, "Hours after a judge ordered that Terri Schiavo was not to be removed from her hospice, a team of state agents were en route to seize her and have her feeding tube reinserted—but they stopped short when local police told them they would enforce the judge's order." The story continued, "Participants in the high-stakes test of wills, who spoke with The Herald on the condition of anonymity, said they believed the standoff could ultimately have led to a constitutional crisis and a confrontation between dueling lawmen."[30]

This is how democracy starts to degenerate—with a breakdown of legal authority, government deadlock, and leaders who use the chaos to seize unwarranted powers. A liberal society (in the classical sense of the word) requires politicians willing to follow their own laws or, if they don't, institutions to hold them accountable. It requires leaders who will abide by the rulings of judges and, conversely, judges free to issue rulings that displease politicians. Otherwise some people are above the law and others, inevitably, are below it.

America is still a liberal democracy, but it is becoming less of one each day. While Christian nationalists have attacked the legitimacy of the courts as arbiters of the Constitution, whole segments of the population have been exiled from the law's shelter. In state after state, gay people have been systematically stripped of legal protections and, along with non-Christians, suffered publicly funded job discrimination thanks to Bush's faith-based initiative. And as the Air Force Academy scandal in Colorado Springs demonstrated, some soldiers are trying to turn America's military into a sectarian Christian army. All of this is taking place in the context of the broader corrosion of democratic institutions and civil rights since September 11, a breakdown symbolized most luridly by the prison at Guantánamo Bay, where the administration has declared itself unbound by any outside law at all. In this febrile, unsettled climate, things that used to seem impossible in America have become possible, and the freedoms so many of us grew up taking for granted have begun to appear terrifyingly tenuous.

As Columbia University history professor Robert O. Paxton pointed out, "We know from tracing its path that fascism does not require a spectacular 'march' on some capital to take root; seemingly anodyne decisions to tolerate lawless treatment of national 'enemies' is enough." An American fascism, according to Paxton, would eschew colored shirts and goosesteps for the comforting iconography of flag and faith. It would seem so familiar that it wouldn't panic most people. "No swastikas in an American fascism, but Stars and Stripes (or Stars and Bars) and Christian Crosses."[31]

If fascism's rise is gradual and subtle, how does one spot it? "Knowing what we do about the fascist cycle, we can find more ominous warning signals in situations of political deadlock in the face of crisis, threatened conservatives looking for tougher allies, ready to give up due process and the rule of law, seeking mass support by nationalist and racialist demagoguery," wrote Paxton. "Fascists are close to power when conservatives begin to borrow their techniques, appeal to their 'mobilizing passions,' and try to co-opt the fascist following."[32]

Substitute "religious" for "racialist," and Paxton could have been describing America in 2005. He wasn't telling us how to recognize a fascist regime. He was telling us how to recognize an emergent movement, and the political conditions that would allow it to grow, before it was too late.

CONCLUSION

Exiles in Jesusland

History, I believe, furnishes no example of a priest-ridden people maintaining a free civil government. This marks the lowest grade of ignorance of which their civil as well as religious leaders will always avail themselves for their own purposes.

—Thomas Jefferson

Whenever I talk about the growing power of the evangelical right with friends and acquaintances, they always ask the same question: What can we do? Usually I reply with a joke: Keep a bag packed and your passport current. I don't really mean it, but my underlying anxiety is genuine. It's one thing to have a government that shows contempt for civil liberties; America has survived such men before. It's quite another to have a mass movement—the largest and most powerful mass movement in the nation—rise up in opposition to the rights of its fellow citizens. The Constitution protects minorities, but that protection is not absolute; with a sufficiently sympathetic or apathetic majority, a tightly organized faction can get around it.

For opponents of the right, one of the most alarming things about the current state of our country is the fact that so many Americans fervently believe things that are objectively false—that Iraq was behind September 11, for example, or that Bill Clinton was a more profligate spender than Bush, or that the world is only a few thousand years old. They wonder how to get through to their fellow citizens, how to find the message or slogan or frame that will make them *see* the perilous condition America has been reduced to. What's lacking, though, isn't just truth—it's the entire social mechanism by which truth is distinguished from falsehood. Blunting Christian nationalism requires turning back toward the Enlightenment and rebuilding a culture of rationalism. Unfortunately, multitudes of Americans no longer find Enlightenment values compelling. A rational politics cannot promise the national restoration so many seem to long for.

I'm not sure that we shall overcome. Those who don't want to live in the country the Christian nationalists would create have no choice but to fight, and I have some suggestions about tactics. But I'm scared by what I've seen happening in America, and I don't want to try to inspire at the expense of sincerity.

Throughout the preceding chapters, I've argued that the Christian nationalist movement has totalitarian elements. I want to be clear, however, that I am *not* suggesting that religious tyranny is imminent in the United States. Our democracy is eroding and some of our rights are disappearing, but for most people, including those most opposed to the Christian nationalist agenda, life will most likely go on pretty much as normal for the foreseeable future. Thus for those who value secular society, apprehending the threat posed by Christian nationalism is tricky. It's kind of like being a lobster in a pot, with the water heating up so slowly that you don't notice the moment at which it starts to kill you.

It is far from inevitable that we will reach the boiling point, but the threat will not simply fizzle out without pressure from a countermovement organized to defend pluralism, religious equality, reason, and personal freedom. If current trends continue, we will see ever increasing division and acrimony in our politics. That's partly because, as Christian nationalism spreads, secularism is spreading as well, while moderate, mainline Christianity is in decline. According to the City University of New York Graduate Center's comprehensive American religious identification survey, the percentage of Americans who identify as Christians has actually fallen in recent years, from 86 percent in 1990 to 77 percent in 2001. The survey found that the largest growth, in both absolute and percentage terms, was among those who don't subscribe to any religion. Their numbers more than doubled, from 14.3 million in 1990, when they constituted 8 percent of the population, to 29.4 million in 2001, when they made up 14 percent. "The top three 'gainers' in America's vast religious market place appear to be Evangelical Christians, those describing themselves as Non-Denominational Christians and those who profess no religion," the survey found. (The percentage of Jews, Muslims, Hindus, Buddhists, and other religious minorities remained small, totaling less than 4 percent of the population).

This is a recipe for polarization. The religious divide in America isn't so much between the faithless and faithful—it's between those who want to maintain a secular, pluralistic society and those who do not. But the growing presence of non-Christians will exacerbate the frightened anger of those desperate to drag the country back to its mythical Christian roots. As the religious historian Karen Armstrong has written, fundamentalism works in symbiosis with secularization; the more it is thwarted, the more extreme it becomes.[1] As Christian nationalism becomes more militant, secularists and religious minorities will mobilize in opposition, ratcheting up the hostility. Thus we're likely to see a shrinking middle ground, with both camps increasingly viewing each other across a chasm of mutual incomprehension and contempt.

I suspect things are going to get worse, at least in the immediate future. As 2005 came to an end, many liberals savored the spectacle of an imploding GOP. But while the Republicans' collapse may frustrate some of the Christian nationalists' long-term ambitions, it also increases the party's dependence on its base, something demonstrated quite clearly when Bush was forced to jettison Harriet Miers's nomination to the Supreme Court in favor of the more reliably anti-abortion Samuel Alito. Meanwhile many Republicans, burdened by the increasingly unpopular war in Iraq, will likely see culture war issues as their best hope of staving off Democratic gains.

In the coming months and years, we will probably see the curtailment of the civil rights that gay people, women, and religious minorities have won in the last few decades. With two Bush appointees on the

Supreme Court, abortion rights will be narrowed; if the president gets a third, it could mean the end of *Roe v. Wade*. Expect increasing drives to ban gay people from being adoptive or foster parents, as well as attempts to fire gay schoolteachers. Evangelical leaders are encouraging their flocks to be alert to signs of homosexuality in their kids, which will lead to a growing number of gay teenagers forced into "reparative therapy" designed to turn them straight. (Focus on the Family urges parents to consider seeking help for boys as young as five if they show a "tendency to cry easily, be less athletic, and dislike the roughhousing that other boys enjoy."[2])

If Bush's faith-based initiative is not rolled back, gay people and non-Christians will be discriminated against by more and more publicly funded social service jobs. The prejudice will be more severe in some places than others—although, as Anne Lown learned at the Salvation Army, people anywhere could be affected. Meanwhile, those seeking government help with drug treatment, job training, or emergency food and housing assistance will learn to expect a degree of proselytization.

From what I've witnessed while researching this book, I'm convinced that Christian nationalist symbolism and ideology will increasingly pervade public life. In addition to the war on evolution, there will be campaigns to teach Christian nationalist history in public schools. An elective course developed by the National Council on Bible Curriculum in Public Schools, a right-wing evangelical group, is already being offered by more than 300 school districts in thirty-six states.[3] Elizabeth Ridenour, a member of the Council for National Policy, founded the organization in 1993; its advisory committee includes David Barton, D. James Kennedy, and Howard Phillips. The course purports to study scripture from a literary and historical perspective, which is permissible under the First Amendment, but it actually teaches biblical literalism and Barton-style revisionism.

Christian nationalists will also continue to challenge the country's universities. In Florida in 2005, House Republicans approved a bill called the Academic Freedom Bill of Rights, which was intended to fight "leftist totalitarianism" by "dictator professors." If passed, the law would have given students grounds to sue if they felt themselves subject to liberal bias. Dennis Baxley, the bill's sponsor, described the kind of victimization he had in mind to the *Sarasota Herald-Tribune*: "The lawmaker recalled his first day in an anthropology class at Florida State University when the professor said, 'Evolution is a fact. There's no missing link. I don't want to hear any talk about intelligent design, and if you don't like that, there's the door.' " Baxley was quoted saying, "The leftists with those viewpoints didn't take our campuses; those in the mainstream just relinquished them for fear of being called bigots."[4]

The Academic Freedom Bill of Rights failed in Florida, but attempts to pass similar measures, aimed primarily at professors thought to be insufficiently patriotic, are under way nationwide. There have also been successful efforts to force public colleges to fund evangelical groups out of student fees, and to exempt such groups from rules banning discrimination against gay men and lesbians.

The influence of Christian nationalism in public schools, colleges, courts, social services, and doctors' offices will deform American life, rendering it ever more pinched, mean, and divided. There's still a long way, though, between this damaged version of democracy and real theocracy. Tremendous crises would have to shred what's left of the American consensus before religious fascism becomes a possibility. That means that secularists and liberals shouldn't get hysterical, but they also shouldn't be complacent. The process by which the unthinkable becomes ordinary takes time, which means there's time to turn it back.

For all its totalitarian resonances—its antirationalism, antiliberalism, conspiracism and claims to a grand, all-encompassing theory of history and politics—Christian nationalism is still constrained by the Constitution, the courts, and by a passionate democratic (and occasionally Democratic) opposition. It's also limited by capitalism. Many corporations are happy to see their political allies harness the rage and passion of the Christian right's foot soldiers, but the culture industry is averse to government censorship. Nor is homophobia good for business, since many companies need to both recruit qualified gay employees and market to gay customers. Biotech firms are not going to want to

hire graduates without a thorough understanding of ev
nomic pressure will militate against creationism's invadin
mass of the public schools.

Worst-Case Scenarios

It would take a national disaster, or several of them, for all these bul-
warks to crumble and for Christian nationalists to truly "take the land,"
as Michael Farris put it. Proto-totalitarian movements have existed and
continue to exist in most Western countries, but they're usually rele-
gated to the margins. Occasionally, they succeed in moving further into
the mainstream, as has happened in America, but that needn't mean
they're poised for victory.[5] Historically, totalitarian movements have
been able to seize state power only when existing authorities prove
unable to deal with catastrophic challenges—economic meltdown,
security failures, military defeat—and people lose their faith in the
legitimacy of the system.[6]

Such calamities are certainly conceivable in America—Hurricane
Katrina's anarchic aftermath offered a terrifying glimpse of how quickly
order can collapse. The attacks of September 11 precipitated tremendous erosion in our constitutional government; there's no guarantee
American democracy would survive another, similarly savage assault.*
If terrorists successfully strike again, we'd probably see significant curtailment of liberal dissenters' free speech rights, coupled with mounting
right-wing belligerence, both religious and secular. Last time around
the right burned CDs by "subversives" like the Dixie Chicks; no one
knows what they'll torch in the future. It's not hard to imagine
apocalypse-minded Christian nationalist militias growing in response
to a new attack, and they would find significant support in at least
some sectors of the Republican party.

---

* Speaking to *Cigar Aficionado* magazine in December 2003, General Tommy
Franks, former head of the U.S. Central Command, said that in the aftermath of a
"massive, casualty-producing event somewhere in the Western world" Americans
might "question our own Constitution and to begin to militarize our country. . . .
Which in fact, then begins to unravel the fabric of our Constitution."

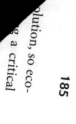

.tem could also be subtler. Many experts
:bt is unsustainable and that economic cri-
In April 2005, Paul Volcker, former chair-
published a piece in *The Washington Post*,
n Ice," in which he wrote that under the
iere are disturbing trends: huge imbalances,
em what you will. Altogether the circum-
erous and intractable as any I can remember,
and I can remember quite a lot. What really concerns me is that there
seems to be so little willingness or capacity to do much about it." A few
months later, *The Atlantic Monthly* published a cover story by James Fal-
lows titled "Countdown to a Meltdown." Written in the form of a memo
to a presidential candidate in 2016 assessing the economic destruction
of the United States, it said, "In retrospect, the ugly end is so obvious
and inevitable. . . . Economists had laid out the sequence of causes and
effects in a 'hard landing,' and it worked just as they said it would."

If there is a hard landing—due to an oil shock, a burst housing bubble, a sharp decline in the value of the dollar, or some other crisis—
interest rates would shoot up, leaving many people unable to pay their
floating-rate mortgages and credit card bills. Repossessions and bank-
ruptcies would follow. Many Americans would lose everything they
have, including their houses. The resulting anger could fuel radical
populist movements of either the left or the right—more likely the
right, since it has a far stronger ideological infrastructure in place in
most of America. Economic hardship incubates hate; as Harvard economics professor Benjamin M. Friedman wrote, "American history
includes several episodes in which stagnating or declining incomes over
an extended period have undermined the nation's tolerance and threatened citizens' freedoms."[7]

A small but genuine Christian fascist movement arose in the United
States during the Great Depression under Father Charles Coughlin, the
Detroit-based "radio priest." One of the first radio celebrities, Coughlin
began his career as a supporter of FDR, but his populism turned sharply
rightward in the mid-1930s, finally degenerating into vicious anti-

Semitism. In 1938, he organized more than one thousand of his followers into a paramilitary outfit called the Christian Front, which carried out attacks on Jewish businesses and plotted political assassinations.[8]

Decades later, the farm crisis that hit the Midwest during the 1980s laid ground for the growth of the Posse Comitatus, the Christian Identity–influenced paramilitary network, which in turn bred the militia movement of the Clinton years. The agriculture crisis was caused by a combination of rising interest rates and falling prices, and it devastated family farmers who had gone into debt in order to expand when interest rates were lower. Tens of thousands of families lost their farms, and the resulting rage and dispossession offered an organizing bonanza for violent right-wing movements that blamed greedy Jewish bankers for preying on humble and hardworking Americans. By the mid eighties, the Posse Comitatus had up to fifteen thousand active members and many times that number of supporters; one poll showed that more than a quarter of Farm Belt respondents blamed "international Jewish bankers" for the farmers' woes.[9]

The militia movement, which was active in several states during the mid-1990s, evolved out of the Posse Comitatus. Militia ideologues often trafficked in an explosive blend of conspiracy theory, survivalism, hatred of the federal government, and Christian Identity; the movement was part of the paranoid and violent demimonde that nurtured terrorists including Oklahoma City bombers Timothy McVeigh and Terry Nichols and Olympic bomber Eric Rudolph. As the decade came to an end, the militia movement splintered and dissipated. Yet its brand of radical religious nationalism, rather than going underground, slithered closer to the mainstream.

People like Howard Phillips are eagerly awaiting the kind of national calamity that would allow hard-right ideas to be actualized. "My friends, it is time to leave the 'political Titanic' on which the conservative movement has for too long booked passage," Phillips said in a 1998 speech to the Council for National Policy. "Instead, it is our task to build an ark so that we can and will be ready to renew and restore our nation and our culture when God brings the tide to flood."

The building has already begun. The Anti-Defamation League reported that in 2004 militia activity was once again on the rise; one Texas cadre described itself as "a group of concerned citizens who feel the need to prepare for an economic collapse caused either by terrorism abroad or within the USA, or a piss poor leadership of our Country. We have lost many of our God Given Rights and see a bad moon rising."[10]

Military disaster may exacerbate such disaffection. As of this writing, America's war in Iraq seems nearly certain to come to an ignominious end. The real victims of failure there will be Iraqi, but many Americans will feel embittered, humiliated, and sympathetic to the stab-in-the-back rhetoric peddled by the right to explain how Bush's venture has gone so horribly wrong. It was the defeat in World War I, after all, that created the conditions for fascism to grow in Germany. The country had entered the war in a frenzy of triumphal, imperialistic pride and was deeply shocked by its military failure and concomitant loss of prestige. Refusing to face the fact that their army had been beaten on the battleground, German conservatives bought into the *dolchstosslegende*, the myth that the military had been stabbed in the back by subversive civilian traitors—especially Jews. This fed into a fierce backlash against liberalism, and the rapid growth of movements that promised to overcome the enervating decadence of the cities and restore their civilization's lost glory.

America, of course, will not be wholly vanquished in Iraq as Germany was in the First World War—it won't lose territory or be burdened with anything approaching the punitive provisions of the Treaty of Versailles. Nevertheless, a humiliating defeat in Iraq could result in nasty spasms of jingoism at home. Some liberals may hope that, in the case of disaster in the Middle East, a nationwide rejection of Bush-style belligerence will form a thin silver lining, but that seems improbable to me, since almost all the social networks that are in place to channel people's anger and disappointment point in other directions. Conservatives are already attempting to explain the unfolding nightmare in Iraq as the result of liberal treachery. According to the new *dolchstosslegende*, a disloyal, appeasement-seeking press has distorted the view of what is actually going on in Iraq in order to weaken the American people's morale and commitment. In April 2005, a month in which violence soared in Iraq, David Limbaugh, author of *Persecution: How Liberals Are Waging War Against Christianity*, wrote, "How can we but conclude that the media simply don't want to promote the good news out of Iraq? But why? Well, obviously, they suppress good news because it vindicates their nemesis, President Bush, and incriminates them and their liberal comrades."[11]

If ideas like Limbaugh's gain momentum, we'll see escalating campaigns against the press, which the right has consistently attacked for undermining American solidarity and giving comfort to the nation's enemies. There may be further attacks on "un-American" professors. We could also see the renascence of the anti-Semitic strains of Christian fundamentalism, which would blame neoconservative Jews for manipulating the country into war in the first place. In such a climate, Christian nationalism could mutate into a real and potent force for theocratic authoritarianism, rather than just a movement with some totalitarian echoes.

Righting the Boat

Perhaps America will be lucky, however, skirting disaster and muddling through its looming problems. In that case, Christian nationalism will continue to be a powerful and growing influence in American politics, although its expansion will happen more fitfully and gradually.

Both the American electoral system and the country's demographics are on the movement's side. There's an antiurban bias built into the structure of our democracy that overrepresents people who live in small, rural states, which tend to be more conservative. Because each state has two senators, the 7 percent of the population that live in the seventeen least-populous states control more than a third of Congress's upper house.[12] Conservative states are also overrepresented in the Electoral College. According to Steven Hill of the Center for Voting and Democracy, the combined populations of Montana, Wyoming, Nevada, North and South Dakota, Colorado, Nebraska, Kansas, Oklahoma, Arizona, and Alaska equal that of New York and Massachusetts, but the former states have a total of nine more votes in the Electoral College (as well as over five times the votes in the Senate).[13] In America, conservatives literally count for more.

At the same time, megachurch culture is spreading. The exurbs where religious conservatism thrives are the fastest growing parts of America; in 2004, 97 of the country's 100 fastest-growing counties voted Republican.[14] The rootlessness and disconnection of the exurbs is a large part of what makes the spread of Christian nationalism's fictitious reality possible, because there is very little to conflict with it. If the only public forums are the mall and the megachurch, then the range of views to which most people are likely to be exposed are very small. Those who want other perspectives can easily find them, but reality doesn't intrude on the movement's lies unless it's actively sought out.

A movement that constitutes its members' entire social world has a grip that's hard to break. Here, too, Hannah Arendt is instructive: "Social atomization and extreme individualization preceded the mass movements which, much more easily and earlier than they did the sociable, nonindividualistic members of the traditional parties, attracted the completely unorganized, the typical 'nonjoiners' who for individualistic reasons always had refused to recognize social links or obligations."[15]

Electing a Democratic president in 2008, crucial as that is to maintaining many liberties, will not reverse the growth of Christian nationalism, although it will conduct the movement's energies in new directions. The Christian right had some of its greatest organizing triumphs under Bill Clinton by focusing on local politics and taking over the Republican party precinct by precinct, district by district. Because Christian nationalists control the party on the ground, and because the GOP has a structural advantage in Congress, the religious right will play a powerful role in government, even if a majority of Americans vote to repudiate its agenda. In Congress, Christian nationalist irredentism would make it very hard for any Democrat to govern. The same forces that went after Clinton—forces that are now stronger than ever—would be massed and ready to attack before a new Democratic president was even sworn in.

Getting out the vote will not be enough. Neither will the protections of the Constitution, or the much mythologized "moderation" that is said to be at the heart of the American character. Those who want to fight Christian nationalism will need a long-term and multifaceted strategy. I see it as having three parts—electoral reform to give urban areas fair representation in the federal government, grassroots organizing to help people fight Christian nationalism on the ground, and a media campaign to raise public awareness about the movement's real agenda.

My ideas are not about reconciliation or healing. It would be good for America if a leader stepped forward who could recognize the grievances of both sides, broker some sort of truce, and mend America's ragged divides. The anxieties that underlay Christian nationalism's appeal—fears about social breakdown, marital instability, and cultural decline—are real. They should be acknowledged and, whenever possible, addressed. But as long as the movement aims at the destruction of secular society and the political enforcement of its theology, it has to be battled, not comforted and appeased.

Similarly, while I support liberal struggles for economic justice—higher wages, universal health care, affordable education, and retirement security—I don't think economic populism will do much to neutralize the religious right. Cultural interests are real interests, and many drives are stronger than material ones. As Arendt pointed out, totalitarian movements have always confounded observers who try to analyze them in terms of class.*

Ideologies that answer deep existential needs are hugely powerful.

---

* Arendt wrote, "Since virtually all of European history through many centuries had taught people to judge each political action by its *cui bono* and all political events by their particular underlying interests, they were suddenly confronted with an element of unprecedented unpredictability. Because of its demagogic qualities, totalitarian propaganda, which long before the seizure of power clearly indi[cated] how little the masses were driven by the famous instinct of self-preserva[tion, was] not taken seriously."[16]

The Christian nationalists have one and their opponents largely do not. Today's liberalism has many ideas and policy prescriptions, but given the carnage born of utopian dreams in the twentieth century, it is understandably distrustful of radical, all-encompassing political theories. It is cautious and skeptical. Liberals don't want to remake the world; they just want to make it a little better. Because it is wise but not exhilarating, liberalism has dogged defenders but few impassioned evangelists. In the short term, there is no changing this—grand optimistic visions cannot be ordered up like policy papers from think tanks, although an intellectual infrastructure is helpful in developing them. Such an infrastructure is just now being built; a new group called the Democracy Alliance is pledging to channel hundreds of millions of dollars to erect liberal idea factories that can compete with outfits like the Heritage Foundation and the American Enterprise Institute. This is encouraging, but it will take years to see the results.

Among some liberals, there's a hope that an emerging religious left might counterbalance conservatives. Since Bush's reelection, Jim Wallis, the progressive evangelical who founded Sojourners, a ministry devoted to peace and social justice, has been frequently feted by Democrats. Along with religious leaders like Bob Edgar, secretary general of the National Council of Churches, and C. Welton Gaddy, the Baptist minister who heads the Interfaith Alliance, Wallis is a powerful and prophetic voice against the right. Shortly before the 2004 election, he published a beautiful statement, signed by more than two hundred theologians and ethicists, titled "Confessing Christ in a World of Violence," which eloquently rejected Christian nationalism in the name of Christianity. The "theology of war," it said, "emanating from the highest circles of ___ an government, is seeping into our churches as well. ___ 'righteous empire' is employed with growing fre- ___ f God, church, and nation are confused by talk of an ___ nd 'divine appointment' to 'rid the world of evil.' ___ lse teaching that America is a 'Christian nation,' ___ ue, while its adversaries are nothing but vicious," ___ t the belief that America has nothing to repent of, even as we reject that it represents most of the world's evil. All have sinned and fallen short of the glory of God (Rom. 3:23)."

Wallis's voice, as well as those of others like him, is enormously important. He's a reminder to secularists not to confuse a transcendent religion with the right's punitive sanctimony, and a reminder to believers that the GOP does not have a monopoly on Jesus. We can hope that Wallis and other leaders on the religious left will find a way to channel some of America's moral fervor into a new social gospel to ameliorate the poverty that's been exacerbated by Republican rule.

Ultimately, though, while religious liberals will be an important part of any movement to combat Christian nationalism, they're no match for it on their own. Progressive Christians are unlikely to consent to turning their churches into auxiliaries of a political party in the way conservative churches like Rod Parsley's World Harvest have done, and they seem to have little appetite for following preachers who take orders from operatives in Washington. Jim Wallis has said that there is no Christian position on the Senate filibuster. The religious right says there's a Christian position on *everything*, a view that, while perhaps spiritually bankrupt, is incredibly powerful politically. There's no greater motivation than the conviction that one is following God's explicit orders.

Ordinary Americans

A countermovement to Christian nationalism needn't be totalistic, but it does have to be ready for ugly political combat. In time, with the right support, such a movement might emerge. Ironically, it is likely to gestate among people who are today mocked and reviled as bitter anachronisms, fated to be left behind by an ever more suburban and pious public.

The fundamentalist counterculture that nurtured Christian nationalism, after all, was a product of deep disaffection, created by those who despised the liberal values then embraced by most of their fellow citizens. It was the home of people who felt angry and embattled, and who sought validation in a culture that seemed to constantly insult them. It was a *rebuke* to the American people. Eventually, of course, savvy operatives turned this nascent community of outraged believers into a mighty political force, but the outrage and the belief came first. A movement has to spring from longings deeper than the longing to create a movement.

Today there also exists a group whose values are routinely trashed by the country's rulers. They are dismissed as dinosaurs, out of touch with "the people" and the inevitable pull of history. They are considered an embarrassment by many of the leaders of their own party, and casually slighted by commentators. People at the highest levels of government blithely accuse them of treason.

I'm talking, of course, about liberals, especially liberals of the urban, secular variety. Progressives, intellectuals, denizens of the most creative and vibrant parts of the country, freethinkers, and cosmopolitans are constantly marginalized and defamed by those who believe "America" is a synonym for the nation's most devout crimson corners. The obloquy that the right pours on America's founding cities and the people who live in them is remarkable, even though the media rarely remarks on it. Campaigning against John Kerry in the 2004 election, George Bush, who was ostensibly running to remain president of the entire country, spit out the word "Massachusetts" like it was something foul, as in, "What would you expect from a senator from *Massachusetts*?" Rick Santorum has gone further, blaming the "decaying culture" of the cities for the Catholic Church's sex abuse scandals. It "is no surprise," he wrote, "that Boston, a seat of academic, political and cultural liberalism in America, lies at the center of the storm."[17]

Most famously, during the Democratic primary season, the right-wing Club for Growth ran an anti–Howard Dean ad featuring an elderly Middle American couple ranting against a type that populates much of the Northeast and Northwest. The man began, "I think Howard Dean should take his tax-hiking, government-expanding, latte-drinking, sushi-eating, Volvo-driving, *New York Times*–reading . . ." His wife continued: ". . . body piercing, Hollywood-loving, left-wing freak show back to Vermont where it belongs." Imagine, for a moment, if

MoveOn had run an anti-Bush ad that called his following a gun-toting, Bible-thumping, McDonald's-eating, gay-bashing, gas-guzzling right-wing freak show. There would have been no end of hand-wringing about the supercilious secular elite and their contempt for so-called ordinary Americans. Having defined Americanism as an amalgam of anti-intellectualism, provincialism, self-righteousness, and bellicosity, conservatives then attack everyone who finds these things repellent as unpatriotic, and few mainstream voices challenge them. (Incidentally, conservative evangelicals are the only religious faction I've encountered who sell lattes *in church*.)

Given all the scorn piled upon them, it is not surprising that a separatist impulse has arisen among some progressives. In the mournful days after the 2004 election, liberals indulged themselves in maps showing Canada gathering the blue states into its social democratic embrace, leaving the red states to form their own "Jesusland." Many passed around a scathing rant from the Web site Fuck the South, which, inverting the sectionalist hostility of the right, lacerated the chauvinism of the heartland: "Take your liberal-bashing, federal-tax-leeching, Confederate-flag-waving, holier-than-thou, hypocritical bullshit and shove it up your ass."

Speaking on *The McLaughlin Group* the weekend after George W. Bush's victory, panelist Lawrence O'Donnell, a former Democratic Senate staffer, noted that blue states subsidize the red ones with their tax dollars, and said, "The big problem the country now has, which is going to produce a serious discussion of secession over the next twenty years, is that the segment of the country that pays for the federal government is now being governed by the people who don't pay for the federal government."

A shocked Tony Blankley asked him, "Are you calling for civil war?" To which O'Donnell replied, "You can secede without firing a shot."

Secession, of course, is not an option, and even if it were, it would be cruel for liberals to leave their progressive allies in right-wing states to the tender mercies of the country's Roy Moores and David Bartons. Indeed, there should be a much greater effort to reach out to liberals living in Christian nationalist strongholds. They're often the people fighting the hardest.

But there's also a need for people in blue states to understand how much our current electoral arrangements disenfranchise them and give disproportionate power to the most reactionary parts of the country. With enough consciousness-raising, perhaps the profound alienation that many feel from red America could fuel a campaign for fair representation. It was a backlash against liberalism that spurred the right to become the best-organized faction in American politics; a backlash against the right could serve as a similar catalyst for liberals and frightened moderates.

Ultimately, a fight against Christian nationalist rule has to be a fight for electoral reform. Liberals should work to abolish the Electoral College and to even out the composition of the Senate, perhaps by splitting some of the country's larger states. (A campaign for statehood for New York City might be a place to start.) It will be a grueling, Herculean job. With conservatives already indulging in fantasies of victimization at the hands of a maniacal Northeastern elite, it will take a monumental movement to wrest power away from them. Such a movement will come into being only when enough people in the blue states stop internalizing right-wing jeers about how out of touch they are with "real Americans" and start getting angry at being ruled by reactionaries who are *out of touch with them.*

After all, the heartland has no claim to moral authority. The states whose voters are most obsessed with "moral values" have the highest divorce and teen pregnancy rates. The country's highest murder rates are in the South and the lowest are in New England.[18] The five states with the best-ranked public schools in the country—Massachusetts, Connecticut, Vermont, New Jersey, and Wisconsin—are all progressive redoubts. The five states with the worst—New Mexico, Nevada, Arizona, Mississippi, and Louisiana—all went for Bush.[19]

Despite the evidence, our culture clings to the *völkisch* myth of Middle American wholesomeness. Liberals have been so intimidated by charges of elitism that they rarely speak up for their own values. How else to explain how little discussion there is in our politics of the feudal backwardness and moral dissipation that results whenever Christian nationalists have the chance to put their policies into practice?

The canard that the culture wars are a fight between "elites" versus "regular Americans" belies a profound split between different kinds of ordinary Americans, all feeling threatened by the others' baffling and alien values. Ironically, however, by buying into right-wing elite-baiting, liberals start *thinking* like out-of-touch elites. Rather than reflecting on what kind of policies would make their own lives better, what kind of country they want to live in, and who they want to represent them—and then figuring out how to win others to their vision—progressives flail about for ideas and symbols that they hope will appeal to some imaginary heartland rube. *That* is condescending.

Building a Movement

When I talk about liberals and progressives, I do not mean the Democratic party, although for now that is the only practical vehicle for their ambitions. It is entirely possible that in the short term, Democrats will have to make concessions to religious conservativism. Support for gay marriage, for example, is obviously just and moral, yet, at the moment, it's electorally suicidal. Reproductive choice is a fundamental Democratic principle, but it makes sense for the party to line up behind Pennsylvania's Robert P. Casey Jr., a popular Democratic pro-lifer, in the 2006 race against Rick Santorum. Those who would rather see Democrats win than reflect liberal idealism in their concession speeches will have to accept some degree of realpolitik. A Casey victory could actually help *protect* reproductive choice, by putting Democrats closer to control of the Senate and robbing the Christian nationalists of one of their firmest allies in government. For people committed to abortion rights, it is a bitter thing to support a candidate devoted to taking those rights away. One hopes that their bitterness will spur activists to try to build a culture where such compromises will be less and less necessary.

If this seems to contradict my call for progressive pride, it is because political parties and social movements operate in different ways. Political parties address the beliefs people already hold. Movements work to change those beliefs. When activists expect parties to do the job of movements—nominating crusading candidates like Barry Goldwater or George McGovern—political disaster ensues. A movement has to shape the culture before candidates who reflect its values will have a chance.

One way for progressives to build a movement and fight Christian nationalism at the same time is to focus on local politics. For guidance, they need only look to the Christian Coalition: it wasn't until after Bill Clinton's election exiled the evangelical right from power in Washington that the Christian Coalition really developed its nationwide electoral apparatus. Writing of that time, Ralph Reed said, "How could the pro-family movement recover from the body blows it had suffered and regain the momentum of the early Reagan years? The way they chose was to focus on local politics and local issues. Thus the Christian Coalition began quietly building a formidable network of grassroots activists, who organized their neighborhoods, sponsored training workshops, identified friendly voters, and passed out voter education literature."[20]

The Christian right developed a talent for crafting state laws and amendments to serve as wedge issues, rallying their base, and forcing the other side to defend seemingly extreme positions. Campaigns to require parental consent for minors' abortions, for example, get overwhelming public support and put the pro-choice movement on the defensive while giving pro-lifers valuable political experience. As governor of Texas, George W. Bush was able to make Texas Democrats' opposition to parental notice an important campaign issue. He eventually got a notice law passed, and then trumpeted it during his first presidential campaign as a way to signal his pro-life bona fides without frightening moderate women.[21]

Liberals can use this strategy too. They can find issues to exploit the other side's radicalism, winning a few political victories and, just as important, marginalizing Christian nationalists in the eyes of their fellow citizens. Progressives could work to pass local and state laws, by ballot initiative wherever possible, denying public funds to any organization that discriminates on the basis of religion. Because so much faith-based funding is distributed through the states, such laws could put an end to at least some of the taxpayer-funded bias practiced by the Salvation Army and other religious charities. (Religious groups would, of course, remain free to refuse to hire people of other faiths—they would just have to make do without government money.) Besides rectifying an immediate injustice, a campaign to end state-financed discrimination would move the issue into the public spotlight. Right now, very few people know that, thanks to Bush, a faith-based outfit can take tax dollars and then explicitly refuse to hire Jews, Hindus, Buddhists, or Muslims, among others. The issue needs far more publicity, and a political fight—or a series of them—would provide it. It would also force Christian nationalists to explain why they *should* be allowed to discriminate on the public's dime. Better still, the campaign would contribute to the creation of a grassroots infrastructure—a network of people with political experience and a commitment to pluralism.

Progressives could also work on passing laws to mandate that pharmacists fill contraceptive prescriptions. (Such legislation has already been introduced in California, Missouri, New Jersey, Nevada, and West Virginia.) The commercials would practically write themselves. Imagine a harried couple talking with their doctor and deciding that they can't afford any more kids. The doctor writes a birth control prescription, the wife takes it to her pharmacist—and he sends her away with a religious lecture. The campaign could use one of the most successful slogans that abortions rights advocates ever devised: "Who decides— you or them?"

In addition to efforts to change the electoral landscape at the state and national level, liberals should create a new organization devoted to intervening in local culture-war battles. For years, a number of groups have done crucial work against the religious right through lobbying, legal challenges, and opposition research—the ACLU, People for the American Way, Americans United for Separation of Church and State, and the Southern Poverty Law Center are some of the most important.

What's been missing is a nationwide citizens' group that can back up those who are fighting the right in their own communities.

Conservatives have a plethora of political operatives providing aid to people working to get creationism in their schools or antigay initiatives passed in their cities and states. According to Jeff Brown—the Dover, Pennsylvania, school board member who quit after his colleagues mandated the teaching of intelligent design—when Bill Buckingham, the chair of the curriculum committee, first made the news with his crusade against Darwin, he bragged that groups all over the country had contacted him offering help. "When anybody makes the wire service for a stupid statement like, 'This biology book is laced with Darwinism,' there is apparently this whole network" that springs into action, Brown said. It was these outside lawyers and political operatives, he believes, who cautioned Buckingham to use the phrase "intelligent design" instead of creationism.

No one came forward to help the Browns. When Buckingham started talking about intelligent design, it took Jeff and his wife, Casey, by surprise—they weren't familiar with the phrase. Imagine, though, if an organization had existed specifically to bolster people who find themselves drafted into the culture wars. As soon as the controversy started, it could have reached out to the Browns and briefed them on how evolution fights usually progress, filling them in on intelligent design, where it comes from and how to refute it.

Such an organization could connect people with others who faced similar challenges in their own towns to discuss which strategies and arguments worked and which fell flat. It could offer campaign training to political novices who want to challenge school board or city council incumbents, and sponsor speaking tours by people who've been in the trenches. Casey Brown, for one, is eager to share her experience. "I want to go out there and I want to say this is what happened to us, this is what you need to do," she said. "Perhaps we can help another community."

The kind of organization that's needed is one that would help people win their neighbors over, not just beat them in court. "If you don't win the grass roots it's going to come back again," Jeff Brown said.

"We've got to get to the grass roots. That's where these people"—the Christian nationalists—"do their recruiting."

Right now, it's hard to find so much as a Web site offering advice to those facing Christian nationalist challenges to their schools. The lack of an infrastructure for fighting local political contests is partly a result of liberals' reliance on the courts to protect minority rights. Ever since *Brown v. the Board of Education*, the left has turned to the Supreme Court to defend civil liberties in the face of hostile majorities. When a school board decides to introduce creationism, the immediate liberal impulse is to sue.

Lacking allies on the high court, the right turned to populist, grass-roots politics instead, reaping the benefit of the backlash against countermajoritarian decisions. A vicious cycle developed—every time the court intervened to protect some unpopular group, the right garnered more popular support.

It's unfair to condemn anyone for seeking redress from the Supreme Court—African-Americans, gay people, and others are entirely justified in not wanting to put their civil rights up for popular vote. But whether or not relying on the courts was wise, it's no longer possible. The bench is filling up with judges who are fundamentally hostile to many rights liberals treasure—from the right to private, consensual sex to the right to a public education free of religious indoctrination. This is a tremendous loss, but progressives can make a virtue of necessity by refocusing on local politics.

It was through local politics, finally, that intelligent design was defeated in Dover. On November 8, 2005—after arguments in the lawsuit had concluded but before the judge issued his ruling—Dover voters narrowly ousted all of the eight school board members who were up for reelection and replaced them with a pro-evolution slate. One of the victors was Bryan Rehm, who, along with his wife, Christy, had been a plaintiff in the suit. (At least, it seems he was one of the victors—as of this writing, the incumbent he defeated was challenging the results, claiming voting machine malfunction). It was as decisive a rebuke as anyone had dared to imagine.

The new board's win didn't come in time to halt the court case. Nor did it mean that the Dover citizenry had been disabused of their doubts about Darwin. Most observers attributed the election result to embarrassment over the international mockery caused by the controversy and, most importantly, mounting anger over the lawsuit's cost. "Some people carry their vote in their shirt pocket right next to their heart, but most people carry it in their hip pocket right next to their wallet," Jeff Brown told me. Nevertheless, the outcome completely changed the local political dynamic, rendering intelligent design momentarily useless as a populist cudgel. Four days after the vote, Rick Santorum flip-flopped on his earlier position, telling a local newspaper that intelligent design doesn't belong in classrooms. "Science leads you where it leads you," he said.[22]

In December 2005, U.S. District Judge John Jones—a George W. Bush appointee—issued a ruling eviscerating the former board's intelligent design policy. "To be sure, Darwin's theory of evolution is imperfect," Jones wrote in his 139-page opinion. "However, the fact that a scientific theory cannot yet render an explanation on every point should not be used as a pretext to thrust an untestable alternative hypothesis grounded in religion into the science classroom or to misrepresent well-established scientific propositions." He continued, "The citizens of the Dover area were poorly served by the members of the Board who voted for the ID Policy. It is ironic that several of these individuals, who so staunchly and proudly touted their religious convictions in public, would time and again lie to cover their tracks and disguise the real purpose behind the ID Policy."

Ordinarily, a decision like Jones's would have been loudly denounced as an elitist attack on the will of the people. But because the will of the people now seemed to be on the judge's side, the right's reaction was muted. Dover's new school board didn't appeal Jones's ruling, so there was no rallying of the troops for the next stage of the legal fight. In an effort to distance himself from the case, a chagrined Santorum publicly resigned from the Thomas More law firm's advisory board. Pundits pronounced intelligent design dead.

The obituaries were, of course, premature. Days after Dover tossed out its school board, the state of Kansas approved new science standards critiquing evolution. Then, less than two weeks after Jones ruled that intelligent design doesn't belong in science classes, California's El Tejon School District introduced intelligent design as a philosophy elective. "This class will take a close look at evolution as a theory and will discuss the scientific, biological, and Biblical aspects that suggest why Darwin's philosophy is not rock solid," said the course description for "The Philosophy of Design." "This class will discuss Intelligent Design as an alternative response to evolution. . . . Physical and chemical evidence will be presented suggesting the earth is thousands of years old, not billions."

Americans United for Separation of Church and State promptly joined with local parents to file a lawsuit, and the school district backed down, agreeing not to offer the course again. Meanwhile, though, statewide anti-evolution initiatives gained momentum in Oklahoma, Utah, and Missouri, and, given the tenacity of the anti-evolution movement, more are likely on the way. If they pass, they'll spur other legal challenges, meaning the battle in Dover will be replayed throughout the country. Not all judges are likely to be as enlightened as Jones, so we may yet see judicial sanction for teaching intelligent design in public schools. As the fight continues, defenders of science and reason need to learn from what happened in Pennsylvania, and try to vanquish intelligent design's proponents in local elections as well as in the courtroom, neutralizing the issue's demagogic appeal.

Fighting Christian nationalism through local campaigns involves more than just playing defense. There are many ways activists can push issues like gay rights forward in a piecemeal fashion through electoral politics in sympathetic states. Victories won this way are incremental, but they're far more durable, since they don't spur demagogic attacks on unelected judges. In April 2005, Connecticut became the third state in the union to offer almost all the benefits of marriage to gay couples through domestic partnerships. Unlike Massachusetts and Vermont, here there was virtually no national outcry, because the change came from the legislature and was signed by the (Republican) governor. There's no reason people in other liberal states can't fight for similar laws. It would be thrilling to see more battles for social justice won with the help of the people, rather than in spite of them.

As long as there's a Republican Congress and a Republican president, Democrats can't accomplish anything positive on the national level; at most, they can temper a few right-wing excesses. That's important work, but it's also demoralizing. By engaging in winnable local and state contests, liberals can achieve some of the small victories necessary to stave off futility and despair. They can build networks, learn how electoral politics is played, and work to turn their cities and states into societies that reflect their values, even if those values aren't shared by the rest of the country.

In conjunction with local initiatives, opponents of Christian nationalism need a new media strategy. Many people realize this. Fenton Communications, the agency that handles public relations for MoveOn, recently put together the Campaign to Defend the Constitution, a MoveOn-style grassroots group devoted to raising awareness about the religious right. With nearly 3.5 million members ready to be quickly mobilized to donate money, write letters, or lobby politicians on behalf of progressive causes, MoveOn is the closest thing liberals have to the Christian Coalition, but its focus tends to be on economic justice, foreign policy, and the environment rather than contentious social issues. The Campaign to Defend the Constitution intends to build a similar network to try to counter Christian nationalism wherever it appears, including attacks on evolution, gay rights, reproductive choice, and separation of church and state.

Much of the work that media strategists need to do simply involves public education. Every time David Barton appears in the news in conjunction with the GOP, liberals should be drawing attention to his connections to white supremacists. Americans need to learn what Christian Reconstructionism means so that they can decide whether they approve of their congressmen consorting with theocrats. They need to realize that the Republican party has become the stronghold of men who fundamentally oppose public education because they think women should school their kids themselves. (In *It Takes a Family*, Rick Santorum calls public education an "aberration" and predicts that homeschooling will flourish as "one viable option among many that will open up as we eliminate the heavy hand of the village elders' top-down control of education and allow a thousand parent-nurtured flowers to bloom."[23])

When it comes to the public relations fight against Christian nationalism, nothing is trickier than battles concerning public religious symbolism. Fights over crèches in public squares or Christmas hymns sung by school choirs are really about which aspects of the First Amendment should prevail—its protection of free speech or its ban on the establishment of religion. In general, I think it's best to err on the side of freedom of expression. As in most First Amendment disputes, the answer to speech (or, in this case, symbolism) that makes religious minorities feel excluded or alienated is *more* speech—menorahs, Buddhas, Diwali lights, symbols celebrating America's polyglot spiritualism.

Things become more complicated when it comes to displays like Roy Moore's Ten Commandments monument, which conflates civil law with the Bible. It aims to convey the *authority* of religion, and allowing it to stand would strengthen the Christian nationalists' theocratic claims. The difference lies in a subtle distinction between images that affirm that many Americans are Christian, and those that declare America a Christian nation.

There are no neat lines, no way to suck the venom out of these issues without capitulating completely. But one obvious step civil libertarians should take is a much more vocal stance in defense of evangelicals' free speech rights when they *are* unfairly curtailed. Although far less common than the Christian nationalists pretend, on a few occasions lawsuit-fearing officials have gone overboard in defending church/state separation, silencing religious speech that is protected by the First Amendment. (In one 2005 incident that got tremendous play in the right-wing press, a principal in Tennessee wouldn't allow a ten-year-old student to hold a Bible study during recess.[24]) Such infringements should be fought for reasons both principled, because Christians have the same right to free speech as everyone else, and political, because these abuses generate a backlash that ultimately harms the cause of church/state separation.

The ACLU already does this, but few ever hear about it, because secularists lack the right's propaganda apparatus. Consider, for example, the Christian nationalist urban legend that Jerry Falwell dubbed "The Case of the Offensive Candy Canes." Falwell described this secularist outrage in a 2003 article: "Seven high school students in Westfield, Mass., have been suspended solely for passing out candy canes containing religious messages. . . . The fact is, students have the right to free speech in the form of verbal or written expression during non-instructional class time. And yes, students have just as much right to speak on religious topics as they do on secular topics—no matter what the ACLU might propagate."[25]

In fact, the ACLU submitted a brief *defending* the students on the grounds that, as the ACLU's attorney said, "students have a right to communicate ideas, religious or otherwise, to other students during their free time, before or after class, in the cafeteria, or elsewhere." Nevertheless, stories about the ACLU and its evil plots against Christian confections proliferated in the right-wing media.

Liberals need to create their own echo chamber to refute these kind of distortions while loudly supporting *everyone's* freedom of speech. Committed Christian nationalists won't be won over, but some of their would-be sympathizers might be inoculated against the claim that progressives want to extirpate their faith, making it harder for the right to frame every political dispute as part of a war against Jesus. The challenge, finally, is to make reality matter again. If progressives can do that, perhaps America can be saved.

AFTERWORD
Solidarity

One way to understand the hatreds tearing up the world today is as a war between East and West, Christendom and Dar El Islam. But this schema ignores the civil wars within both houses, and the alliances across spiritual and geographic lines. At a time when religious extremism seems everywhere ascendant, I see a different struggle, one between modernity, humanism, reason, and progress on one hand, and fundamentalism, tribalism, Puritanism, and obscurantism on the other. Liberals the world over are fighting religious tyranny.

In the summer of 2005 I interviewed Marjane Satrapi, an Iranian graphic novelist whose books, *Persepolis* and *Persepolis 2*, chronicle her childhood during the revolution that instituted religious rule. Part of a cosmopolitan, politically engaged family, Satrapi captures their terrified disbelief as theocrats obsessed with sex and death took over Iran. I thought secularists in America might be feeling some faint shadow of that same horror, but I was reluctant to make comparisons between Iran's despotic mullahs and our Christian nationalists, because I didn't want to trivialize her country's exponentially greater suffering. Satrapi had no such qualms. "They are the same!" she said over the phone from Paris, before spontaneously launching into a plea for solidarity among all enemies of fundamentalism. "The secular people, we have no country. We the people—all the secular people who are looking for freedom—we have to keep together. We are international, as they"—the zealots of all religions—"are international."

Indeed they are. The alliance between Christian Zionists and the most fanatical Israeli settlers is well-known. Less remarked upon is the way American evangelicals have made common cause with Islamists at the United Nations against international accords protecting women's and children's rights. Under Bush, U.S. delegations to United Nations conferences mimic the lineup at the Reclaiming America for Christ conference: the group sent to a 2002 U.N. summit on children included Concerned Women for America's Janice Crouse; Paul Bonicelli, dean of academic affairs at Patrick Henry College; and John Klink, a former advisor to the Vatican. They worked with delegates from authoritarian Islamic countries to scuttle a reference to "reproductive health care services" in the declaration that came out of the meeting. In a story headlined, "Islamic Bloc, Christian Right Team Up to Lobby U.N.," *The Washington Post* wrote of U.S. and Iranian officials huddled together during coffee breaks, presumably plotting strategy. (In 2005, Bonicelli was appointed to oversee the U.S. Agency for International Development's democracy and government programs.)

According to the *Post*, partnering with conservative Muslims "provided the administration an opportunity to demonstrate that it shares many social values with Islam." It quoted an American official noting, "We have tried to point out there are some areas of agreement between [us] and a lot of Islamic countries on these social issues."[1]

The things so many Islamic fundamentalists hate about the West—its sexual openness, its art, the possibilities it offers for escaping the bonds of family and religion, for inventing one's own life—are what the Christian nationalists hate as well. And so, in a final grotesque irony, we come full circle and see defenders of American chauvinism speaking the language of anti-American radicals. At another U.N. meeting, this one in March 2005, Janice Crouse made the connection pointedly.

Held to review the progress made since the 1995 Fourth World Conference on Women in Beijing, the gathering offered another opportunity for the administration to pack its delegation with people like

Christian radio broadcaster Janet Parshall (who, incidentally, was the narrator of David Balsiger's fawning documentary, *George W. Bush: Faith in the White House*). Crouse wasn't an official part of the team this time, but toward the end of the conference, she gave a talk at the United Nation's nongovernmental organization building about how feminism and "sexual liberation" have been an "unmitigated disaster" for women. Her bizarre slide show compared feminism to communism by interspersing pictures and quotes from Mao Zedong ("All power comes from the barrel of a gun") and Josef Stalin ("A single death is a tragedy, a million is a statistic") with one of Betty Friedan ("Women, all you have to lose, is your vacuum cleaner"). And then, the climax—a slide of bodies piled up at a Nazi concentration camp, followed by a picture of a fetus's hand reaching out of an incision in a woman's womb.

The audience was split among American evangelicals, Latin American Catholics, and Muslims from the Middle East and Asia. Addressing them, Crouse made it as clear as any feminist could have that banning abortion means curtailing women's autonomy: "To what end has this plague of abortion, this massacre of innocents, been directed?" she asked. "The pursuit of hedonistic pleasure? Women's liberation? Liberation from what? So that a woman can engage in the pleasure of sexual intercourse without the demands of motherhood? No, this horrible slaughter has little to do with pleasure, but it has a great deal to do with the demands of motherhood. Radical feminists accurately see abortion as a woman's ultimate weapon in the battle to escape the control of men. The issue is of power, of having the power to call the shots. With abortion as an option, a woman can escape pregnancy. Abortion gives her the power to escape giving birth to a man's child, a child she would otherwise be connected to for that child's whole life, and who would likewise connect her to the child's father."

The blatancy of her appeal to patriarchy surprised me, because in speaking to American audiences Christian nationalists usually imitate the language of female empowerment. What shocked me, though, were Crouse's comments during the Q&A following her performance. A Turkish woman in a head scarf stood up and declared that American culture and communism are "the same," because both are colonialist forces that assault traditional norms. And amazingly, Janice Crouse agreed.

"I think you're very much on target when you say that modern-day feminism is colonialism in disguise," she said. "I get very short-tempered with American feminists today, because I see much of what they emphasize as importing decadent Western culture into third world nations." Frantz Fanon—or Osama bin Laden—couldn't have said it better. The crowd applauded.

This is what we are up against. Christian nationalists worship a nostalgic vision of America, but they despise the country that actually exists—its looseness, its decadence, its maddening lack of absolutes.

Writing just after September 11, Salman Rushdie eviscerated those on the left who rationalized the terrorist attacks as a regrettable explosion of understandable third world rage: "The fundamentalist seeks to bring down a great deal more than buildings," he wrote. "Such people are against, to offer just a brief list, freedom of speech, a multiparty political system, universal adult suffrage, accountable government, Jews, homosexuals, women's rights, pluralism, secularism, short skirts, dancing, beardlessness, evolution theory, sex."[2] Christian nationalists have no problem with beardlessness, but except for that, Rushdie could have been describing them.

It makes no sense to fight religious authoritarianism abroad while letting it take over at home. The grinding, brutal war between modern and medieval values has spread chaos, fear, and misery across our poor planet. Far worse than the conflicts we're experiencing today, however, would be a world torn between competing fundamentalisms. Our side, America's side, must be the side of freedom and Enlightenment, of liberation from stale constricting dogmas. It must be the side that elevates reason above the commands of holy books and human solidarity above religious supremacism. Otherwise, God help us all.

—Michelle Goldberg
January 2006

After the Fall:
The Future of Christian Nationalism

It all fell apart so fast. When I finished *Kingdom Coming*, Ted Haggard, former head of the National Association of Evangelicals, was a respected spokesman for the sanctity of heterosexual marriage. Mel Gibson was revered as a hero of the faith, and those who saw anti-Semitism in *The Passion* were dismissed as paranoid Christophobes. Ralph Reed was better known for his boy-wonder days at the Christian Coalition than for his ties to Indian casinos and Jack Abramoff. Tom DeLay ran the House and Bill Frist, a man who purported to diagnose Terri Schiavo via cable TV, ruled the Senate.

This book was written in the ugly year following the 2004 election, when much of what was decent in America seemed swamped by the forces that returned Bush to office and elevated a cadre of reactionary congressmen to buttress him. Now, though, some equilibrium has been restored to this country, and Christian nationalism is, for the moment, in retreat. First Roy Moore, once the great political hope of the religious right, self-destructed, losing his primary bid to be the GOP candidate for Alabama governor by a devastating 67 to 33 percent. (His candidacy wasn't helped when he speculated that the state's first case of mad cow disease was part of a government conspiracy to impose a livestock tracking system "more identifiable with communism than free enterprise.")[1] DeLay left Congress after being indicted on charges of criminal conspiracy in a campaign finance probe. A drunken Gibson revealed himself as more nakedly anti-Semitic than most of his critics could have imagined. Haggard was disgraced in a sex scandal involving a gay prostitute and crystal meth. Sweeping away the Republican majority in Congress, the 2006 midterm elections brought the defeat of some of the religious right's most stalwart supporters, including Senator Rick Santorum and Congressmen John Hostettler. In 2004, the Christian nationalist movement pushed Bush over the top in Ohio, but in 2006, Ken Blackwell, the Ohio gubernatorial candidate closely allied with figures like Rod Parsley and James Dobson, was annihilated in his race against Democrat Ted Strickland (himself a Methodist minister).

Most heartening of all were the victories in statewide ballot initiatives. When South Dakota attempted to ban all abortions except to save a woman's life—a campaign led by Leslee Unruh of the Abstinence Clearinghouse—activists decided to appeal directly to voters rather than simply relying on the courts. They forced a referendum, and the people of South Dakota rejected the abortion ban 56 to 44 percent. Arizona saw the first electoral defeat of a statewide anti-gay-marriage amendment, largely because voters realized that it also precluded benefits for domestic partnerships. Missourians chose to defend stem cell research, and citizens in California and Oregon voted against requiring parental notification for minors seeking abortion. Rights were protected, and right-wingers lost the chance to demagogue about activist judges.

Among some Republicans, a backlash against the religious right has begun. Months before the election, former House majority leader Dick Armey, an evangelical and a Texan, blasted James Dobson and his "gang of thugs" as "real nasty bullies" in an interview with journalist Ryan Sager.[2] Armey then took to the *Wall Street Journal* editorial page to opine, "The national representatives of the social conservative movement used to be sophisticated and tolerant. Today, they are sophomoric and angry."[3] The recriminations only increased following the Democrats' November sweep. The day after the vote, an Iowa County Republican chairman named Steve Salem made news for fulminating against the "Christian fascists" within his party. "You've heard of IslamaFascists— I think we now have Christian fascists," he was quoted saying in the *Sioux City Journal*. "What is the definition of a fascist? Not only do they want to beat you, but they want to destroy you in the process."[4]

There has also been a reaction against Christian nationalism within evangelical Christianity. The same month that this book was published, Minnesota megachurch pastor Gregory Boyd came out with *The Myth of a Christian Nation: How the Quest for Political Power Is Destroying the Church*, in which he argued that militant nationalism and ideological fervor both have a "demonic dimension."[5] A few months later saw the release of *Thy Kingdom Come: How the Religious Right Distorts the Faith and Threatens America: An Evangelical's Lament* by Randall Balmer, who is both a believer and a professor of religious history at Columbia University.

Then, shortly before the election, David Kuo, the former deputy director of the White House Office of Faith-Based and Community Initiatives, published *Tempting Faith: An Inside Story of Political Seduction*, in which he accused the administration of selling out its evangelical supporters. Writing of the staff at the faith-based office, he said, "We were good people forced to run a sad charade, to provide political cover to a White House that needed compassion and religion as political tools."[6]

Kuo criticized the administration for offering little new money to faith-based programs, instead simply loosening regulations to make already-appropriated funds more easily available to religious groups. An ardent supporter of the faith-based idea, Kuo regards this as terribly insufficient. As should be obvious from this book, I find the effort to channel public money to religious groups deeply troubling, so I can't lament the fact that it wasn't even more extensive. Despite this fundamental disagreement, though, Kuo's book confirms my criticism of the faith-based initiative for favoring conservative evangelicals. He describes a conversation with a woman who reviewed grant applications for the Compassion Capital Fund: "She talked about how the govern-

ment employees gave them grant review instructions—look at everything objectively against a discreet list of requirements and score
accordingly. 'But,' she said with a giggle, 'when I saw one of those non-
Christian groups in the set I was reviewing, I just stopped looking at
them and gave them a zero.' "[7]

A disillusioned Kuo is now recommending that evangelicals take a
two-year "fast" from politics.[8]

So have we reached the end of Christian nationalism? I would like to
report that we have, but despite the avalanche of setbacks the movement
has suffered, I don't believe so. Certainly, I'm more optimistic than I was
a year ago. As resistance to Christian nationalism has grown, the power
of its atavistic appeals has weakened. Despite the movement's most
ardent efforts, women's health advocates succeeded in making emergency contraception available over the counter, at least for those over
eighteen. With a Democratic majority in Congress, it will be harder for
the Christian right to handpick federal judges.

But obituaries for the Christian right have been written many times
before—after the televangelist scandals of the late 1980s, for example,
and after Clinton's election and reelection. In 1988, following the collapse of Pat Robertson's presidential campaign, William Safire penned a
New York Times column titled "Demise of the Fundies." "[T]he Fundies
are not a serious political force and their current hero is not a serious
political candidate," he wrote. "They are a minor force; their pet peeves
will be given lip service at the convention."[9] Safire was right, of course,
that Robertson was never a serious political candidate. He was very
wrong about his followers being a "minor force." In 1999, just before the
Christian nationalists would achieve unprecedented power in the Bush
administration, *The Economist* wrote of their decline: "The armies of
righteousness, which once threatened to overwhelm the Republican
Party, are downcast and despondent."[10]

This is a movement that knows how to resurrect itself. In the 1990s,
the Christian right was rejected by a majority of Americans, just as it was

in 2006. That didn't stop it from helping to force the crisis of impeachment, and I doubt it will neuter it now.

Indeed, one of the great ironies of the last election is that, while it
was a massive defeat for Christian nationalism, it also left the GOP more
dependent on the movement than ever. Contrary to some initial reports,
there was no significant evangelical shift toward the Democrats. A CNN
poll found that 70 percent of white evangelicals voted for Republican
House members in the last election, compared to 74 percent in 2004.[11]
That was a decline, but it was hardly a realignment. Polls also showed
that evangelicals made up about the same percentage of the electorate
that they did two years ago. The base turned out for the Republicans, but
independents turned away.

Meanwhile, although some prominent Christian nationalists were
tossed out, the more significant defeats were among moderate
Republicans from the Northeast, where they lost nearly a third of their
House seats, and the Midwest, where they lost 15 percent. There is now
only one Republican congressman, Chris Shays, from New England.
Thus the center of gravity among the rump GOP has moved even further
to the right. Christian nationalist causes will continue to be championed
by people like Indiana representative Mike Pence, a handsome darling of
the movement who describes himself on his congressional Web site as "a
Christian, a conservative and a Republican, in that order." He'll have
allies like freshman Minnesota congresswoman Michele Bachman, who,
in an October speech at the Living Word Christian Center, explained
how after three days of fasting and praying, God commanded her to
enter the race.

The movement will also continue its push for power at the local
level. During the Clinton years, the Christian Coalition made great
strides by focusing on the grass roots—Ralph Reed once said he'd rather
elect a thousand school board members than one president. Now the
campaign to inject Christian nationalism into the public schools is once
again accelerating, though it doesn't receive nearly as much attention as
fights over evolution. The Texas Freedom Network, an invaluable
organization that fights the religious right where it's strongest, recently

surveyed the state's thousand-plus school districts to find out which were teaching the kind of revisionist history and biblical literalism propagated by the National Council on Bible Curriculum in Public Schools. (According to the council, the Bible "was the foundation and blueprint for our Constitution, Declaration of Independence, our education system, and our entire history until the last 20 to 30 years.") They found twenty-five school districts offering public school Bible classes, most of them steeped in Protestant fundamentalism. One school district was using David Barton's video *America's Godly Heritage*. Two screened the film version of *Left Behind*. Students in Amarillo were shown a chart explaining that the various races are descended from Noah's sons. In a report on its findings, the Texas Freedom Network explains, "According to the chart, 'Jews, Semitic people, and Oriental races' are descended from Shem; 'African races' and Canaanite nations from Ham; and 'Western Europeans' and 'Caucasians' from Japheth." As the group notes, this typology has been integral to many racist movements: "The belief that Africans, like Canaanites, descended from Ham figured prominently in nineteenth-century defenses of slavery and has often been cited as evidence of the racial inferiority of African Americans."[12]

The Texas Freedom Network reported that while such courses are still relatively uncommon, they appear to be spreading both inside and outside the state. In 2006, Georgia passed a law establishing elective Bible classes in public schools. It was written with the help of the National Council on Bible Curriculum in Public Schools, and the lawmaker who sponsored it later joined the group's advisory board.[13] Similar bills have been introduced in other states. Thus the ideology I've tried to describe in this book is being passed on in a small but growing number of classrooms, where it comes with the imprimatur of official truth.

Some of my book's critics have accused me of hyping the possibility of a theocracy. That was never my intention—America is certainly not about to morph into some version of Margaret Atwood's dystopian

Gilead. What I've attempted to describe in *Kingdom Coming* isn't an imminent theocratic takeover but a slow, often subtle, but ultimately profound change in our country's life and government. One aspect of such change has been the influx of members of the religious right into the federal bureaucracy. Bush hasn't brought about a theocracy by filling the government with Christian nationalists and conservative ideologues, but he has greatly elevated the role of faith in policymaking, and downplayed reason, evidence, and expertise.

The 2006 elections didn't stop him—just eight days after the midterms, he named Eric Keroack, an apparent opponent of birth control, to oversee Title X, the government program that provides $283 million in annual grants for family planning programs, primarily for poor women. (It was signed into law by Richard Nixon, who declared, "no American woman should be denied access to family planning assistance because of her economic condition.") At the time of his appointment, Keroack was a member of the medical advisory council of the Abstinence Clearinghouse and the medical director of A Woman's Concern, a network of anti-abortion crisis pregnancy centers. Like most CPCs, A Woman's Concern opposes contraception as well as abortion; according to its Web site, the group "is persuaded that the crass commercialization and distribution of birth control is demeaning to women, degrading of human sexuality, and adverse to human health and happiness." The outfit also distributes misleading information about sexual health—its Web site claims that abortion increases the risk for breast cancer by fifty percent and that "50% of post-abortive women report experiencing emotional and psychological disturbances lasting for months or years."

Again, that such a man is now in charge of the federal government's primary family planning program is not evidence that America is becoming an evangelical version of Iran. It is evidence that the Christian nationalist movement has gained significant administrative and policy-making influence, and that it is changing the way our country works.

In October 2006, I gave a talk in New York with Deborah Lauter, the civil rights director of the Anti-Defamation League. She spoke about the changes wrought in the texture of American life by an increasingly assertive evangelical culture, and she said that many of these changes fall outside the bounds of law and politics. In some schools and workplaces, for example, Bible study and prayer groups play a crucial part in social life, and while there's no official pressure to join, the imperative to conform, especially at work, can be quite strong. Legally, there's probably nothing that can or should be done about this—people have the right to free speech and free association. But it makes some people anxious all the same.

Afterward, a woman came up to me and said that her daughter worked in such a place. I expressed my sympathy, and asked where. "The Justice Department," she said.

It's too early to tell what role Christian nationalism will have in the 2008 election. Arkansas governor Mike Huckabee, whom we met at the covenant marriage rally in Little Rock, is being touted as a possible presidential contender. Last year he spoke at D. James Kennedy's Reclaiming America for Christ conference. Two years out, it's hard to estimate his chances. Perhaps he won't even run, or maybe he'll implode like Senator George Allen, once a conservative favorite for the nomination. It seems quite unlikely, though, that the GOP will nominate someone the movement disapproves of, which is why Rudy Giuliani's bid is quixotic at best. Because we're now probably one judge away from the end of *Roe v. Wade*, the next presidential election or Supreme Court confirmation battle—whichever comes first—is going to tear the country in half over choice.

No matter what happens in 2008, there will be a crucial difference between that presidential campaign and the one in 2004. During Bush's reelection drive, little attention was paid to the political organizing happening in churches all over the country. This time, many people will be watching. Since this book was published, I've been invited to address groups all over the country—Christians, Jews, freethinkers, feminists, civil libertarians, and others, all of them concerned about the growing power of religious absolutism in American politics. I've met people like Marji Mendelsohn and Janice Weiss, two suburban Cincinnati mothers who, frightened by the growing influence of Christian fundamentalism in their state's politics, began spending time at local megachurches and right-wing rallies to educate themselves about the players and their messages. They learned that instructors from an anti-abortion crisis pregnancy center were teaching abstinence-only sex ed at their local public middle school, and they pressured the principal to hire a health teacher instead. They brought speakers to Ohio to address local interfaith leaders and concerned residents, and in 2005 they launched We Unite, a nonprofit dedicated to combating Ohio's religious right and promoting religious pluralism.

As it gets up and running, We Unite could eventually serve the same kind of watchdog function as the Texas Freedom Network. Perhaps someday there will be similar organizations in states throughout America. If others worried about Christian nationalism can mobilize just as conservatives have mobilized, maybe these past few febrile years really will be remembered as the religious right's peak.

—December 2006

Notes

Introduction: Taking the Land

1. Michael Farris, *The Joshua Generation* (Nashville: Broadman & Holman, 2005), pp. 11–12.

2. The National Center for Education Statistics in the U.S. Department of Education estimated there were 1.1 million students being homeschooled in 2003, a 29 percent increase from 1999. The National Home Education Research Institute claims that 1.7 million to 2.1 million children were homeschooled during the 2002–2003 academic year.

3. David Kirkpatrick, "College for the Homeschooled Is Shaping Leaders for the Right," *The New York Times*, March 7, 2004.

4. John Green, for the Pew Forum on Religion and Public Life, American Religious Landscapes and Political Attitudes, September 9, 2004.

5. In 2005, the Associated Baptist Press reported on a growing nationwide divide between those Christians who want to "re-establish Christendom" and those who "refuse to wrap the cross in the flag." See Ken Camp, " 'Nationalism' New Culture Split for Churches, Says Prof," July 26, 2005.

6. Kimberly H. Conger and John C. Green, "Spreading Out and Digging In; Christian Conservatives and State Republican Parties," *Campaigns and Elections*, February 2002.

7. Quoted in Daniel Levitas, *The Terrorist Next Door* (New York: Thomas Dunne Books/St. Martin's, 2002), p. 27.

8. Sara Diamond, *Roads to Dominion: Right-Wing Movements and Political Power in the United States* (New York: Guilford Press, 1995), p. 209.

9. David Kirkpatrick, "Club of the Most Powerful Gathers in Strictest Privacy," *The New York Times*, August 28, 2004.

10. Diamond, *Roads to Dominion*, pp. 221–25; Sara Diamond, *Spiritual Warfare: The Politics of the Christian Right* (Boston: South End Press, 1989), pp. 16–17; Scott Anderson and John Lee Anderson, *Inside the League* (New York: Dodd, Mead, 1986), pp. 179–80.

11. Michael Lind, "Rev. Robertson's Grand International Conspiracy Theory," *New York Review of Books*, February 2, 1995.

12. *The Collected Works of Pat Robertson* (New York: Inspirational Press, 1994), pp. 256–57; Pat Robertson, *The New World Order* (Nashville: Word Publishing, 1995), p. 257; Lind, "Rev. Robertson's Grand International Conspiracy Theory."

13. Garry Wills, *Under God: Religion and American Politics* (New York: Simon and Schuster, 1990), p. 174.

14. Frederick Clarkson, *Eternal Hostility* (Monroe, Me.: Common Courage Press, 1997), p. 110.

15. Ibid. p. 122.

16. Balsiger is another veteran of the Christian right's Cold War campaigns. During the 1980s, he organized the RAMBO Coalition, which supported right-wing guerillas in southern Africa. See Diamond, *Roads to Dominion*, p. 223.

17. "Intolerance Complaints Bubble over at Air Force Academy," Associated Press, May 12, 2005.

18. Hannah Arendt, *The Origins of Totalitarianism* (1951; reprint, New York: Harcourt, 1994), p. 353.

1: This Is a Christian Nation

1. *Ex parte H.H.*, 830 So.2d 21 (2002).

2. Matt Labash, "God and Man in Alabama," *The Weekly Standard*, March 2, 1998.

3. Dahleen Glanton, "Crusading for a Christian Nation; Groups Across the Country Are Defying the Courts and Invoking Patriotism as They

Fight for Displays of the Ten Commandments and School Prayer," *Chicago Tribune*, December 10, 2001; Americans United for Separation of Church and State, " 'Take Back Our Land,' Alabama's Judge Moore Urges Christian Rally," January 2002.

4. The Glenmary Research Center's study "Religious Congregations and Membership: 2000" found that during the 1990s, the fastest-growing denominations were the Mormons (19.3 percent), the conservative, evangelical Christian Churches and Churches of Christ (18.6 percent), and the Pentecostal Assemblies of God (18.5 percent). The steepest declines were registered by the liberal Presbyterian Church (U.S.A.) (11.6 percent) and the United Church of Christ (14.8 percent). See Laurie Goodstein, "Conservative Churches Grew Fastest in 1990s, Report Says," *The New York Times*, September 18, 2002.

5. Rick Scarborough, *In Defense of . . . Mixing Church and State* (Houston: Vision America, 1999), p. 9.

6. Thomas Frank, *What's the Matter with Kansas?* (New York: Metropolitan Books/Henry Holt, 2004), p. 6.

7. Isaac Kramnick and R. Laurence Moore, *The Godless Constitution* (New York: W. W. Norton, 1996), p. 143.

8. James G. Lakely, "President Outlines Role of His Faith," *Washington Times*, January 12, 2005.

9. David Frum, *The Right Man* (New York: Random House, 2003), pp. 3–4.

10. Fritz Stern, *The Politics of Cultural Despair: A Study in the Rise of the Germanic Ideology* (Berkeley: University of California Press, 1989), p. xx.

11. Roger Griffin, *The Nature of Fascism* (New York: Routledge, 2003), p. 38.

12. Quoted in a 1994 Anti-Defamation League report, "The Religious Right: The Assault on Tolerance and Pluralism in America," p. 121.

13. William Edgar, "The Passing of R.J. Rushdoony," *First Things*, August/September 2001.

14. Francis Schaeffer, *A Christian Manifesto* (Westchester, Ill.: Crossway Books, 1981), p. 18.

15. Ibid. p. 121.

16. Ibid. p. 131.

17. Tim LaHaye, *Battle for the Mind* (Old Tappan, N.J.: Fleming H. Revell, 1980), p. 9.

18. Alan Cooperman, "DeLay Criticized for 'Only Christianity' Remarks," *The Washington Post*, April 20, 2002.

19. George Grant, *The Changing of the Guard* (Ft. Worth: Dominion Press, 1987), pp. 50–51.

20. D. James Kennedy, *Character and Destiny: A Nation in Search of Its Soul* (Grand Rapids, Mich.: Zondervan, 1995), p. 59.

21. Ibid., pp. 56–57.

22. Quoted in Kramnick and Moore, *The Godless Constitution*, p. 105.

23. Anti-Defamation League, "The Religious Right," pp. 55–56.

24. Rob Boston, "Naked Power Grab," *Church & State Magazine*, November 2004.

2: Protocols of the Elders of San Francisco:
The Political Uses of Homophobia

1. "Alabama Bill Targets Gay Authors," *CBS Evening News*, April 27, 2005.

2. "Tenn. County Officials Seek to Ban Gays," Associated Press, March 17, 2004.

3. Alan Sears and Craig Osten, *The Homosexual Agenda* (Nashville: Broadman & Holman, 2003) p. 10.

4. Richard J. Evans, *The Coming of the Third Reich* (New York: Penguin, 2005), p. 376.

5. Sears and Osten, *The Homosexual Agenda*, p. 14.

6. Scott Lively and Kevin Abrams, *The Pink Swastika* (Sacramento: Veritas Aeterna Press, 2002), p. 13.

7. Marvin Olasky, "We the People," *World Magazine*, November 13, 2004.

8. Luisa Kroll, "Megachurches, Megabusiness," *Forbes*, September 17, 2003; William C. Symonds, "Earthly Empires: How Evangelical Churches Are Borrowing from the Business Playbook," *BusinessWeek*, May 23, 2005.

9. Symonds, "Earthly Empires."

10. Susan Page, "Shaping Politics from the Pulpits," *USA Today*, August 2, 2005.

11. Walter Shapiro, "Ohio Churches Hope Marriage Ban Prods Voters to Polls," *USA Today*, September 26, 2004.

12. "Heartbroken," *The Economist*, August 15, 2002.

13. Pam Belluck, "To Avoid Divorce, Move to Massachusetts," *The New York Times*, November 14, 2004.

14. Richard Hofstadter, *The Paranoid Style in American Politics and Other Essays* (Cambridge, Mass.: Harvard University Press, 1996), p. 31.

15. Tim LaHaye and Jerry Jenkins, *The Remnant* (Wheaton, Ill.: Tyndale House, 2002), p. 318.

16. Max Blumenthal, "Justice Sunday Preachers," *The Nation* online, April 26, 2005.

17. Bronwyn Turner, "Undoing Racism Task Force Calls for Reconciliation During Evening to Honor Black Leaders," *Lufkin* [Tex.] *Daily News*, April 17, 2004.

18. Walter Shapiro, "Presidential Election May Have Hinged on One Issue: Issue 1," *USA Today*, November 4, 2004.

19. LaHaye and Jenkins, *The Remnant*, p. 323.

20. Hanns Oberlindober, *Ein Vaterland, das allen gehört! Briefe an Zeitgenossen aus zwölf Kampfjahren* (Munich: Zentralverlag der NSDAP, 1940), pp. 152–67; translation by Randall Bytwerk, posted at the German Propaganda Archive at Calvin College, http://www.calvin.edu/academic/cas/gpa/oberlindober1.htm.

3: Lord of the Laboratory: Intelligent
Design and the War on the Enlightenment

1. *Kitzmiller et al. v. Dover Area School District*, complaint, p. 13; Joseph Maldonado, "Dover Schools Still Debating Biology Text," *York* [Pa.] *Daily Record*, June 9, 2004.

2. Neela Banerjee, "Christian Conservatives Turn to Statehouses," *The New York Times*, December 13, 2004.

3. Jonathan Wells, "Darwinism: Why I Went for a Second Ph.D.," posted at

http://www.tparents.org/library/unification/talks/wells/DARWIN.htm. See also Peter Slevin, "In Kansas, a Sharp Debate on Evolution," *The Washington Post*, May 6, 2005.

4. Phillip Johnson, *The Wedge of Truth* (Downers Grove, Ill.: InterVarsity Press, 2000), pp. 157–58.

5. Ibid., p. 158.

6. Hannah Arendt, *The Origins of Totalitarianism* (1951; reprint, New York: Harcourt, 1994), p. 350.

7. Rick Santorum, "Illiberal Education in Ohio Schools," *Washington Times*, March 14, 2002.

8. Percival Davis and Dean H. Kenyon, *Of Pandas and People* (Richardson, Tex.: Foundation for Thought and Ethics, 1989), p. 14.

9. Kitzmiller *v.* Dover transcript, October 27, 2005.

10. Joseph Maldonado, " 'Intelligent Design' Voted In," *York Daily Record*, October 19, 2004.

11. Ronald Numbers, *The Creationists* (Berkeley: University of California Press, 1992), p. 44.

12. Edward J. Larson, *Summer for the Gods: The Scopes Trial and America's Continuing Debate over Science and Religion* (New York: Basic Books, 1997), pp. 231–33.

13. Anna Badkhen, "Anti-evolution Teachings Gain Foothold in U.S. Schools," *San Francisco Chronicle*, November 30, 2004.

4: The Faith-Based Gravy Train

1. See transcript of Bush's speech, "President Highlights Faith-Based Initiative at Leadership Conference," on the White House Web site, http://www.whitehouse.gov/news/releases/2005/03/20050301–4.html.

2. Amy Sullivan, "Faith Without Works," *Washington Monthly*, October 2004.

3. Alan Cooperman, "An Infusion of Religious Funds in Fla. Prisons," *The Washington Post*, April 25, 2004.

4. Marvin Olasky, *Renewing American Compassion* (New York: Free Press, 1996), p. 26.

5. Marvin Olasky, *The Tragedy of American Compassion* (Washington, D.C.: Regnery Gateway, 1992) p. 230.

6. Marvin Olasky, "God and Sinner Reconciled," *World Magazine*, December 14, 1996.

7. David Grann, "Where W. Got Compassion," *The New York Times Magazine*, September 12, 1999.

8. Olasky, *Tragedy of American Compassion*, p. 220.

9. Grann, "Where W. Got Compassion."

10. David C. Hammack, review of *The Tragedy of American Compassion*, by Marvin Olasky, *Nonprofit and Voluntary Sector Quarterly*, Spring 1996; abridged version published online by H-State, February 1996.

11. Molly Ivins and Lou Dubose, *Bushwhacked* (New York: Random House, 2003), pp. 215–18.

12. Subcommittee of International Organizations of the House Committee on International Relations, *Investigation of Korean American Relations*, 95th Cong., 2d sess., October 31, 1978. Full speech available online at http://www.tparents.org/Moon-Talks/sunmyungmoon73/SM730517.htm.

13. Marc Fisher and Jeff Leen, "A Church in Flux Is Flush with Cash," *The Washington Post*, November 23, 1997.

14. Ibid.

15. Hamil R. Harris, "Moon Tries to Connect with Black Pastors," *The Washington Post*, April 21, 2001.

16. John Gorenfeld, "Bad Moon on the Rise," *Salon.com*, September 24, 2003.

17. Don Lattin, "Moonies Knee-Deep in Faith-Based Funds," *San Francisco Chronicle*, October 3, 2004.

18. Laura Meckler, "U.S. Gave $1 Billion in Faith-Based Funds," Associated Press, January 3, 2005.

19. Ron Suskind, "Why Are These Men Laughing?" *Esquire*, January 2003.

20. Ibid.

21. Ernest Herndon, "A Light in Louisiana," *Charisma*, October 23, 2003.

22. Sullivan, "Faith Without Works."

23. Richard B. Schmitt, "Justice Unit Puts Its Focus On Faith," *Los Angeles Times*, March 7, 2005.

24. Dana Milbank, "Charity Cites Bush Help in Fight Against Hiring Gays," *The Washington Post*, July 10, 2001.

25. Daniel J. Wakin, "Charity Reopens Bible, and Questions Follow," *The New York Times*, February 2, 2004.

5: AIDS Is Not the Enemy:
Sin, Redemption, and the Abstinence Industry

1. Frederick Clarkson, *Eternal Hostility* (Monroe, Me.: Common Courage Press, 1997), p. 37.

2 Christina Larson, "Pork for Prudes," *Washington Monthly*, September 2002.

3. The 30 percent figure comes from a 2004 poll commissioned by National Public Radio, the Kaiser Family Foundation, and Harvard's Kennedy School of Government.

4. Hannah Brückner and Peter Bearman, "After the Promise: The STD Consequences of Adolescent Virginity Pledges," *Journal of Adolescent Health 36* (2005), pp. 271–78.

5. Laura Beil, "Abstinence Programs: Lessons in Futility?" *Dallas Morning News*, January 29, 2005.

6. Janice M. Irvine, *Talk About Sex: The Battles over Sex Education in the United States* (Berkeley: University of California Press, 2004) p. 51.

7. Laura P., as told to Teresa Theophano, "Anti-choice 'Crisis Pregnancy Centers': A Personal Account," *PlannedParenthood.org*, June 23, 2005.

8. Sexuality Information and Education Council of the United States (SIECUS), Texas state profile.

9. Joneen Krauth, *WAIT Training Manual* (Greenwood Village, Colo.: WAIT Training, 2004), p. 295.

10. Deborah D. Cole and Maureen G. Duran, *Sex and Character* (Richardson, Tex.: Foundation for Thought and Ethics, 1998), p. 24.

11. Krauth, *WAIT Training Manual*, pp. 275–76, 291.

12. *ACLU of Massachusetts v. Leavitt*, complaint, p. 12.

13. Cole and Duran, *Sex and Character*, p. 80.

14. James R. Coughlin, *Facing Reality Student Manual* (Golf, Ill.: Project Reality, 1998), p. 11.

15. Bruce Cook, *Choosing the Best Student Manual* (Atlanta: Choosing the Best Publishing, 1993), p. 25.

16. Damien Cave, "Panic in the Sheets: Abstinence Crusaders Are Exploiting Fears of a Mysterious Virus to Scare Teens Away from Having Sex," *Salon.com*, October 8, 2002.

17. Debora MacKenzie, "Will Cancer Vaccine Get to All Women?" *New Scientist*, April 18, 2005.

18. Rob Stein, "Cervical Cancer Vaccine Gets Injected with a Social Issue," *The Washington Post*, October 31, 2005.

19. Ayelish McGarvey, "Dr. Hager's Family Values," *The Nation*, May 30, 2005.

20. "FDA Official Quits over Morning After Decision," Associated Press, August 31, 2005.

21. Quoted in Marc Kaufman "Memo May Have Swayed Plan B Ruling," *The Washington Post*, May 12, 2005.

22. Hannah Arendt, *The Origins of Totalitarianism* (1951; reprint, New York: Harcourt, 1994), p. 371.

6: No Man, No Problem: The War on the Courts

1. "Moralists at the Pharmacy," *The New York Times*, April 3, 2005.

2. Liz Austin, "Firings in Morning-After Pill Flap," Associated Press, February 12, 2004.

3. "Pharmacy Refusals 101" fact sheet, National Women's Law Center.

4. Rob Stein, "Pharmacists' Rights at Front of New Debate," *The Washington Post*, March 28, 2005.

5. "Sen. Rick Santorum's Comments on Homosexuality in an AP Interview," Associated Press, April 22, 2003.

6. R. J. Rushdoony, "Christian Reconstructionism as a Movement," *The Journal of Christian Reconstruction*, Fall 1996, p. 21.

7. Dana Milbank, "And the Verdict on Justice Kennedy Is: Guilty," *The Washington Post*, April 9, 2005.

8. Dan Smoot, *Judicial Oligarchy* (pamphlet reprinted from the John Birch Society magazine, *The Review of the News*, April 26, 1972).

9. Frederick Clarkson, *Eternal Hostility* (Monroe, Me.: Common Courage Press, 1997), p. 86.

10. Jean Hardisty, *Mobilizing Resentment* (Boston: Beacon Press, 1999), pp. 107–8; Rob Boston, "If Best-Selling End-Times Author Tim LaHaye

Has His Way, Church-State Separation Will Be . . . Left Behind," *Church & State Magazine*, February 2002.

11. Russ Bellant, *The Coors Connection* (Cambridge, Mass.: Political Research Associates, 1991), pp. 45–46.

12. Chip Berlet and Matthew Lyons, *Right-Wing Populism in America* (New York: Guilford Press, 2000), p. 178.

13. Tim LaHaye and David Noebel, *Mind Siege* (Nashville: Word Publishing, 2001).

14. Hubert Kregeloh, *There Goes Christmas?!* (Belmont, Mass.: American Opinion), May 1959.

15. John Gibson, *The War on Christmas: How the Liberal Plot to Ban the Sacred Christian Holiday Is Worse Than You Thought* (New York: Sentinel, 2005), p. 160.

16. Sara Diamond, *Roads to Dominion: Right-Wing Movements and Political Power in the United States* (New York: Guilford Press, 1995), p. 57.

17. Rick Perlstein, *Before the Storm* (New York: Hill and Wang, 2002), p. 322.

18. Richard T. Cooper, "General Casts War in Religious Terms," *Los Angeles Times*, October 16, 2003; Andrea Shalal-Esa, "U.S. General Violated Rules with 'Satan' Speeches," Reuters, August 18, 2004; "The Holy Warrior," *60 Minutes*, September 15, 2004.

19. William D. Graves, "The Case for Curbing the Federal Courts," *The Journal of Christian Reconstruction*, Fall 1996, pp. 168–69.

20. Ralph Reed, *Active Faith* (New York: Free Press, 1996), p. 261.

21. Sara Diamond, *Not by Politics Alone: The Enduring Influence of the Christian Right* (New York: The Guilford Press, 2000), p. 107.

22. R. J. Rushdoony, *The Institutes of Biblical Law* (Nutley, N.J.: The Craig Press, 1973), pp. 725, 425.

23. Bob Moser, "Our Terrible Swift Sword," *Southern Poverty Law Center Intelligence Report*, Fall 2003.

24. John Nickerson, "Red Mass Breakfast Visited by Filibuster Controversy," *Stamford Advocate*, April 25, 2005.

25. "Frist: Schiavo Case Won't Affect Dispute over Judges," Associated Press, April 5, 2005.

26. Leon Holmes and Susan Holmes, "Gender Neutral Language: Destroying an Essential Element of Our Faith," *Arkansas Catholic*, April 12, 1997.

27. Max Blumenthal, "In Contempt of Courts," *The Nation* online, April 11, 2005.

28. Paul Gigot, "Miami Heat: A Burgher Rebellion in Dade County," *The Wall Street Journal*, November 24, 2000.

29. Lou Dubose and Jan Reid, *The Hammer* (New York: PublicAffairs, 2004), pp 210–13; Adam Cohen, "For Partisan Gain, Republicans Decide Rules Were Meant to Be Broken," *The New York Times*, May 27, 2003.

30. Carol Marbin Miller, "Police 'Showdown' over Schiavo Averted," *Miami Herald*, March 26, 2005.

31. Robert O. Paxton, *The Anatomy of Fascism* (New York: Vintage, 2005), pp. 202, 220.

32. Ibid. p. 205.

Conclusion: Exiles in Jesusland

1. Karen Armstrong, *The Battle for God: A History of Fundamentalism* (New York: Ballantine, 2001), p. 178.

2. "Helping Boys Become Men, and Girls Become Women," on the Focus on the Family Web site.

3. Figures taken from the National Council on Bible Curriculum's Web site.

4. Joe Follick, "Lawmakers Tangle over 'Free Inquiry' Law for Universities," *Sarasota Herald-Tribune*, March 23, 2005.

5. Roger Griffin, *The Nature of Fascism* (New York: Routledge, 2003), p. 61: "Even the progression to the columns of large-circulation newspapers and well-attended public meetings represents a quantum leap for the diffusion of fascism which is still far removed from nation-wide mass rallies, extensive paramilitary violence and the 'seizure' of state power."

6. Ibid., pp. 196, 210–11. "Fascism," Griffin writes on p. 211, "can only break out of its marginalized position as part of the 'lunatic' right if it operates in a secularizing and pluralistic society struck by crisis. It will

only stand a chance of carrying out a successful revolution in a liberal democracy caught in a particularly delicate stage of its evolution: mature enough institutionally to preclude the threat of a direct military or monarchal coup, yet too immature to be able to rely on a substantial consensus in the general population that [classical] liberal political procedures and the values which underpin them are the sole valid basis for a healthy society."

7. Benjamin M. Friedman, "Meltdown: A Case Study," *The Atlantic Monthly*, July/August 2005.

8. Alan Brinkley, *Voices of Protest: Huey Long, Father Coughlin, and the Great Depression* (New York; Vintage, 1982), pp. 266–67. "In January of 1940 an FBI raid on a New York branch of the Front uncovered a cache of weapons," wrote Brinkley. "J. Edgar Hoover claimed that the members had planned to 'eliminate' Jews and Communists and 'knock off about a dozen Congressmen.' "

9. Daniel Levitas, *The Terrorist Next Door* (New York: Thomas Dunne Books/St. Martin's, 2002), pp. 9, 253.

10. Quoted in Anti-Defamation League, "The Quiet Retooling of the Militia Movement," September 7, 2004.

11. David Limbaugh, "Old Media on Iraq: Good News Not Newsworthy," *WorldNetDaily*, April 12, 2005.

12. Francis E. Lee and Bruce I. Oppenheimer, *Sizing Up the Senate: The Unequal Consequences of Equal Representation* (Chicago: University of Chicago Press, 1999), p. 2.

13. Steven Hill, *Fixing Elections: The Failure of America's Winner Take All Politics* (New York: Routledge, 2002), p. 8.

14. Jonathan Mahler, "The Soul of the New Exurb," *The New York Times Magazine*, March 27, 2005.

15. Hannah Arendt, *The Origins of Totalitarianism* (1951; reprint, New York: Harcourt, 1994), pp. 316–17.

16. Ibid., p. 348.

17. Rick Santorum, "Fishers of Men," *Catholic Online*, July 12, 2002.

18. James Alan Fox and Marianne W. Zawitz, "Homicide Trends in the

United States," U.S. Department of Justice Bureau of Justice Statistics, September 28, 2004.

19. Morgan Quinto Press 2004–2005 Education State Rankings, available at http://www.morganquitno.com/edrank04.htm.

20. Ralph Reed, *Active Faith* (New York: Free Press, 1996), p. 7.

21. William Saletan, *Bearing Right: How Conservatives Won the Abortion War* (Berkeley: University of California Press, 2003), pp. 249–51.

22. Bill Vidonic, "Santorum: Don't put intelligent design in classroom," *Beaver County Times & Allegheny Times*, November 13, 2005.

23. Rick Santorum, *It Takes a Family* (Wilmington, Del.: ISI Books, 2005), pp. 386–87.

24. "Let Bible Study Be Allowed at Recess, Suit Says," Associated Press, June 4, 2005. For the conservative reaction, see "Intolerance in the Bible Belt," *Washington Times*, June 8, 2005.

25. Jerry Falwell, "The Case of the Offensive Candy Canes," *WorldNetDaily*, January 11, 2003.

Afterword: Solidarity

1. Colum Lynch, "Islamic Bloc, Christian Right Team Up to Lobby U.N.," *The Washington Post*, June 17, 2002.

2. Salman Rushdie, "Fighting the Forces of Invisibility," *The Washington Post*, October 2, 2001.

Epilogue: After the Fall: The Future of Christian Nationalism

1. Phillip Rawls, "Roy Moore Challenges Tracking of Mad Cow," *The Decatur Daily*, March 29, 2006.

2. Ryan Sager, "Q&A with Dick Armey," posted on Sager's blog at http://www.rhsager.com/blog/index.php/2006/09/15/qa-with-dick-armey/.

3. Dick Armey, "The Pocketbook Conservative Is Up for Grabs," *The Wall Street Journal*, September 23, 2006.

4. Bret Hayworth, "Local GOP Chairman Blasts Own Party," *Sioux City Journal*, November 9, 2006.

5. Gregory Boyd, *The Myth of a Christian Nation: How the Quest for Political Power Is Destroying the Church* (Grand Rapids, Mich.: Zondervan, 2006), p. 24.

6. David Kuo, *Tempting Faith: An Inside Story of Political Seduction* (New York: Free Press, 2006), p. 242.

7. Ibid., pp. 215–16.

8. Ibid., pp. 262–63.

9. William Safire, "Demise of the Fundies," *The New York Times*, March 7, 1988.

10. "Lexington: Gary Bauer's Glass Door," *The Economist*, October 30, 1999.

11. 2006 CNN poll posted at http://www.cnn.com/ELECTION/2006/pages/results/states/US/H/00/epolls.0.html; 2004 CNN exit poll posted at http://www.cnn.com/ELECTION/2004/pages/results/states/US/H/00/epolls.0.html. In 2004, Bush's share of the national white evangelical vote was higher (78 percent) than that of Republican congressmen.

12. Texas Freedom Network, "Reading, Writing and Religion: Teaching the Bible in Texas Public Schools," September 2006.

13. Ibid.

Index